Fried Chicken

Fried Chicken

THE WORLD'S BEST RECIPES FROM
MEMPHIS TO MILAN, FROM BUFFALO TO BANGKOK

DAMON LEE FOWLER

BROADWAY BOOKS   NEW YORK

BROADWAY

Broadway Books titles may be purchased for business or promotional use or for special sales.
For information, please write to: Special Markets Department, Random House, Inc.,
1540 Broadway, New York, NY 10036.

BROADWAY BOOKS and its logo, a letter B bisected on the diagonal, are trademarks of Broadway Books, a division of Random House, Inc.

LIBRARY OF CONGRESS CATALOGING-IN-PUBLICATION DATA

Fowler, Damon Lee.
Fried chicken : the world's best recipes from Memphis to Milan, from Buffalo to
Bangkok / Damon Lee Fowler.–1st ed.
p.   cm.
Includes bibliographical references and index.
ISBN 0-7679-0183-5
1. Cookery (Chicken) 2. Frying. 3. Cookery, International.
I. Title.
TX750.5.C45F69   1999
641.6965–dc21   98-19140
                                                                CIP

FIRST EDITION

DESIGNED BY VERTIGO DESIGN

99 00 01 02 10 9 8 7 6 5 4 3 2 1

FOR MY FATHER AND

IN MEMORY OF HIS MOTHER

ADDIE GILLESPIE FOWLER

WHO SET THE STANDARD

Contents

Preface — viii

Acknowledgments — xi

The Chicken Fryer's Kitchen — 1

    EQUIPMENT — 2

    TECHNIQUES — 5

    INGREDIENTS — 9

The Deep End: Deep- and Pan-Fried Chicken — 19

    BATTERED BIRD — 19

    BREADED BIRD — 29

    CHICKEN CUTLETS — 40

    THE NAKED BIRD — 50

    DEEP-FRYING A WHOLE BIRD — 62

    THIS BIRD IS FULL OF IT — 65

    THE PARTY BIRD — 75

The Developed Art: Southern Fried Chicken   97

The Shallow End: Sautés and Stir-Fries   117
  SAUTÉING   118
  STIR-FRYING   129
  CHINESE STIR-FRIED CHICKEN   131
  STIR-FRIED PIECES AND PARTS   147

On the Side   153
  SAUCING THE BIRD   154
  BREAD, RICE, GRITS, POTATOES,
  AND SALADS   167

Bibliography
    183
Index   187

Preface

I suppose it seems obvious that a Southerner should write a book on fried chicken. What isn't obvious—at least it wasn't to me and to many other Southerners when I started the thing—is that, dearly as we love and prize it, and like to think we have perfected it, we Southerners don't have a gridlock on fried chicken. I have discovered that wherever in the world there are chickens and fat, cooks are, and probably always have been, frying the bird in one form or another.

Consequently, whenever I mentioned the subject of this book, the inevitable question it generated was "Well—are you sure you can fill up a whole book with nothing but that? Just how many ways are there to fry a chicken, anyway?" My answer quickly became the counter-question: "How many countries are there in the world?" It might as easily (and truthfully) have been "How many cooks are there in the world?" It did not take me long to realize that my real worry would not be finding enough recipes to fill a book, but whether or not that book would have room for everything that I did find.

It didn't.

For every recipe that I've included here, there were at least two that had to be laid aside. Some (only a few) were frankly not very wonderful and many were subtle variations on a recipe that was already represented. But many were great dishes that there just wasn't any room to include.

Some of the recipes were historical ones that had fallen out of use, and, historian that I am, those were the hardest of all for me to lay aside. But what I was after here was not history, but to filter the myriad ways that the world's cooks fry chicken into a representative collection of the way it is done throughout the world today. Historical recipes that have vanished from the modern cook's repertory, fascinating and tasty though they were, had to be laid aside for the time being.

But historically speaking for a moment, just how old is fried chicken? Recipes dating back to the late Medieval period in northern Europe can be found, and that was without really digging. Certainly it can be said to predate the colonization of the American South by centuries. Cooks have been frying for thousands of years, long before the Christian era—in fact, ever since pots were developed that could withstand the heat of boiling fat. My guess is that cooks have been frying chicken ever since they had chickens to fry and a pot to fry them in.

As universal as it is, however, there are a few of the world's cuisines in which fried chicken has developed more than others. For variety and sheer volume, China indisputably leads the way, which should come as no surprise to anyone, since China has one of the world's most ancient and highly developed cuisines. Chinese cooking has shaped much of the cooking of all of Asia. There are literally hundreds of varieties of fried chicken in China—both deep- and stir-fried. Next after China is probably the United States, where, in the South, it is almost a state religion. But fried chicken is popular all over America, and because of the many cultures that have shaped ours, it is almost as infinite in variety as China's. Next is Italy and France, two more venerable cuisines, where dozens of variations on deep-fried and sautéed chicken can be found, varying from region to region within each country. India, which enjoys another ancient and highly developed cuisine, and is believed by some historians to be the part of the world where chickens originated, predictably has many variations on fried chicken. Indian cookery was influential all over Southeast Asia and westward into the Arab world, Africa, and even as far as the American West Indies.

The Arab world offers an ancient cuisine where fried chicken is much less prevalent. Though chickens are a popular food throughout the region, most Middle Eastern cooks prefer to grill, roast, or bake their chickens, or else to put them into stews (tagines) and rice pilafs (pilaus). In Africa, older birds tend to be used for fried chicken, and so the chicken is often cooked in a sort of reverse fricassee—that is, it is first stewed and then fried. The exact flavorings may vary, but the core method remains pretty much the same.

In South America, as in North America, the cuisine tends to be derivative of all the cultures that have colonized it and is highly influenced by Spanish, Portuguese, and, in many places, even African cooking. Consequently, the fried chicken dishes from this part of the world have distinctive and telling Spanish and African elements. One dish is almost universal in Latin America—*chicharrones de pollo*—literally, "chicken cracklings," a picturesque name for chicken fried in cornmeal breading.

But why, you may well ask, is it a chicken above other birds? Well, naturally, other birds are fried, some of them are even domesticated; but the truth is, we humans are a lazy bunch and chickens are easy. The longest recorded flight of a modern domestic chicken is only 13 seconds; in other words, the little suckers just can't get away fast enough. And besides, let's face it—chickens are not exactly renowned for their intelligence.

Yet, chickens have not always been the inexpensive, taken-for-granted food source that they have become with modern breeding. In the not-too-distant past (as late, in fact, as World War II), chickens were a luxury food for most of the world—hence that hackneyed politician's promise of a chicken in every pot became symbolic of ultimate prosperity. Fried chicken, in those days, was a strictly seasonal delicacy available only while chickens were breeding in the spring and summer. Young hens were kept for their eggs. Only older hens that had stopped laying and the tough old roosters could be readily dispatched to the kitchen. The more common way of cooking these older, tougher birds in a frying pan was a fricassee, the half-fried method in which the bird could be put through a slow, tenderizing stewing stage, either before—or, more frequently, after—it is fried. Even so, a fricassee with young birds was considered much nicer than one with an old hen. Today, chickens are relatively inexpensive and young ones are plentiful year-round, but the downside is that these mass-produced birds do not have as much flavor.

Well, whatever. No matter that the birds have become plentiful and less flavorful; never mind that fast food restaurants have turned our Sunday luxury into a weekday quick and cheap meal. Wherever chickens are still fried in the world—and in whatever way that they are fried, whether in deep fat in a pot, in shallow fat in an iron skillet, or in very little fat in a wok—we have never tired of them. From ancient India, where chickens may have originated, to the modern South, where we like to think the bird has been perfected, fried chicken might arguably be called the world's favorite food.

These recipes are a few of the world's favorite ways to make it.

Acknowledgments

It is no accident that two of the chapter titles of this book are swimming pool puns. Beginning this book was like stepping off into the deep end of a pool without knowing much more than how to float. Southern fried chicken, I can handle (and darn well, thank you very much), but branching out into other cuisines was another story. Without a lot of help, advice, and guidance, I probably would have drowned in lard by now. As always, thanks to my editor, Harriet Bell, who made hard work seem like play, and to my agents, Elise and Arnold Goodman, for staying with me and behind me.

As I grow as a food writer, so does the number of professionals that I am privileged to know and respect, but Karen Hess and John Martin Taylor remain the foundation and inspiration for everything that I do. Karen opened her library to me, and John was never too busy with his own work to stop and give me advice on sources and techniques. John's *The Fearless Frying Cookbook* has been my textbook for the last oil-slicked year.

My thanks also to the many cooks who took the time to talk about their own fried chicken traditions, including Joan Cobitz, Jack Coburn (who also opened his own library), Nita Dixon, Chi Ezekwueche, Jim Fobel, Mary Ellen Greenwood, Vertemae Grosvenor, Jessica B. Harris, Marie Huntington, Zarela Martinez, Anne Mendelson, Marie Rudisill, and Michele Scicolone. My parents helped me piece together my grandmother's Sunday fried chicken (and we got very close), still my standard for the best.

The folks at Han Me Oriental Foods here in Savannah were very patient with me and my bad pronunciation as I learned about, and came in looking for, the Asian ingredients that were foreign to my experience as a Southern cook.

Several patient friends helped taste and critique all this chicken, but Jim King sampled almost every one of the test runs, and only twice said "Not chicken again!"

The Chicken Fryer's Kitchen

Before you tackle frying a chicken, there are a few things that you need to know about frying in general, especially if you have never done much of it before. In this chapter we'll review frying basics—the necessary equipment, the techniques (none of which are complicated), the ingredients, and a few hints and tricks of the fry-cook's trade.

EQUIPMENT

The only real equipment you "need" to fry chicken is a deep cast-iron skillet. And a heat source. If you know how to handle the former and control the latter, you can successfully execute just about every recipe in this book—even the stir-fries. There are, however, a few things that make the job easier. This is not, naturally, a comprehensive kitchen equipment list. I'm assuming you are already equipped with the basics.

First, it is not essential to own an electric deep-fat fryer to successfully fry chicken (or anything else). Commercial kitchens all have special deep-fat fryers because they fry huge quantities of food and must keep large amounts of grease clean and hot for hours at a time. Unless you fry food in huge quantities every day as a restaurant would, you really don't need a deep-fat fryer. Just make sure that you have a good exhaust system over your range, or set up an outdoor area where you can fry without worrying about grease and odors. I almost never deep-fry indoors.

Home deep fryers are convenient, however, since they usually have a thermostat, and many of them have filtration systems that keep that greasy steam from getting all over your house. Their advantage is that the thermostat makes controlling the temperature of the fat easier. However, don't take for granted that the thermostat is accurate. Test it with a candy thermometer that you know is correct (to test a thermometer's accuracy, see Thermometer, page 4) and adjust accordingly. I find it easier to regulate a deep fryer by keeping a thermometer in the fat while frying.

Regardless of whether you invest in (or have already invested in) an electric deep fryer, here are a few other basics.

CAST-IRON AND OTHER SKILLETS: Cast-iron is the best for Southern fried chicken and for pan-frying in small amounts of fat. The poor conductivity of the metal means that the pans are slow to heat up; but once heated, they hold a steady temperature more evenly than any other cookware. I have an array of different sizes from 14 to 6 inches in diameter. If you only have room for one or two, settle on one large skillet (at least 12, but preferably 14 inches in diameter). Anything smaller than 12 inches won't be large enough to fry a whole chicken at once. It should be at least 2½ inches deep.

Enameled cast iron is fine for braising and baking, but I prefer regular cast iron for frying. Stainless steel, copper, and aluminum pans should have very heavy bottoms (thin pans almost guarantee that food will stick to them and they don't heat evenly). Never use uncoated aluminum or copper with acidic food. That usually isn't a problem with frying, unless you are finishing a sauté with wine, vinegar, tomatoes, or lemon juice. In that case, make sure that the pan you use is nonreactive or, if it is coated with a nonstick or tin surface, that this coating is intact.

Many professional cooks like French steel frying pans for their durability, low conductivity, and relatively light weight. They must be seasoned like a cast-iron pan.

Seasoning and caring for a cast-iron pan: To season a new cast-iron pan, preheat the oven to 275°F. Wash the pan thoroughly with soapy water. Rinse it well, dry it, and rub the entire inside surface with lard, olive, or peanut oil. Put the pan in the oven for an hour. Turn off the oven and let the pan sit in it until the oven is cold, or overnight. Wipe out the pan, rub it with fresh fat, and repeat this process. The pan is now ready to use for frying and will get better with every batch of chicken that you cook in it.

Never use detergent on a cast-iron pan once it has been seasoned, and never put it in the dishwasher. If food sticks, use a plastic scrubber or a little salt to scrub it loose, then wash the pan in mild soapy water. Wipe it dry and rub the inside with a cloth dipped in lard or olive or peanut oil.

A CAST-IRON DUTCH OVEN: While we're on cast iron, an iron Dutch oven is just about the best deep fryer you'll ever own. It will hold the temperature evenly once it heats up and, unlike an electric deep fryer, can be used for many other cooking jobs—stewing, braising, and baking, for example. Choose a Dutch oven that is at least 5 inches deep and 12 inches in diameter. Any heavy-bottomed pot of similar size can be used for deep-frying if you prefer.

Cast-iron Dutch ovens are seasoned and cared for exactly as you would any other cast-iron pan (see above). Another great way to season one is to use it to render a batch of lard (see page 13 for the method).

SAUTÉ PANS: Though a classic French sauté pan has straight sides, many professional cooks like pans with sloping sides for sautéing. The curved or sloping sides catch the food as you toss it and throw it back toward the center of the pan. Again, look for pans with a heavy bottom. Aluminum and copper make the best sauté pans because they are lightweight and heat up evenly, but both should have a coated interior. The jury is still out on the safety of uncoated aluminum cookware.

WOK: A wok can take up a lot of space in your kitchen. A large sauté pan with a tight-fitting, domed lid will suffice for most of your stir-frying needs. If, however, you stir-fry a lot (and once you get the hang of the technique, you will), a wok is a great thing to have. The advantage is that its broad sloping steel surface not only super-heats, it makes it possible for all the food in the pan to be in constant direct contact with a hot surface, so that it cooks more quickly and evenly.

One caution: In countries where woks are the principal cooking utensil, they do just about everything in it, including deep-frying. If you own a wok and plan to use it for deep-frying, it must have a stable bottom. Because the sides slope up from a very narrow bottom, it can tip easily. Chinese ranges actually are designed with a well for holding the wok. Unless you have such a range, always make sure the wok is set inside a ring stand

and is very stable before you add fat and begin to heat it, and make sure it is safely away from small hands or an elbow that might accidentally jar it. Otherwise, save the wok for stir-fries and use a cast-iron Dutch oven for all your deep-frying.

THERMOMETER: For deep-frying, even if you have an electric fryer with a thermostat, you'll need a reliable frying or candy thermometer, preferably one that can be clamped to the side of the pot. The thermometer should be designed specifically for this use and be made in such a way that the thermometer itself does not touch the pan directly. To test a thermometer for accuracy, dip it into water that has just come to a boil. It should register exactly 212°F.

MISCELLANEOUS TOOLS: In addition to spatulas in a couple of different sizes, you will find it convenient to have a couple of wooden spatulas for tossing stir-fries, a sturdy pair of long-handled tongs, a perforated or wire frying skimmer for lifting out and draining small batches of food, and a deep-frying basket that will fit snugly into the Dutch oven or deep pot that you use for deep-frying. Electric deep fryers usually come with their own basket. You will also need a large wire cooling rack for draining and holding fried food.

If you stir-fry a lot and have a thing for authenticity, you may want a pair of kitchen chopsticks (they're larger than the ones you eat with, and are sometimes tied together at the top), but a couple of spatulas and a good set of tongs answer the demands of wok cooking just fine.

A few of the recipes in this book call for chicken to be soaked in an acidic marinade (lemon juice, wine, vinegar, buttermilk, and so forth). You will need a large glass or non-reactive stainless steel bowl for this process.

TECHNIQUES

Chances are, if you cook at all, you already know more about frying than you think you do. It does not require any special technique on the part of the cook. In spite of the fact that the word "fry" originally derived from boiling or frothing liquid, frying is nonetheless a dry heat (moistureless) cooking method. In most cases, the outside moisture vaporizes the instant it hits the fat, which is why the food "sizzles" when you first put it into a pan, but subsides after a minute or two. Deep-frying cooks food faster than moist-heat methods because the food is surrounded by heat that is more than a hundred degrees hotter than boiling water or steam (vaporized water). Pan-frying, sautéing, and stir-frying are usually done at temperatures that are well above the boiling point as well.

This means that the cooking goes very quickly and the heat, though intense, does not have to be maintained for more than a few minutes. That makes it an especially attractive medium where fuel is expensive or where the ambient temperature makes long, slow moist-heat processes like braising, baking (yes, baking), and stewing less feasible.

Here are a few notes and tips on the basic techniques involved in frying food. They apply universally—whether you are frying chicken or broccoli—with few exceptions; there are no special frying rules for each different type of food. We'll begin with the lightweight or shallow-end frying technique—sautéing—and work up to the deep pool stuff: deep-frying.

SAUTÉING: Many of our commonplace kitchen terms are French, and this is one of them. *Sauter* in this case (it has other meanings in France besides, but never mind) means "to jump" and that is exactly what happens in the pan. There is debate about whether sauté is derived from actually tossing the food or because the food jumps from the heat, but we can leave that to the etymologists. For our purposes here, in sautéing the food is tossed in the pan with a little fat. Professional cooks often prefer a pan with sloping sides that catch the food as the pan is jerked and throw it back into the center. Sauté can also designate a kind of light pan-frying, where the food has to be turned and cooked one side at a time; again, professional cooks will often flip the food by tossing the pan.

For home cooks, such time-saving maneuvers are not as important. The tossing maneuver for sautéing is not complicated, though it does take getting used to. The pan is jerked firmly toward you, throwing the food to the back of the pan. The lip of the sloping side catches it and tosses it back toward the center. If you've never done this, practice it in a dry pan with some large dried beans before you start trying to toss hot food around, and keep your arm and body protected and well away from the edge of the pan in case something gets tossed over the side. If the movement still intimidates you, or if you aren't able to lift and jerk the pan, don't worry about it. Just keep the food tossed with a spatula or wooden spoon, scooping and flipping it as often as indicated by the recipe. The end result will be the same.

As a rule, very little fat is involved in sautéing, and its principal job is not so much to carry the heat (as in deep-frying) as it is to add flavor and lubrication. It keeps the food gliding smoothly and prevents it from sticking to the bottom of the pan. Oddly enough, sautéed dishes are not usually lighter than deep-fried ones, since a proper deep-fry sears the outer surface and seals out most of the fat and, after frying, the fat is carefully drained away, whereas the fat of a sauté is an integral part of the final sauce.

STIR-FRYING: Stir-frying, as its name implies, is the Eastern version of sautéing. The food is constantly moving in the pan. Occasionally, a little liquid will be introduced to the wok, and the wok may be covered briefly for a quick steaming at the end, but the real action is in the tossing stage. The food itself is cut up into bite-sized pieces, not only because it is easier to eat with chopsticks, but because it cooks more evenly. It's critical to keep things moving. The heat for stir-frying is lively and intense, and if the food sits still, it cooks unevenly and can't burn on the bottom. Consequently, stir-frying requires all the cook's attention while it is going on, but it goes very quickly. There are no special techniques for stir-frying, but you will find a few tips on the process on pages 129 to 131.

PAN-FRYING: This is a generic term that gets applied to anything from a sauté to frying in enough fat to half-cover the food, cooking first one side and then the other. What a lot of people call pan-frying more accurately might be called pan-broiling. A fatty food is added to a dry pan, or a steak or similar food is added to a super-heated, virtually dry pan to sear the outside quickly and evenly. Neither of these techniques is really frying, though they are a similar dry-heat process. For our purposes here, when I refer to pan-frying, it means frying in a skillet or frying pan with the food half-submerged in the fat.

DEEP-FRYING: Deep-fat frying means that the food cooks completely submerged in boiling fat. The heat is transferred through the fat directly to all sides of the food, cooking it quickly and evenly. Deep-fat fried food should never be greasy; when properly done, the outside of the food caramelizes almost instantly, sealing out the heating fat and sealing in the succulent juices.

Deep-frying requires caution and a certain amount of care on the part of the cook, but it doesn't require any special skill. Even if you have never done much frying, if you follow a few rules and pay attention to what is going on in the pot, you'll be frying like a pro in no time.

1 Be prepared. Everything should be ready to go before you begin heating the fat for frying. Also, especially if it's an unfamiliar dish, it's a good idea to read through the

entire recipe both before you start the preparation, and after you are ready to begin heating up the fat. Once the grease is hot, it won't wait for you to figure things out.

2 Use the right equipment (page 2). You need a deep heavy-bottomed pan that will hold enough fat to completely cover the food you are cooking and give it plenty of room both to move around and to be constantly surrounded by fat. Never, ever, use a pan that is smaller than your heat source as splatters or accidental spills could cause a fire, and never fill that pan more than half full of fat. Keep in mind that the fat level will rise as the fat is displaced by the food, and it will bubble up as the moisture evaporates. If you introduce too much food into the pot and it looks as if the fat is going to boil over, lift the food out of the fat at once, using a fryer basket or skimmer, and re-introduce it in smaller batches.

3 Use good, clean fat. This is no place to be cheap with inexpensive oil or old grease that you have used repeatedly for frying. Though frying fat often can be used more than once, its smoking point is lowered every time it gets heated, which means that every time you use it, it becomes less stable and cannot get as hot as it did before without burning. Not only will it give a burned taste to the food and transfer absorbed flavors from the last batch of whatever you fried, more of the fat will be absorbed into the food, making it taste heavy and greasy.

4 Keep firm control over the fat. The heat must be steady, but don't let the fat begin to smoke. Frying fats, like any other organic substance, will burn, most of them at temperatures higher than 375° to 450°F. If the fat begins smoking, it is beginning to burn. The next stage will be heavy smoke, closely followed by a burst of flames. Don't wait for that to happen: Take it off the heat at once and let it cool—then throw it away. If you try to reuse fat that has begun smoking, it will be far more likely to burn at a lower temperature, and will make the fried food taste heavy and burned. If, by the way, you ever have a grease fire, turn off the heat and quickly cover the pan with a tight-fitting lid. Do not try to douse the flame or put it out with a fire extinguisher, since it could splatter and spread. And don't try to move the pan; you could seriously burn yourself if it splatters.

But while it is critical to prevent the fat from burning, it is equally important to maintain a steady high temperature. Usually the fat is heated to a temperature that is slightly higher than the maintained temperature for frying, so that the food doesn't cool it down too much when it is added to the pan. That's especially critical with chicken, which is generally in large pieces when it is introduced to the fat. If, for example, the temperature at which you need to fry chicken is 365°F, the fat should be at around 375° to 385°F when you introduce the chicken.

Use a candy or deep-fry thermometer (see page 4) to monitor the temperature, modulating the heat to keep it at the proper temperature. Put the thermometer into the fat before you start heating it. It should be completely suspended in the fat, and should not touch the pot at any point; otherwise, you'll be getting the temperature of the metal of the pot, not the fat.

Note: Even if you have a thermostatically controlled deep-fryer, it is still a good idea to monitor the temperature with a reliable thermometer.

5 Add the food a little at a time, always in a single layer, and never crowd the pan. Overcrowding could cause the fat to boil over, lower the overall temperature of the fat too much, causing the fat to be absorbed into the food, or keep the food from cooking evenly both because of uneven contact with the fat and because you have created hot and cool spots.

Don't put a great pile of food that you are planning to fry (like an entire chicken) in a fryer basket and lower it into the boiling fat all at once. This is inviting disaster. The fat could easily boil over and the food, especially if it is covered with batter, may stick to the fryer basket and to the other pieces of food surrounding it. It is better to lower an empty basket into the fat, then add the food a few pieces at a time until you have put in all that can be fried in a single batch, then use the basket to lift it out. There are exceptions to this, the second frying for french fries, for example; but as a general practice, it is the way to go.

6 Lift the food from the fat with tongs, a wire or perforated skimmer, or the fry basket. Don't use a fork, which will pierce the food, or a spoon—even a slotted spoon—since they retain too much of the fat.

7 Always drain the fried food thoroughly and keep it warm. Fried food should always be greaseless and is almost always served hot. (The exception is occasions when fried chicken is served at room temperature or cold at picnics and family reunions.) Since home equipment is seldom large enough to fry a complete recipe all at once, you'll need to keep the first batch warm while the second one fries. Before you start frying, set the oven at 150°F (or Warm setting) as a matter of routine, and have ready a wire rack set on a cookie sheet.

Hold the food over the fat until it is no longer dripping, then transfer it to the wire rack and hold it in the warm oven while you fry the second batch. In a few instances, I call for the food to be blotted briefly on absorbent paper. Where that is the case, briefly is the operative word. Don't let the food sit on the paper or it will draw out the internal moisture and make the bottom crust soggy.

INGREDIENTS

When a group of Southerners come together and talk about fried chicken, you will usually hear a lively debate about such things as the *"only proper"* marinade, spices and other seasonings, breading, and fat. Seldom is the most important ingredient in fried chicken ever debated—that is, the bird itself. But if it isn't very good to begin with, no amount of art will make it good when it comes to the table.

Choosing and Handling the Bird

In all cases, a young chicken is the choice for frying. There was a time when fried chicken was strictly seasonal, that is, it could only be made when there were very young birds (weighing under 2 pounds) around. This was mostly in the spring and summer breeding season, which is where that expression about "spring chickens" came from. Older, more mature birds can't be fried because their muscles are too large and tough. An old stewing hen or a barnyard rooster will have to be slow-baked or stewed to be tender. Asian and Middle Eastern cooks compensate for this by employing a twice-cooked method; they steam or stew an older bird to make it tender and then fry it.

Today, commercial birds are bred year-round and have an accelerated youth; that is, they are much larger than a naturally raised or "free-range" chicken would be at the same age. You will have trouble finding a commercial bird weighing less than 2 pounds—even less than 3. But use the smallest chickens you can, since smaller birds cook more quickly and evenly, and for frying, that is preferable. If you can get true free-range chickens, they are worth the price.

The chicken should be very fresh, with clear, pink-white (not yellowish) skin. It should not smell or have yellow or gray-looking flesh. Try to use chickens that have never been frozen. Chicken stands up fairly well to freezing, but it loses flavor and some

Chicken Safety The USDA's recommendations for the safe handling of poultry have become more stringent as a result of outbreaks of salmonella and other food-borne bacterial contaminants. To be absolutely safe, all poultry should be well cooked. The guidelines recommend that the meat should reach an internal temperature of 180°F. when measured with a meat thermometer at the thickest part of the thigh. Careful handling before the bird goes into the fat is just as important as making certain that the chicken is thoroughly cooked.

All poultry is susceptible to airborne contaminants. Keep raw poultry well chilled. USDA guidelines recommend never leaving the poultry out at room temperature for any length of time. After handling the raw poultry, always thoroughly wash your hands and any surface or tool that has touched the poultry (knives, cutting boards, sink, etc.) with soap and hot water. Scrub porous cutting boards with a disinfectant. And whatever you do, don't let the cooked chicken or any other foods come into contact with a surface where raw chicken has been.

texture in the process. If you must freeze chicken, thaw it slowly in the refrigerator, and never keep it in the freezer for more than two months.

With salmonella becoming the health buzzword of the decade, I caution you not to be careless with the bird. Don't leave it sitting out at room temperature. If marinating, put it in the refrigerator. Use the chicken within a day or two (and no more than three days) of buying it. Always wash the bird well inside and out with running water, and wash your hands and work surfaces with a disinfectant, such as vinegar or an antibacterial cleanser, after you have handled raw chicken. Finally, make sure that the chicken is cooked well. Salmonella bacteria die when the meat reaches an internal temperature of 165°F.

CUTTING, DISJOINTING, AND BONING TECHNIQUES: Though most markets sell cut-up chickens and packages of individual parts and boneless breast fillets, it is useful to know how to cut up a bird yourself. Not only is it cheaper, markets seldom do a good job of cutting the bird into the right portions. Moreover, you'll never feel at a loss when you are confronted with a whole bird.

Cutting up a chicken is very easy; joints in the muscle and fat leave natural guidelines that show you exactly where to cut. Once you get the hang of it, you'll be able to cut up a whole bird in about 2 minutes. I know chefs who can do it in less than half that time. For many of the recipes in this book, skinning the chicken is optional; however, for several of them, the skin must remain intact, as it acts as a natural casing to protect the inner flesh or hold in a stuffing.

There are two basic ways of cutting up a chicken. Both employ disjointing, but in the Far East, cooks go a step further and chop the disjointed parts into smaller pieces so that it cooks more quickly. This method is occasionally used in the West (in Italy, for example), but it is more prevalent in Southeast Asia, India, and China.

DISJOINTING THE CHICKEN: Outside the United States, and even in some ethnic markets in our country, chickens are often sold with the head and feet still attached. Most of our birds have already been trimmed of these parts. If you have a whole bird, cut the neck just above the shoulders, leaving the flap of skin at the crop intact. Remove the feet from the leg at the joint between the scaly skin and the drumstick. If the bird is already trimmed, begin by removing the packet containing the giblets and neck and set it aside for broth. Lay the chicken flat on its back on the work surface and bend back a leg. Under the skin, you will see a line where the thigh muscles join the hip. Cut through this line, bend back, cut through the hip joint, and remove the entire leg. Lay it flat, outer side down. You'll see another line between the muscles of the thigh and drumstick, marking the joint. Cut through it with a cleaver or heavy chef's knife. Set the thighs and drumsticks aside. The wings have a similar ball joint at the shoulder. Cut through it, and set the wings aside with the leg pieces. The rib cage of the bird has joints up both sides where the back and breast rib bones meet. Cut through these joints and bend back the breast until the joints at the shoulder are exposed. Separate them with a cleaver or chef's knife.

CUTTING UP A DISJOINTED CHICKEN WESTERN-STYLE: Turn the breast skin side up on the work surface. At the collarbone is the little Y-shaped bone that we call the wishbone. Southern cooks usually cut this piece out as a separate treat. Reach under the collarbone and feel for the joint of the bones. Cut through them with a sharp knife, then find the joint at the neck end of the keel bone. Cut straight down and then cut the meat away from the collarbone. Turn the breast over and, using a cleaver or heavy chef's knife, chop through the center breast or keel bone and its long, pointed cartilage. Now take the cleaver or knife and cut each breast half in half crosswise. If you are using a very small bird, you may elect to leave the breast halves in one piece. Many traditional cooks split the back crosswise in halves and fry it, too, but most modern cooks put the backs and necks into the stockpot.

Your bird is now ready to be fried in any of the recipes calling for chicken "cut up for frying."

CUTTING UP A DISJOINTED CHICKEN CHINESE-STYLE: Do not skin the chicken. Using a heavy cleaver, chop the drumsticks and thighs in half crosswise (this is also sometimes done lengthwise down the center of the bone). Chop the wings into drumettes by chopping through the joints. Chop the breast in half, and then chop each half crosswise into 3 or 4 pieces about 1 inch thick. Chop the meaty parts of the back into 1-inch by 2-inch pieces. Remove any loose bone splinters and discard them. Chinese cooks use every scrap of the bird, but you may set aside the wing tips, bony back parts, neck, and giblets for broth.

The chicken is now ready to be used in any of the recipes calling for chicken "cut up Chinese-style."

Note: In some Chinese recipes, the chicken is not disjointed, but is chopped so that the joints remain intact. Instructions for this method are included with the specific recipe.

BONING: A number of recipes in this book call for boneless breasts or thighs or drumsticks. Though boneless breasts are widely available, thighs and drumsticks are seldom sold boneless, so you will need to do this yourself. And while boneless breasts are widely available, it is still useful to know how to bone them yourself.

It is easier to bone a whole breast than one that has been split at the keel bone, but if you are buying breasts in packages, they will probably be split. If you don't need the skin to remain intact for the given recipe, then work your fingers underneath it to loosen the connective membrane and then pull the skin off. If the breast is whole, work the flesh loose from the ribs with a fillet knife and your fingers, beginning on the sides. When the flesh is loosened all the way to the keel bone, scrape it away from the center bone and the collar and wishbone, then pull it off the pointed, nose-shaped piece of cartilage. You will now have both lobes of the breast with their "tenders" (a feather-shaped muscle that lies against the rib) still attached to them. If the breasts are to be used whole, just trim away the fat and leave the connective cartilage that runs down the center intact. Otherwise, cut along either side of this cartilage and discard it.

To bone a split breast, start at the keel bone side, cutting it away from the bone and cartilage, then the collar and wishbone, then scrape and pull it away from the ribs. In most of the recipes, it won't matter if the breast has been split into halves and the tenders have been removed.

When you are boning the thighs and legs, if they are to be skinned for a specific recipe, it should be done first. Slip your fingers under the skin and loosen the connective tissue, then pull it off. To bone the thigh, place it skin-side down on a cutting board. You'll see a line running vertically down the inside where the fat and muscle tissue connect to the bone. Cut along this line and then cut the flesh away from the hip ball joint, exposing the bone. Scrape downward until all the muscle has been loosened from the bone, then cut it away from the knee joint. To bone the drumstick, put it skin-side down on the cutting board. Cut along the vertical line in the joint of the fat and muscle, then scrape the flesh from the bone beginning at the small end and working toward the large knee joint. There are two bones in this part of the leg—the large drumstick and a thin needle-like bone running parallel to it. Be careful to remove the smaller bone, too. Finally cut the flesh loose from the knee joint and trim away any excess fat. The leg meat is now ready to be cup up and used as directed in the individual recipes.

12

The Frying Fat:

The most usual fats for pan- or deep-frying chicken are lard (rendered fresh pork fat) and some type of vegetable oil. The most usual fats for sautés are those that are loaded with flavor—butter, olive oil, and rendered bacon fat. Each has its own advantages and disadvantages.

ANIMAL FATS: Lard, clarified butter, and rendered beef or chicken fat are the most commonplace animal fats used for frying. They are not as frequently used for deep-fat frying as they once were when animal fat and olive oil were pretty much the only fats available. Beef and rendered chicken fat are almost never used for frying chicken; lard and clarified butter are used both for frying and sautéing.

LARD: For Southern fried chicken, lard, or rendered pork fat, is the best and most traditional fat. No other fat will give you the right crispness or flavor. Look for it in butcher shops or markets that either make their own or sell fresh, clean lard without preservatives. It should be creamy white, with a pleasant, slightly oily smell. If the package has brown splotches, it means the lard has been stored at too high a temperature and will probably be rancid. The best insurance for quality is to render your own.

RENDERING LARD: Wash and pat dry 4 pounds of fresh pork fat (preferably leaf fat from the saddle around the kidneys). Cut it into small dice or put it through a meat grinder (if you have one, or see if the butcher will do this for you). Place the fat in a deep, heavy-bottomed pan such as a cast-iron Dutch oven. Over low heat, let it cook until the fat is dissolved and the solids sink to the bottom. When the solids turn brown, turn off the heat, lift them out with a skimmer, and drain them well on absorbent paper. These are the cracklings, which can be used in place of shortening as a flavorful addition to Southern cornbread and certain kinds of Italian and French country loaves. Let the lard cool enough to handle and strain it into a clean container with a tight-fitting lid.

BUTTER AND CLARIFIED BUTTER: Use the best that you can find. Where the flavor of browned butter is critical to a sauté, the butter is used whole. The solids that it contains will brown and add flavor and color to the dish. But sometimes, one wants the flavor of butter without the caramelized taste of the solids, or else, the butter needs to be heated to a high temperature. In this case, clarified butter is used. Clarified butter is simply butter from which all the milk solids and liquids have been removed. Since the solids have a much lower burning temperature than the pure fat, clarifying raises the burning temperature of butter, making it possible to fry with it at much higher temperatures than with whole butter. It is the classic fat for breaded Milanese cutlets. It is also useful for high-temperature sautés where the flavor of browned butter is not essential or desirable.

TO CLARIFY BUTTER: Put unsalted butter in a heavy-bottomed pan over low heat and heat until it is completely melted, but don't let it bubble up or begin to brown. As soon as it is melted, turn off the heat and let it sit in a warm spot for a few minutes. The solids and any whey that the butter may contain will sink to the bottom of the pan. Carefully pour the fat into a container with a tight-fitting lid, making sure that the solids remain in the pan. Discard the solids, or use them for flavoring other dishes where fat isn't important.

The solid and moisture content of American butter can vary wildly, but in general, you can count on losing about an eighth of the volume in the process. In other words, 1 stick (8 tablespoons) of butter will produce about 7 tablespoons when clarified; a pound (2 cups) will produce about 1¾ cups.

VEGETABLE OILS: Of all vegetable oils, probably the best-known and most ancient (at least in the West) is olive oil. I love extra virgin olive oil and use it frequently for sautéing, broiling, for drizzling over cooked vegetables or fish, or as the simplest and most sublime dipping sauce imaginable. It has a distinctive flavor that varies from country to country, region to region, and often within regions, depending on the olives, the soil conditions, and a number of other factors. For sautéing, where the flavor of the fat is important, use the best quality extra virgin oil you can afford. For stir-frying, I prefer peanut oil but any vegetable oil is suitable.

For deep-frying, however, using an extra virgin oil is an extravagance that few of us could afford. Many Mediterranean cooks therefore use cheaper, lesser grades of olive oil for frying. Peanut oil has a higher smoking point than most other oils and animal fats, a mild but distinctive flavor, and gives fried food a crispness that no other fat except possibly lard can quite duplicate. However, you may use any vegetable oil that you prefer for any of the deep-frying recipes in this book that don't call for a specific fat.

14

Batters, Meals, Crumbs, and Other Breadings

There are two reasons to coat food that is to be fried. The first and most obvious is to create a protective shell on the outside of the food to seal it and keep it from absorbing fat. The second is to provide a dry surface. Foods that are fried without a coating (such as french fried potatoes, potato chips, and some of the chicken recipes in this book) must be perfectly dry when they go into the fat, or they'll boil up too much and the outside won't sear and caramelize properly. The results will be limp and greasy, not crispy.

The simplest coating is a dusting of flour, meal, or a similar starch (such as cornstarch or potato starch). The moisture of the food reacts with the coating, creating a paste. The paste dries and caramelizes when it hits the hot fat, sealing the outer surface. For many foods, including chicken, this light coating is sufficient.

For dusting flour, any all-purpose flour will work, but I prefer unbleached flour because I think it browns better. For cornmeal dusting, use fine, preferably stone-ground cornmeal or corn flour.

More delicate foods, such as vegetables, and foods that are naturally rather dry often need a more substantial coating. In such cases, the food is dipped in an egg wash and then rolled in breading: dry bread crumbs, nuts, cheese mixed with crumbs, and powdered cracker or matzoh meal. Breadings give fried foods a lively crunch and are common to most of the world's cuisines.

MAKING YOUR OWN CRUMBS: Crumb breadings are available ready-made, and they will work in any of the recipes in this book, but once you take the trouble to make your own, you will never be satisfied with commercial crumbs again. Save the ends and leftover bits of rolls and crusty French loaves, store them in the freezer until you have enough, and grate them with a box grater or in a food processor fitted with a steel blade. For cracker or matzoh meal, put the crackers or matzoh between 2 layers of wax paper or into a ziplock bag and crush them with a rolling pin, or pulverize them in the food processor as you would bread crumbs. Directions for making other crumb mixtures are included in the individual recipes that call for them.

BATTERS AND DOUGHS: The exception to the rule requiring a dry surface are batters and doughs, both of which can be very wet indeed. A batter, in fact, is always thin enough to pour and is sometimes poured directly into the pan and fried all by itself. But while batter coatings are thin, they are still thick enough to make a solid covering, and the moisture evaporates immediately, leaving behind a crisp shell that completely seals the outer surface.

Most batters are made by beating eggs with flour or a similar starch and sometimes another liquid. The character of the batter is determined by the kind of starch, the kind of liquid (milk reacts differently than wine, wine than water, and so forth), and whether or not some kind of leavening is introduced—egg whites beaten separately and added just before frying, beer or wine, and sometimes yeast or baking powder. These last make the batter puff up spectacularly, resulting in an airy coating that is very crisp and delicate. The recipes for individual batters are included in the recipes that use them.

BROTH: The foundation of a good gravy and the essential moisture of many sautés and stir-fries, good broth may seem to have nothing to do with frying, per se, but it is a critical element in many a fried-chicken meal. Canned and frozen commercial broths are a convenience, but for the best flavor, color, and texture, there is no substitute for homemade broth. Whenever I am cooking a chicken, whether I'm frying, roasting, or poaching it, the scraps are always put to use in a pot of broth on the back of the range.

Why is the breading sometimes put into a bag, sometimes a bowl?

Well, when a coarse breading, such as bread crumbs, nuts, or seeds, is used, the breading has to be patted into the surface of the chicken; the breading wouldn't be evenly distributed if it were shaken onto the bird in a bag. The answer is less obvious when the breading is a powder such as flour, cornstarch, or fine meal, but it's no less simple. When the bird is rolled in the breading in a bowl, the coating will be lighter than it will be if it is shaken together with the bird in a bag. When a lighter breading is required, then, it goes into a bowl and the chicken is lightly rolled in it; when one wants a more substantial coating, it goes into a bag. So wherever the recipe calls for one method, follow it for best results.

Quick Broth

THE BEST BROTH is simmered for a long time and jellies handsomely when cold, but when you are caught short, this quick broth makes a fine substitute and still tastes better than canned broth. It can be made with the giblet packet and scrap pieces from a whole chicken, or you can pick up an extra package of backs or necks to throw into the pot. The more meat and bones you have, the quicker the broth will be flavored.

It must simmer for at least 45 minutes; however, you can put the broth on first and let it cook while you prepare and cook the remainder of the meal. Or put it on the night before, refrigerate overnight, and skim and strain it the next morning.

MAKES ABOUT 1 QUART

The giblet packet (including the neck) from a whole fryer, plus the back and any other scrap pieces, or 1 pound backs or wing tips left over from chicken drumettes (page 88)

1 large yellow onion, thinly sliced

1 large carrot, thinly sliced

1 large celery rib, including the leafy top, strung and thinly sliced

1 quarter-sized fresh ginger slice

2 large garlic cloves, lightly crushed but left whole

1 cup green leek tops, sliced thin (optional)

6 whole black peppercorns

3 whole cloves

1 large parsley sprig (at least 3 inches leafy top)

1 large thyme sprig (at least 3 inches leafy top)

1 bay leaf

Salt

one Combine all the ingredients in a 3-quart pot with a couple of large pinches of salt. Add 5 cups cold water and bring it to the boiling point over medium-high heat, but before it breaks into a full boil, reduce the heat to medium-low. Let simmer for at least 45 minutes or as much as 1½ to 2 hours, if you have the time.

two Turn off the heat. Let the broth settle for 2 or 3 minutes, then carefully strain it through a wire-mesh sieve. Let the fat come to the surface and skim away as much of it as possible. Quick Broth will keep for several days, covered, in the refrigerator.

NOTE: It's better to strain the broth, but I'm very lazy on this point. Sometimes, when I'm short of time, I just dip it directly from the pot with a ladle.

Chicken Broth

FORTUNATELY, INEXPENSIVE SCRAPS are the best choice for making broth, and packages of necks and backs are usually available in the market. Wing tips (left over from making chicken drumettes; see page 88) and feet (unfortunately, hard to find) produce the best jelly. When using fatty scraps, don't trim off the excess fat. It'll help flavor the broth. It can be easily skimmed off if you strain the broth and chill it until the fat solidifies on top.

MAKES ABOUT 4 QUARTS

5 pounds chicken scraps and bones

2 large yellow onions, 1 thinly sliced, the other left whole, then stuck with 4 whole cloves

2 large carrots, thickly sliced

2 large celery ribs, including the leafy tops

1 large leek, split and sliced (including the green top)

3 to 4 large garlic cloves, lightly crushed but left whole

2 quarter-sized fresh ginger slices

1 large parsley sprig (at least 3 inches of leafy stalk)

1 large thyme sprig (at least 3 inches long)

2 bay leaves

8 whole black peppercorns

2 tablespoons salt

one Combine all the ingredients in an 8-quart kettle and add 5 quarts of cold water. Cover loosely. Over low heat, bring the broth slowly to a simmer—it will take 30 to 45 minutes.

two Adjust the heat so that the liquid simmers very slowly, the bubbles not quite breaking the surface of the broth. With the pot lid askew, let the broth simmer for a minimum of 2 hours; 3 or 4 hours will only improve it.

three Turn off the heat and let the broth settle for 30 minutes. Strain it carefully through a wire-mesh sieve and let it cool completely. Cover and refrigerate until the broth is jellied and the fat on the surface is congealed. Skim off the fat before using the broth. It will keep for up to a week in the refrigerator, indefinitely if frozen in small portions.

Okay, those are the basics. As you can see, there is nothing mysterious or complicated about the process. Though only practice will make you a great fry-cook, it doesn't require any special skill to be a good one. All it requires of you is a little care and attention. As with playing a piano or a decent game of tennis, practice is the only thing standing between you and great fried chicken. So don't be afraid of it: Roll up your sleeves, tie on an apron, and let's get started.

You're ready to do some serious frying.

BATTERED BIRD

Batter-frying seems like a contradiction. The purpose of a coating on the outside of fried food is to create a dry surface to hold the juices in and keep the grease out. Yet a batter coating is very wet indeed. This seeming contradiction is easily explained: The moisture in the batter vaporizes almost immediately and is quickly carried away from the outer surface by the boiling fat. This quick vaporization causes the solids in the batter to harden and caramelize, forming a crisp shell that effectively encapsulates the food. Rather than relying on the moisture in the chicken's flesh to bind the coating, the batter provides its own moisture, and the chicken remains exceptionally juicy. The exploding moisture also makes the solids of the batter expand, creating a light, lacy coating on the chicken—the most elegant finish imaginable.

Because of the extra moisture, however, more care is needed when you are frying with a batter. Add the chicken carefully, one piece at a time, and allow the fat to settle between each addition. Don't overcrowd the pan: You could cause the fat to boil over and if the pieces of chicken touch, the batter will stick them to one another like glue.

The following recipes are only a small sample of the batter-fried repertory. There are literally hundreds of variations from all around the globe. Choosing the best was no easy job. Aside from this sampling, other great batters that are included elsewhere in this book include Southern Batter-Fried Chicken (page 100), Golden Coin Chicken (page 80), Beer-Battered Chicken Drumettes (page 88), and Sesame Chicken Fingers (page 84).

Florentine Fried Chicken

Pollo Fritto alla Fiorentina

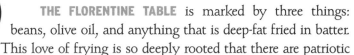 THE FLORENTINE TABLE is marked by three things: beans, olive oil, and anything that is deep-fat fried in batter. This love of frying is so deeply rooted that there are patriotic Florentines who claim it to have been practically invented in their city. As is true of Southern-fried chicken, there's no single, definitive recipe for *pollo fritto alla fiorentina*. There are as many versions as there are Florentine cooks. The breading ranges from the simplicity of a light coating of flour and beaten egg to a complex fritter batter laced with nutmeg and white wine. Cooking teacher Lorenza dei Medici insists that what sets a Florentine *fritto* apart is not so much the batter as it is the fat—extra virgin olive oil—but many cooks use a less expensive oil.

When boneless pieces of chicken are fried in this manner and mixed with batter-fried calves' brains, lamb chops, rabbit, sweetbreads, trimmed artichoke wedges, zucchini, and zucchini blossoms (either all of these or only a few), they compose one of the city's most celebrated dishes, *fritto misto alla fiorentina*.

SERVES 4 TO 6

one Preheat the oven to 150°F (or Warm setting). Fit a wire cooling rack over a cookie sheet and set aside. Sift together the flour, a large pinch of salt, and a grating or so of whole nutmeg into a large mixing bowl. Make a well into the center, add the olive oil, and mix it into the flour. Add and mix in the egg yolks, then the wine, then 1 cup water. Beat the batter thoroughly after each addition. Cover the batter and set it aside at room temperature for at least 2 hours.

two Wash the chicken pieces, pat dry, and remove the skin. If you like, you may bone the chicken pieces, but this isn't necessary. Set aside.

three Fill a deep-fat fryer or cast-iron Dutch oven with oil at least 2 inches deep, but no more than halfway up the sides of the pot. Over medium-high heat, bring the oil to 375°F (hot but not smoking).

four While the oil is heating, beat the reserved egg whites until they form soft peaks and fold them gently into the batter.

five When the oil is very hot, lightly dip the chicken pieces one at a time into the batter, completely coating them. Allow the excess batter to flow back into the bowl. Slip them into the hot fat and cook, maintaining a cooking temperature of 355° to 365°F, until golden brown and the meat is just cooked through, 12 to 15 minutes. (If you have boned the chicken, it should be done in less time—about 8 minutes.)

six Lift the chicken from the fat, drain it briefly on absorbent paper, then transfer the chicken to the wire rack to drain completely. Keep the cooked chicken in the warm oven while you fry the remaining pieces. Arrange the chicken on a serving platter, surround it with the lemon wedges, and serve at once.

NOTE: Arguments over the batter, oil, and seasonings aside, the real secret of a good *fritto* is to serve it piping hot, the instant it comes out of the fat. Plan a simple first course and side dish that won't require any last-minute attention, and have the batter and chicken ready to cook while your guests are letting the first course settle.

You may, if you prefer them, use boneless chicken breasts for this recipe; cut them into strips about 1 inch wide before battering and frying them. They will cook in 3 to 5 minutes.

About 2 cups all-purpose flour
Salt
Whole nutmeg in a grater
¼ cup extra virgin olive oil
2 large eggs, separated
½ cup dry white wine
1 frying chicken, weighing no more than 3 pounds, cut up for frying Chinese-style as on page 11
Peanut or vegetable oil, for frying
2 lemons, cut into wedges

21

French Marinated Batter-Fried Chicken

Poulet en Marinade, Frit

THIS IS THE very old, classic French way of frying chicken, but "marinade" is actually the operative word here: The marinating is more important than the frying. The recipes appear in French cookbooks titled *marinade de poulet* or *poussin en marinade* (marinated spring chicken)—not *poulet frit* (fried chicken). An interesting thing that it tells us is that the Southern method of marinating the chicken in acid (in our case, buttermilk) is very old indeed and probably has European roots. The old recipes marinated the chicken in verjuice—the juice of unripe grapes—but lemon juice is more usual today.

This is a thin batter that makes a delicate, lacy crust on the chicken. When you dip the chicken, the batter will be almost transparent on its surface. However, it shouldn't be too thin or it won't stick. Since the moisture content of flour can vary, you may need a little more than the amount called for here; if the batter seems too thin, sift in a little more flour, a tablespoon at a time. Because of the high moisture content of the batter, the fat will foam up more than usual when you begin frying. The fat must be not quite half the depth of the pot, and the chicken must be added one piece at a time.

SERVES 4

6 to 8 large parsley sprigs

1/2 cup freshly squeezed lemon juice (2 to 3 lemons)

1 small yellow onion, thinly sliced

1 large garlic clove, minced

4 whole cloves, roughly crushed in a mortar or with the flat side of a knife

2 bay leaves, chopped if fresh, crumbled if dried

1 tablespoon chopped fresh thyme or 1 teaspoon dried

Salt and freshly milled black pepper

1 frying chicken, weighing no more than 3 pounds, skinned and cut up for frying as on page 11

1 3/4 cups all-purpose flour

2 cups dry white wine

2 large egg yolks

Lard or peanut or vegetable oil, for frying

1 lemon, cut into wedges

one Wash and thoroughly dry the sprigs of parsley. Set aside in a dry place so that all the moisture can evaporate. Combine the lemon juice, onion, garlic, cloves, bay leaves, thyme, a healthy pinch of salt, and several liberal grindings of pepper in a large nonreactive glass or stainless steel bowl. Stir until the salt is dissolved and the marinade is evenly mixed.

22

two Wash the chicken, pat dry, and add to the marinade. Turn and toss until uniformly coated. Cover and marinate for at least 3 hours, refrigerated, or overnight. Turn the chicken periodically in the marinade to insure an even contact.

three Sift the flour and a healthy pinch or so of salt together into a mixing bowl. Make a well in the center and pour in the wine. Gradually beat the flour into the liquid with a wire whisk until it is incorporated and smooth. Beat in the egg yolks, one at a time. Cover and set aside for at least 30 minutes.

four Fit a wire cooling rack in a cookie sheet and set aside. Fill a Dutch oven or deep-fat fryer with lard or peanut oil to at least 2 inches deep, but no more than halfway up the sides. Over medium-high heat, bring the oil to 375°F (hot but not smoking).

five While the fat is heating, thoroughly drain the marinade from the chicken and pat dry (otherwise the batter won't stick properly).

six When the fat is hot, put in the parsley a sprig at a time and fry until it is crisp but still bright green and the sizzling stops—20 to 30 seconds. Lift it out with a skimmer and drain thoroughly. Dip the chicken pieces, beginning with the thighs, legs, and wings, one at a time in the batter, coating all sides. Let the excess flow back into the bowl and slip the battered chicken carefully into the fat. Repeat with each piece of chicken until the pan is full but not crowded. When all the chicken is in the pot, adjust the temperature to maintain the fat at 325°F and fry, turning once, until the chicken is cooked through and golden brown, about 20 minutes.

seven Lift the chicken from the fat and drain thoroughly on a wire rack. Serve hot, garnished with lemon wedges and the fried parsley.

NOTE: This is better if the chicken can be cooked all at once and served right away, but if you don't have a pot large enough to hold all the chicken at once or you are doing a double batch (double the marinade but not the batter—it should be enough for two batches), keep the cooked chicken warm in a 150°F (or Warm setting) oven on a wire rack set over a cookie sheet.

General Tsao's Chicken

YOU WOULD THINK, with a name as specific as this one, that this popular Western Chinese restaurant dish would have a very specific recipe. It doesn't. About the only constants are the fact of General Tsao, a real Chinese historical figure and poet, and the fact that "his" chicken is battered and deep-fried. Everything else—the Western spelling of the General's name, the marinade, batter, and accompanying hot-sour sauce—varies wildly from cook to cook. Often the chicken is coated with sauce just before serving, but sometimes it isn't. I like the crust to be crispy, and so I prefer to pass the sauce separately.

SERVES 4

1 pound boneless chicken (about 4 boned thighs or 2 large whole breasts), skinned

2 tablespoons soy sauce

2 tablespoons rice vinegar or dark Chinese vinegar

3 tablespoons rice wine

3 quarter-sized fresh ginger slices, minced

3 large garlic cloves, minced

2/3 cup cornstarch

2 teaspoons toasted sesame oil

1 tablespoon Demerara, turbinado, or light brown sugar

Salt

Peanut or vegetable oil, for frying, plus 2 tablespoons for the sauce

1 large egg white

1 to 2 dried small hot red chiles, seeded and julienned

2 tablespoons finely julienned orange zest

4 scallions or other green onions, cut into 1-inch lengths

1/2 cup Chicken Broth (page 18)

one Wash the chicken and pat dry. Cut across the grain into thin strips about ¼ inch thick. Cut the strips into pieces about 1 inch wide by 2 inches long. Combine 1 tablespoon each of the soy sauce, vinegar, and rice wine, half the ginger, and 1 garlic clove in a large nonreactive glass or stainless steel bowl. Add 2 teaspoons of the cornstarch and stir until dissolved. Add the chicken and toss until it is uniformly coated. Marinate for 30 minutes, refrigerated.

two Meanwhile, combine the remaining soy sauce, vinegar, and rice wine with 2 teaspoons of cornstarch and stir until dissolved. Add the sesame oil, sugar, and a large pinch of salt. Stir until the sugar and salt are dissolved and set aside.

three Fit a wire cooling rack over a cookie sheet and set aside. Fill a deep-fat fryer or cast-iron Dutch oven with enough oil to come halfway up the sides. Over medium-high heat, bring the oil to 375°F (hot but not smoking).

24

FRIED CHICKEN

four Meanwhile, beat the egg white until it is frothy. Fold it into the chicken and marinade. Put the remaining cornstarch into a sieve and gradually add enough to the chicken, tossing constantly, to form a thin batter coating. You may not need all of it.

five When the oil is hot, lift the chicken pieces out of the batter, allowing the excess to flow back into the bowl, and slip carefully into the fat. Fry until golden, about 2 minutes. Lift them out, drain thoroughly, and transfer to the rack to finish draining. Turn the heat down to medium.

six Heat a wok or sauté pan over medium-high heat. When it is hot, drizzle in 1 tablespoon of oil around the edges. Add the chiles, remaining ginger, the orange zest, and remaining garlic, one at a time, in that order. Stir and add the scallions. Stir-fry for 30 seconds. Stir the soy mixture to redistribute the cornstarch and add it to the wok. Stir-fry until thickened, then gradually add the broth. Continue cooking, stirring constantly, until thick, about a minute more. Remove it from the heat, taste, and adjust the seasonings.

seven Raise the heat under the frying pot to medium high and reheat the oil to 375°F. Put the chicken back into the oil and fry until very crisp and golden brown, 1 to 2 minutes more. Drain thoroughly and transfer to the wire rack to finish draining. Toss the chicken in the sauce or pass them separately.

Demerara or Turbinado Sugar These are partially refined cane sugars, sometimes labeled "raw" sugar. They are not the same product as regular brown sugar, which is fully refined white sugar with molasses added back to it. The flavor of "raw" sugar is more subtle and delicate than that of brown sugar, making them a much better substitute for exotic sugars such as palm sugar. If you are not able to find them, light brown sugar may be substituted.

Deep-Fried Chicken Livers Beijing-Style

CHICKEN LIVERS HAVE a natural affinity for soy sauce, ginger, and garlic, and the marinade here makes them especially moist and savory. The batter is a light flour and water dip without eggs. If you prefer a dry breading, omit the batter and roll the livers in dry flour or cornstarch just before frying.

SERVES 4 TO 6

2 pounds chicken livers

3 tablespoons soy sauce

2 tablespoons rice wine or extra-dry sherry

1 medium scallion or other green onion, minced

1 garlic clove, minced

2 quarter-sized fresh ginger slices, minced

1 tablespoon Demerara, turbinado, or light brown sugar

Peanut or vegetable oil, for frying

1 cup all-purpose flour

1 large egg, lightly beaten

Chinese vinegar, Hot Chinese Mustard (page 162), and/or Sweet-and-Sour Sauce (page 165)

one Drain the livers well and rinse under cold running water. Remove any fat and cut out any greenish spots. Cut the livers into individual lobes if they are large and whole; leave smaller livers in one piece.

two In a large nonreactive glass or stainless steel bowl, mix together the soy sauce, wine, scallion, garlic, ginger, and sugar, stirring until the sugar is dissolved. Add the livers and toss until they are coated with the marinade. Cover and set aside to marinate for at least 30 minutes, refrigerated.

three Fit a wire cooling rack in a cookie sheet and preheat the oven to 150°F (or Warm setting). Fill a Dutch oven or deep-fat fryer with oil to come halfway up the sides, at least 2 inches deep. Over medium-high heat, bring the oil to 375°F (hot but not smoking).

four Meanwhile, gradually beat 1 cup cold water into the flour until it forms a smooth batter. Beat in the egg.

five Thoroughly drain the livers, discarding the marinade. When the oil is heated, dip a few livers into the batter until they are thoroughly coated, lift them out one at a time, letting the excess flow back into the bowl, and slip them into the hot fat until the pan is full but not crowded. Fry until they are golden brown, 3 to 4 minutes. Lift them from the fat, drain thoroughly, and transfer them to the wire rack. Keep them in the warm oven while you fry the remaining livers. Serve hot, with Chinese vinegar, Hot Chinese Mustard, and Sweet-and-Sour Sauce passed separately for dipping.

Rice Wine and Sake As is true of Western grape wine, rice wines, including Japanese *sake*, vary in sweetness, potency, and flavor, depending on the kind of rice used, the region, the exact method of fermenting and aging the wine, and whether or not it has been fortified. They have no Western equivalent, but the following substitutions come close. For *sake* or other fairly dry rice wine, use an extra-dry sherry (sometimes labeled dry "cocktail" sherry) such as Tio Pepe. For sweet rice wine such as *mirin,* use a medium dry sherry such as an amontillado.

Chicken Tempura

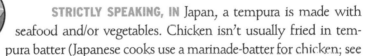

STRICTLY SPEAKING, IN Japan, a tempura is made with seafood and/or vegetables. Chicken isn't usually fried in tempura batter (Japanese cooks use a marinade-batter for chicken; see Toriniku Tatsuta-age, page 83). In the United States, however, chicken tempura is frequently found on Japanese restaurant menus. Just because it is not traditional in Japan, there's nothing to prevent us from giving the tempura treatment to chicken, pork, or even beef; the batter is delicious on just about anything.

Though boneless chicken breast is the most convenient cut to use for this recipe, it is not the most flavorful. If you take the time to prepare chicken thighs as directed on page 11, you will not be sorry.

The secret to a good tempura is to use good, clean oil and keep it very hot, frying in very small batches so that the temperature of the fat is never diminished by the addition of the chicken. And don't overcook. The thin slices of chicken cook in a flash.

SERVES 4

one Wash the chicken and pat dry. Cut across the grain of the muscle into thin, wide strips no more than ¼ inch thick. Set aside.

27

two Combine 1¼ cups all-purpose flour and a large pinch of salt in a large bowl. In a separate bowl, beat the egg whites until they form stiff but not dry peaks. Set aside.

three Set a wire cooling rack in a cookie sheet and preheat the oven to 150°F (or Warm setting). Fill a cast-iron Dutch oven or deep-fat fryer with enough oil to come halfway up the sides. Over medium-high heat, bring the oil to 375°F (hot but not smoking).

2 pounds boneless chicken breasts or thighs (preferably thighs), skinned

1¼ cups all-purpose flour, plus ¼ cup (see Note)

Salt

2 large eggs, separated

Peanut or vegetable oil, for frying

Soy sauce

Tempura Sauce (page 166)

four While the oil is heating, beat 1 cup ice water into the egg yolks. Gradually beat this into the flour mixture until the batter is smooth. Fold in the beaten egg whites. Spread the remaining ¼ cup of flour on a plate.

five Lightly roll the chicken in flour, and dip the chicken pieces one at a time into the batter, making sure that all surfaces are well coated. Allow the excess to flow back into the bowl and then slip the chicken into the hot fat. Fry a few pieces (about 1 serving) at a time until golden, 3 to 5 minutes.

six Lift the chicken from the fat, drain well, transfer to the wire rack, and keep them in the warm oven while you fry the remaining chicken. Serve hot with salt, soy sauce, and Tempura Sauce for dipping.

NOTE: A mixture of ¼ cup of rice flour and 1 cup of all-purpose flour can be used.

BREADED BIRD

A dry coating, or breading, is the most commonplace coating for fried foods, especially chicken. Most often, it is some kind of starch such as wheat flour, cornstarch, or potato flour (or starch). Also common are crumb breadings (whence comes the name) made from dry stale bread, crackers, matzoh meal, dry cereal, or even nuts. The breading may stick to the surface because of the moisture of the chicken's flesh or skin, or the chicken may be dipped first in a liquid to coat its surface—a marinade, beaten eggs, or milk, for example.

These recipes represent a broad cross-section of the world's breaded birds. Other breaded fried chicken recipes can be found elsewhere in this book: see also "The Developed Art" (Southern Fried Chicken, pages 97 to 116), "This Bird Is Full of It" (stuffed fried chicken, pages 65 to 74), and "The Party Bird" (pages 75 to 96). For more on breading ingredients, see "The Chicken Fryer's Kitchen" (pages 15 to 16).

Bajan Fried Chicken

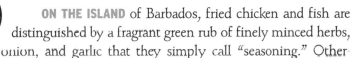

ON THE ISLAND of Barbados, fried chicken and fish are distinguished by a fragrant green rub of finely minced herbs, onion, and garlic that they simply call "seasoning." Otherwise, the chicken is pretty much the same as its close cousins in the American South. The seasoning mix will keep for several days if it is stored in a well-sealed jar and refrigerated, but is best made as you need it.

This recipe comes from Jessica Harris's classic cookbook on the African diaspora, *Iron Pots and Wooden Spoons*.

SERVES 4

one Mix together the garlic, onion, scallion, and herbs in a glass container and sprinkle a generous pinch of salt over the top. Cover and set aside for 30 minutes (refrigerate for longer storage; you may make the seasoning a day or two ahead).

two Wash the chicken pieces and pat dry. Partially loosen the skin but don't remove it. With a sharply pointed paring or fillet knife, cut several deep gashes in each piece of chicken. Pack the seasoning mix into the gashes and rub a little under the loosened skin.

three Combine the flour, cornmeal, a healthy pinch or so of salt and cayenne, and several liberal grindings of black pepper in a paper or large plastic ziplock bag. Close the top and shake until the seasonings are evenly distributed. Set aside.

four Fit a wire cooling rack on a cookie sheet. If your pan won't hold all the chicken at once and you plan to serve the chicken hot, preheat the oven to 150°F (or Warm setting). Fill a large cast-iron skillet with enough lard or oil along with the bacon drippings, if using, to come halfway up the sides of the pan, at least 2 inches deep. Over medium-high heat, bring the oil to 375°F (hot but not smoking).

five When the oil is hot, drop several pieces of chicken, beginning with the dark meat pieces, into the seasoned flour-and-meal mixture. Close the top of the bag and shake until the chicken is well coated. Lift the pieces out one at a time, shake off the excess flour, and slip them into the hot fat. Repeat until the pan is full. Fry the chicken, turning once until lightly browned, about 10 minutes. Reduce the heat to medium and fry, turning once, until it is cooked through and nicely browned on all sides, 15 to 20 minutes, maintaining the fat temperature at 325°F.

six Lift the chicken out of the fat one piece at a time, allow it to drain thoroughly, and transfer to the wire rack. If you are frying in batches, keep it warm in the oven while you fry the remaining chicken. Serve hot or at room temperature.

NOTE: This chicken can also be deep-fried (I prefer it that way, in fact). Half-fill a Dutch oven or deep-fat fryer with the lard or oil and add the bacon fat, if using. Preheat to 375°F over medium-high heat, then fry, maintaining a frying temperature of 365°F. throughout, for 20 to 25 minutes.

FOR THE SEASONING (MAKES ABOUT 1 CUP):

2 large or 3 small garlic cloves, minced

2 tablespoons minced yellow onion

2 tablespoons minced scallion or other green onion, both white and green parts

2 tablespoons minced fresh thyme

2 tablespoons minced fresh chives

2 tablespoons minced parsley, preferably flat-leaf parsley

Salt

FOR FRYING THE CHICKEN:

1 frying chicken, weighing no more than 3 pounds, cut up for frying as on page 11, but not skinned

1½ cups all-purpose flour

½ cup fine stone-ground cornmeal

Salt, ground cayenne pepper, and freshly milled black pepper

Lard or peanut oil, for frying

2 to 4 tablespoons bacon drippings (optional)

Cuban Fried Chicken, Creole Style

Pollo Frito a la Criolla

ONE OF THE trademark flavors of Cuban cooking is the sour juice of the Seville or bitter orange. Here, that distinctive juice does double-duty, first as a tenderizing marinade, then as the steaming liquid for a young frying chicken. Unfortunately, Seville oranges aren't grown commercially. Most Floridians who use them, especially those of Cuban ancestry, grow their own. If you can't get Seville oranges, a close substitute can be made by combining regular orange juice with lime juice.

In this recipe, the chicken fries briefly to seal the outside, then liquid is introduced, the pan is covered, and the chicken steams until it is tender. Finally, it fries again to crisp the outside. This double-frying method is used by many Southern cooks and makes an exceptionally moist chicken that still has a satisfyingly crispy skin.

SERVES 4

1 frying chicken, weighing no more than 3 pounds, cut up for frying as on page 11, but not skinned

2 teaspoons salt

3 large garlic cloves, lightly crushed

Freshly milled black pepper

1 Seville (bitter) orange, or 1 regular juice orange and 1 to 2 limes

1 cup all-purpose flour

Lard or peanut oil, for frying

Parsley and 1 thinly sliced orange, for garnish

one Wash the chicken and pat dry. Combine the salt and garlic in a mortar and work it with the pestle until it is a smooth paste. (The salt acts as an abrasive and will help grind the garlic to a smooth pulp. You can also do this with the flat side of a chef's knife on a cutting board.) Grind a teaspoon of black pepper into the paste and mix it in.

two Grate the zest from the orange, then split the orange and squeeze the juice from it. You will need ½ cup of juice, so if there is more, set it aside for another use. If you cannot get bitter oranges, use the zest from a regular juicing orange and combine 3 tablespoons of the orange juice with 2 tablespoons freshly squeezed lime juice. Combine the garlic paste, juice, and grated zest in a large nonreactive glass or stainless steel bowl. Stir well and add the chicken. Toss until it is uniformly coated. Cover and marinate, refrigerated, for 4 to 6 hours, occasionally turning and basting the chicken. Let the chicken return to room temperature for 30 minutes before frying it.

three Fit a wire cooling rack in a cookie sheet and set aside. Remove the chicken from the marinade and set the marinade aside. Spread the flour on a plate. Fill a cast-iron lidded skillet with enough lard or oil to coat the bottom with about ⅛ inch of fat. Turn the heat to medium-high.

four When the oil is hot, lightly roll the chicken in the flour, beginning with the dark meat, thoroughly shake off the excess flour, and add the chicken to the pan. Fry, turning once, until it is lightly browned on all sides, about 8 minutes. Slowly pour the reserved marinade into the center of the pan, lower the heat to medium-low, and loosely cover the pan. Cook, turning the chicken occasionally, until tender and cooked through, about 20 minutes.

five Uncover the pan, and raise the heat to medium-high. Cook until the liquid is evaporated and the chicken crisp, gently turning the chicken frequently so that it doesn't get overly browned on one side. Be careful; after the steaming stage, the crust will be very fragile and sticky until it is crisped again.

six When the chicken is nicely crisped all over, lift it from the fat, draining well on the wire rack. Transfer it to a serving platter, garnish with the parsley and orange slices, and serve hot.

NOTE: While there is no substitute for bitter oranges, some oranges are more acid than others. Avoid juice oranges such as Valencias and honeybells; blood oranges, especially when they are a little underripe, are a good substitute, but you will still need to add lime juice. If you find that the oranges you are using are very sweet, up the proportion of orange juice to lime juice to equal parts of each.

South American Fried Chicken

Chicharrones de Pollo

CHICHARRONES ARE CRACKLINGS—the flavorful solids that are left over from making lard; the resemblance these little morsels of chicken bear to them accounts for the name "chicken cracklings." *Chicharrones de pollo* is a typically South American dish, variations of which can be found all over that continent and up into the Central American peninsula. The chicken is chopped up Chinese-style—bones, skin, and all—into small pieces. Then it is usually marinated, rolled in wheat or corn flour, and deep-fried—although sometimes it is not marinated, and sometimes it is fried without any breading at all.

SERVES 4

1 frying chicken, weighing no more than 3 pounds, cut up for frying Chinese-style as on page 11, or 8 chicken thighs, chopped in half crosswise

1/2 cup freshly squeezed lime juice

2 garlic cloves, minced

Salt and freshly milled black pepper

1 cup corn flour (very fine cornmeal—not cornstarch)

Lard or peanut or vegetable oil, for frying

Hot sauce

2 limes, cut into wedges

one Wash the chicken and pat dry. Put the pieces into a large nonreactive glass or stainless steel bowl and pour the lime juice over them. Sprinkle with the minced garlic, a large pinch of salt, and several liberal grindings of black pepper. Toss until the seasoning is uniformly distributed and set aside to marinate for at least 1 hour, refrigerated. (Or cover and marinate overnight in the refrigerator; remove from the refrigerator 30 minutes before you are ready to cook the chicken.)

two Place the corn flour in a paper or large plastic ziplock bag. Shake to coat the inside. Fit a wire cooling rack over a cookie sheet and place it in the center of the oven. Preheat the oven to 150°F (or Warm setting). Fill a deep cast-iron skillet, Dutch oven, or deep-fat fryer with enough lard or oil to come halfway up the sides, at least 2 inches deep. Over medium-high heat, bring the fat to 375°F (hot but not smoking).

three When the fat is hot, lift the chicken pieces a few at a time from their marinade, allowing the excess to flow back into the bowl. Drop them into the bag of corn flour, close the top, and shake until the chicken is well coated. Lift them

33

out of the corn flour, shake off the excess, and slip them into the fat. Repeat until the pan is full without crowding. Fry, maintaining a temperature of 365°F, turning once, until the chicken is a rich golden brown and cooked through, 12 to 15 minutes.

four Lift the chicken from the fat, drain well, and transfer to the wire rack in the oven while you fry the remaining chicken. Serve hot, with hot sauce and lime wedges passed separately.

NOTE: If you like, you can spice up the marinade with a few hot red pepper flakes or with a few shots of hot sauce. Other common additions to the marinade are minced fresh ginger (about 2 quarter-sized slices, minced fine), rum, sugar, and chopped cilantro.

Greek Marinated Fried Chicken

Kotopoulo Tiganito Marinato

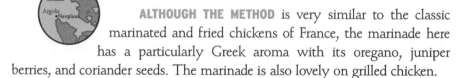

ALTHOUGH THE METHOD is very similar to the classic marinated and fried chickens of France, the marinade here has a particularly Greek aroma with its oregano, juniper berries, and coriander seeds. The marinade is also lovely on grilled chicken.

SERVES 4 TO 5

one Wash the chicken and pat dry. Put it in a large nonreactive glass or stainless steel bowl. In a separate bowl, combine the olive oil, lemon juice, wine, garlic, onion, bay leaf, oregano, juniper berries, coriander seeds, and a few liberal grindings of pepper. Whisk until well mixed and pour over the chicken, turning the chicken until it is uniformly coated with the marinade. Cover and refrigerate, marinating for 2 hours or overnight.

two Fit a wire cooling rack in a cookie sheet and set aside. Drain the chicken, pat dry, and sprinkle liberally with salt. Spread the flour on a plate or place it in a paper or large ziplock plastic bag. Fill a large cast-iron skillet with enough oil to come halfway up the sides, about 1 inch deep. Over medium-high heat, bring the oil to 375°F (hot but not smoking).

three Beginning with the dark meat, roll the chicken in the flour or drop it a few pieces at a time into the bag of flour, close the top, and shake until it is coated. Shake off the excess flour and slip the chicken into the hot fat.

four Fry until the bottom is sealed and beginning to color, about 4 minutes. Turn, and brown the second side. Reduce the heat to medium (325°F) and fry, turning once, until the chicken is cooked through and golden, about 15 minutes more.

five Lift the chicken from the fat and drain well on the wire rack. Transfer to a platter and garnish with the sprigs of herb and lemon wedges and serve at once.

NOTE: The Greeks also half-fry and bake this chicken, which is a good way to prepare it when you have company or are preparing another dish that will require all of your attention. Position a rack in the center of the oven and preheat the oven to 350°F. Fry the chicken in step 4 until it is lightly browned on both sides, about 3 minutes per side. Transfer it to a baking sheet and bake it in the center of the oven until the chicken is cooked through, 45 to 50 minutes.

1 frying chicken, weighing no more than 3 pounds, skinned and cut up for frying as on page 11

1/4 cup extra virgin olive oil

1/2 cup freshly squeezed lemon juice

1/2 cup dry white wine

2 large garlic cloves, minced

1 small onion, thinly sliced

1 bay leaf, crumbled if dried, chopped if fresh

1 tablespoon chopped fresh oregano or 1 teaspoon dried

6 juniper berries, crushed

6 coriander seeds, crushed

Freshly milled black pepper

Salt

1 cup all-purpose flour

Olive or peanut or vegetable oil (or a combination), for frying

Parsley or fresh oregano sprigs and 1 lemon cut into wedges, for garnish

Israeli Fried Chicken with Sesame

COOKING IN THE modern state of Israel is a rich mélange, owing to the diverse origins of its settlers. This recipe shows distinct East Indian influences and is not substantially different from the sesame fried chicken of China and Thailand. The recipe is adapted from *The Complete Middle East Cookbook* by Tess Mallos.

SERVES 4

1 frying chicken, weighing no more than 3 pounds, skinned and cut up for frying as on page 11

Salt

1 cup sesame seeds

1 cup all-purpose flour

Fresly milled white pepper

1 teaspoon paprika

1 large egg

¼ cup Chicken Broth (page 18) or water

Peanut oil, for frying

one Wash the chicken and put it in a large non-reactive glass or stainless steel bowl. Completely cover with cold water and add a couple of large pinches of salt. Toss gently until the salt is dissolved and set aside for 30 minutes. In a large shallow bowl, combine the sesame seeds, flour, a large pinch or so of salt, several liberal grindings of white pepper, and the paprika. Toss with a fork until thoroughly mixed. Break the egg into a separate shallow bowl, add the broth or water, and lightly beat until the mixture is smooth.

two Lift the chicken pieces one at a time from the salted water, lightly roll them in the sesame-flour mixture, then dip into the diluted egg. Allow the excess egg to flow back into the bowl and then roll the chicken a second time in the sesame mixture until it is well coated. Shake off the excess and lay the breaded chicken on a clean dry plate. Set aside.

three Fit a wire cooling rack over a cookie sheet and set aside. Fill a large cast-iron skillet with enough oil to come halfway up the sides, at least ¾ inch deep. Over medium-high heat, bring the oil to 375°F (hot but not smoking). Add the chicken a few pieces at a time, beginning with the dark meat. Fry, turning once, until the chicken is golden brown on all sides, about 4 minutes per side. Reduce the heat to 325°F and fry, turning once, until the chicken is golden brown and cooked through, 12 to 15 minutes more.

four Lift the chicken from the fat, drain thoroughly, and transfer to the wire rack set over a cookie sheet to finish draining. Serve hot or at room temperature.

Nepali Fried Chicken

Kukhurako Bhutuwa

NEPAL
Kathma
Lucknow

TUCKED INTO THE Himalayan Mountains on India's northern border, Nepal has a style of cookery that shares much of the perfume of its southern neighbor. Many of the same spices and flavor combinations of India are found in the Nepali versions of fried chicken, of which this is one of many. Nepali cooks waste absolutely nothing; another fried chicken delicacy from this country is made from the entrails of the bird—including the gizzard, liver, heart, and cleaned intestines. I've included a variation, made with gizzards and livers, on page 150.

1 frying chicken, weighing no more than 3 pounds, cut up for frying Chinese-style as on page 11

3 large garlic cloves

4 quarter-sized fresh ginger slices

Salt

1 teaspoon cumin seeds

1½ cups all-purpose flour

1 teaspoon powdered chiles (see Note)

Peanut oil, for frying

SERVES 4 TO 6

one Wash the chicken, pat dry, and put it into a shallow bowl. Make a paste with the garlic, ginger, and salt using a very sharp knife, mortar and pestle, blender, or food processor fitted with a steel blade. Rub the paste over the chicken until all pieces are uniformly coated and set aside to marinate for about half an hour, refrigerated.

two Grind the cumin to a powder in a spice mill or mortar. Combine it with the flour and chile powder and a large pinch or so of salt in a paper or large plastic ziplock bag. Close the top and shake until the seasonings are uniformly distributed.

three Fit a wire rack in a cookie sheet and set aside. Fill a large, deep cast-iron Dutch oven or deep-fryer with enough oil to come halfway up the sides of the pan, at least 2 inches deep. Over medium-high heat, bring the oil to 375°F (hot but not smoking). Without wiping off any of the marinade, drop the chicken a few pieces at a time into the seasoned flour, close the bag, and shake until they are coated. Lift them out, shaking off the excess flour, and slip them into the hot fat. Repeat until the pan is full without crowding. Fry, turning once, until the chicken is golden brown and cooked through, 15 to 20 minutes.

four Lift the chicken out of the fat, drain thoroughly, and transfer to the wire rack. If you have to fry the chicken in batches, preheat the oven to 150°F (or Warm setting) and keep the cooked chicken in the warm oven while the second batch fries. Serve hot.

NOTE: Powdered dried chiles can be found in Asian and ethnic markets. If you cannot get them, you can grind your own chiles in a spice mill. Stem and seed them first. Or you may substitute 2 rounded teaspoons commercial chili powder for the cumin and chile.

Viennese Fried Chicken

THE VIENNESE LOVE almost anything rolled in crumbs and deep-fried, and they are masters at it. Their version of fried chicken is justifiably celebrated all over Europe. It is made with very young chickens weighing less than 2 pounds. The chicken is quartered, marinated briefly in lemon juice, then breaded and deep-fried in exactly the same way as a Viennese cutlet. The frying fat for really authentic *backbendl* is lard, but you can substitute clarified butter for a more elegant and delicate crust, or use vegetable oil if you prefer it, or if the lard available to you is not of very high quality.

The classic accompaniment for *backbendl* is buttered egg noodles.

SERVES 4

1 frying chicken, weighing no more than 3 pounds, cut up for frying as on page 11, or 1 very small, young chicken, weighing under 2 pounds, cut into quarters (2 leg-thigh quarters, 2 breast-wing quarters)

1/4 cup freshly squeezed lemon juice

Salt

1/4 cup all-purpose flour

2 large eggs, beaten

2 cups dry bread crumbs

Lard or clarified butter (page 14) (or vegetable oil, if you prefer), for frying

1 lemon, cut into 8 wedges

one Wash the chicken, pat dry, and place it in a large nonreactive glass or stainless steel bowl. Pour the lemon juice over and toss until the chicken is coated. Marinate for 1 to 2 hours, covered and refrigerated.

two Drain the marinade from the chicken and pat it dry. Sprinkle liberally with salt. Place the flour in one shallow bowl, the eggs in another shallow bowl, and the crumbs on a plate or in a shallow bowl. Roll each piece of chicken lightly in the flour. Shake off the excess and dip each piece into the egg until it is coated. Allow the excess egg to flow back into the bowl. Roll the chicken in the crumbs, patting them well into all sides, and lay the breaded pieces onto a clean, dry platter or wire rack. Let stand for 15 minutes. (You may make the chicken several hours ahead up to this point. Refrigerate the chicken if it is to sit for more than half an hour, but remove it from the refrigerator 30 minutes before cooking.)

three Position a wire cooling rack over a cookie sheet and set aside. Preheat the oven to 150°F (or Warm setting). Fill a deep cast-iron skillet with enough lard or clarified butter to come halfway up the sides. Over medium-high heat, melt the fat and bring to 375°F (hot but not smoking). Add enough chicken to fill the pan and fry, turning once, until the outside is lightly browned. Reduce the heat to medium (325°F) and continue frying until the chicken is cooked through and a rich golden brown.

four Lift the chicken from the fat, drain, and transfer to the rack in the oven to keep it warm while you fry the remaining chicken. Serve hot with the lemon wedges passed separately.

CHICKEN CUTLETS

The boned breast halves of a chicken, alternately called fillets and cutlets, have many advantages. Aside from their convenience, they are lean, have no waste, and cook quickly. Unfortunately, they are also the least interesting meat on the bird and have a tendency to be dry, tough, and tasteless when they are not properly prepared. The only part of the bird that is any easier to cook—and even easier to ruin—is an egg. When cutlets are dipped in egg, rolled in breading, and fried to crisp perfection, however, their shortcomings vanish and they become an elegant and very satisfying thing to eat.

To prepare boneless chicken breasts for cutlets, skin them and separate the tender from the main muscle of the breast (if it is still attached to the breast). Remove the tendon by laying the tender on a flat surface. Place a knife blade against the tip of the tender on top of the tendon and grasp the tendon with your free hand. Pull it until it slips out, scraping against the knife blade. You may set it aside for another use or use it in any of the recipes that call for the cutlet to be pounded flat. Split the breast into halves by cutting out the connective cartilage that runs down the center and trim away any fat.

Cutlets may be either pounded flat to a consistent thickness or they may be split horizontally. The method required is described in the individual recipe.

Boning your own cutlets is very easy and is the most economical route. Not only are whole breasts much less expensive, the skin, bones, and scraps can be frozen and used for making broth. The method is described on page 11. When you are pinched for time or the market has boned breasts on sale, don't feel guilty about buying them. The perfect-home-chef police are not going to come break down your door.

The following are a few of the world's great classic breaded chicken cutlets, but boneless breasts need not be reserved only for cutlets. They are also ideal for sautés (pages 118 to 128), for stir-frying (pages 129 to 146), and as a casing for all kinds of savory fillings (see "This Bird Is Full of It," pages 65 to 74).

Milanese Cutlets

Cotolleta di Pollo alla Milanese

IN ITALY, a *cotolleta* is more an idea than it is a particular cut of meat or poultry. Commonly it is a slice of meat (veal, chicken, or turkey) dipped in egg, rolled in crumbs, and pan-fried. But it can also be made from a vegetable, such as eggplant or mushrooms. Golden and crispy on the outside, moist and tender inside, cutlets are one of the glories of the Italian table. Because the muscle of the chicken breast is smaller and thinner at one end than at the other, when they are used for cutlets, they are sliced into thin, flat pieces and lightly beaten to a more even thickness.

The tastiest and most luxurious fat for frying a *cotolleta* is clarified butter, but Italian cooks frequently mix butter with a less expensive oil, which raises the burning temperature of the fat without going through the extra step of clarifying the butter.

From *Wiener Schnitzel* to *escalope a l'anglaise,* the variations on the basic theme of Milanese Cutlets are legion. Though veal is the most commonplace meat for most of these variations, chicken breasts take beautifully to all of them. A few such variations are included at the end of the recipe.

SERVES 4

2 large whole boneless chicken breasts prepared for cutlets as on page 40

1 large egg, lightly beaten

2 cups dry bread crumbs (preferably homemade page 15)

1 cup clarified butter (page 14) or ¹/₂ cup unsalted butter mixed with 1 cup olive or peanut oil

1 lemon, cut into 8 wedges

Salt and freshly milled black pepper

one Lay each chicken breast on a flat work surface and press it flat with the palm of your hand. Using a sharp knife, carefully cut through the entire breast horizontally, separating it into 2 equal slices. Set them aside. Place the breasts in one layer between 2 sheets of wax paper or plastic wrap. Lightly pound them to a uniform thickness—a little under ¼ inch. Set aside.

two Beat the egg in a shallow bowl and beat until it is uniformly mixed. Spread the crumbs on a dinner plate. Dip each slice of breast in the egg until it is completely covered, allow the excess to flow back into the bowl, and then roll the meat in the crumbs, patting them to form an even coating. Lay the cutlets on a clean, dry platter or a wire cooling rack and leave them for at least 15 minutes to set the breading. (They can be prepared several hours ahead of time up to this point. If they are to sit for more than half an hour, refrigerate them. Take them out of the refrigerator and let them sit for a half hour to come back up to room temperature before cooking them.)

three Preheat the oven to 150°F (or Warm setting). Fit a wire rack in a cookie sheet and place it in the oven. Put the clarified butter or butter and oil in a large cast-iron skillet that will hold about half the cutlets at once. Over medium-high heat, melt the fat and bring it to 365° to 375°F (hot but not smoking). Add enough of the cutlets to fill the pan without crowding it. Fry until the bottoms are golden brown, about 2 minutes, turn, and fry until they are uniformly browned and cooked through, about 2 minutes longer. Remove the cooked cutlets from the pan, drain them briefly on absorbent paper, and place them on the cooling rack in the warm oven. Cook the remaining cutlets in the same manner.

four Arrange the cutlets on a warm serving platter, scatter the lemon wedges among them, and serve at once, passing salt and black pepper in a peppermill separately. The cutlets must come to the table piping hot.

COTOLETTA ALLA SICILIANA: After dipping the cutlets in the egg, sprinkle them with 2 tablespoons of chopped fresh rosemary before rolling them in the crumbs. Use all olive oil for the frying fat and flavor it by frying 2 crushed (but whole) cloves of garlic in it before frying the cutlets. When the garlic is colored a rich golden brown, remove and discard it, then proceed with cutlets.

COTOLETTA ALLA BOLOGNESE: This is for those who like gilding lilies. Have ready a thin slice each of Parmesan and prosciutto and 2 thin slices of white truffles for each cutlet. When the cutlets have fried on one side, top them first with the ham, then the truffles, and finally the cheese. Cover the pan and cook until the bottoms are golden and the cheese is just melted, about 2 minutes longer. There is also *petti di pollo alla bolognese:* The cutlets are sliced as directed for Milanese Cutlets, floured and sautéed in butter like *scalloppine,* then finished as above with prosciutto, cheese, and truffles.

GEORGIA CUTLETS: An old, old antebellum recipe. Cook the cutlets as for Milanese Cutlets using lard or clarified butter for the frying fat. Arrange on a serving platter, top each cutlet with a spoonful of Curry Sauce (page 157), and pass the remaining sauce separately.

Indian Cutlets

BRITISH RULE OF India during the eighteenth and nineteenth centuries led to a unique mingling of cuisines among the British ruling class and the Indian upper classes. Indian cooks who were employed by the English began adapting Indian food to Western palates, while upper-class Indians eagerly adapted fashionable British cookery, spicing it up to suit their own tastes. The result is a delicious jumble exemplified by these cutlets—a wholly Western idea infused with the heady aromas of ancient India.

The recipe is adapted from Madhur Jaffrey's *An Invitation to Indian Cooking*. It is not fundamentally different from a Milanese cutlet, but note that you will need to start preparing them a day ahead.

SERVES 4

2 large whole boneless chicken breasts, prepared for cutlets as on page 40

3 garlic cloves, lightly crushed

2 quarter-sized fresh ginger slices, roughly chopped

1 small yellow onion, thinly sliced

1 small fresh serrano, jalapeño, or cayenne chile, seeded and thinly sliced

2 tablespoons roughly chopped fresh cilantro or flat-leaf parsley

1/4 cup freshly squeezed lemon juice

Salt and freshly milled black pepper

1 large egg, lightly beaten

2 cups dry bread crumbs (preferably homemade, page 15)

Peanut, olive, or vegetable oil, for frying

1 lemon, cut into 8 wedges

Cilantro or parsley sprigs, for garnish

one Rinse the chicken breasts under cold running water and pat dry. Set aside in a shallow nonreactive glass or stainless steel bowl. In a blender, combine the garlic, ginger, onion, chile, cilantro, and lemon juice. Add a healthy pinch of salt and a few light grindings of pepper. Cover and pulse at high speed until the mixture breaks down, then process on high until it is a smooth paste. You may have to stop the machine periodically and scrape down the sides.

two Rub the paste over the chicken breasts, cover with plastic wrap, and refrigerate overnight or for as long as 24 hours. Remove from the refrigerator 30 minutes before cooking.

three One at a time, lift the chicken breasts out of the marinating paste but don't shake off the excess. Dip the breast into the egg until it is coated, let the excess flow back into the bowl, then roll it in the crumbs, patting them carefully to form an even coating. Lay them on a clean, dry plate or wire rack for 15 minutes.

43

THE DEEP END

four Put the remaining marinating paste in a covered saucepan, add a few spoonfuls of water to thin it to a thin sauce consistency, cover, and place it over medium-low heat. Simmer until the sauce is thick, but for at least 15 minutes. Turn off the heat. Taste and adjust the seasonings.

five In a large cast-iron skillet that will hold all 4 cutlets at once without crowding, heat ½ inch oil over medium heat. When the oil is hot (sizzling when you dip the edge of a cutlet into it), add the cutlets and fry until the bottoms are browned, about 6 minutes. Turn carefully (the breading is fragile because of the marinade) and fry until the cutlets are uniformly golden brown and cooked through, 6 to 7 minutes more.

six Drain thoroughly and transfer to a warm platter. Scatter lemon wedges and cilantro or parsley among them and serve hot with the marinade sauce passed separately.

Savannah Cutlets with Curry Sauce

PECANS ARE NATIVE to the South and are grown commercially in Georgia; consequently, they are relatively economical throughout our region (indeed, for those with their own pecan tree, they are free). So we Georgians tend to use them in prodigal quantities. In this recipe, the basic idea of a Milanese cutlet remains intact, but the chicken breasts are not sliced, and the breading is laced with a healthy portion of those pecans and a bit of Parmesan. The ideal accompaniment is Curry Sauce but you may serve the cutlets plain if you prefer.

44 SERVES 4

one Wash the chicken and pat dry. Spread a sheet of wax paper or plastic wrap on a work surface and lay the breasts on it. Cover with a second sheet and lightly pound the chicken until it is flattened to a uniform thinness of just under ¼ inch. Put the breasts into a shallow nonreactive stainless steel or glass bowl that will hold them in one layer and pour the bourbon over them. Set aside to marinate for 30 minutes, or up to 1 hour, covered and refrigerated.

two In a food processor fitted with a steel blade or blender, grind the nuts fine, but don't over-process them; they should be like very coarse meal. If you process them too much, you'll release the oils and get pecan butter. Transfer to a shallow bowl and mix in the bread crumbs and Parmigiano.

three Break the egg into a second bowl and spread the flour on a dinner plate. Drain the marinade from the chicken, shake off the excess, and roll the breasts in the flour. Shake off the excess and dip into the egg. Let the excess egg flow back into the bowl and then roll the breasts in the crumb mixture one at a time, patting the mixture well into all sides. Lay each breaded breast on a clean, dry plate. Set aside for at least 15 minutes to set the breading. (You can make the cutlets several hours ahead up to this point. Refrigerate until you are ready to cook them, but take them out and let them sit at room temperature for 30 minutes before finishing them.)

four Fit a wire rack over 2 cookie sheets and set aside. In a large cast-iron skillet, heat the clarified butter or butter and oil mixture over medium-high heat. When the butter is melted and hot and the foaming has subsided, add the cutlets to the pan. Fry until the bottoms are golden brown, about 3 minutes, turn, and continue frying until the cutlets are cooked through and uniformly browned, about 3 minutes more. Lift them from the fat, draining thoroughly, and set on the wire rack to finish draining.

five Serve hot with lemon wedges and pass the Curry Sauce separately

2 large whole boneless chicken breasts, prepared for cutlets as on page 40

$^1/_4$ cup bourbon

$^1/_2$ cup pecans, picked over for bits of shell

$^1/_2$ cup dry bread crumbs (preferably homemade, page 15)

$^1/_2$ cup plus 2 tablespoons freshly grated Parmigiano-Reggiano

1 large egg

$^1/_2$ cup flour

1 cup clarified butter (page 14) or $^1/_2$ cup unsalted butter mixed with 1 cup peanut or vegetable oil

1 lemon, cut into 8 wedges

Curry Sauce (page 157)

South African Cutlets in Curry Sauce

SOUTH AFRICA SHARES with the United States the distinction of being a culinary melting pot. Centuries of colonization and international trade have molded a very eclectic cuisine with no single cuisine dominating. This quick, tasty recipe for curried chicken cutlets, from South African Gillian Seymour, is exemplary of the cuisine's Euro-Asian/African mix of Dutch, English, Indian, West African, and Middle Eastern influences.

In South Africa, Indian immigrants sell spices for curry specially blended to order. Most South Africans are accustomed to a hotter, headier blend than domestic commercial curry powders will provide.

SERVES 6

FOR THE BÉCHAMEL SAUCE:

1½ cups whole milk

1 small yellow onion, thinly sliced

2 bay leaves

1½ tablespoons unsalted butter

2 teaspoons all-purpose flour

Salt and freshly milled white pepper

FOR THE CHICKEN:

6 whole boneless chicken breasts, prepared for cutlets as on page 40

4 tablespoons unsalted butter

I large garlic clove, minced

2 teaspoons curry powder (or more to taste)

Juice of ½ lemon

Salt

½ cup Chicken Broth (page 18), Quick Broth (page 17), or ¼ cup canned broth and ¼ cup water

4 tablespoons cream

Sugar

one Combine the milk, onion, and bay leaves in a heavy-bottomed saucepan over medium heat. Stirring frequently, bring the milk almost to a boil. Turn off the heat and set aside for 5 minutes. Strain, discarding the onion and bay leaves, and set aside.

two Melt the 1½ tablespoons butter in a saucepan over medium heat. Add the flour and stir until the flour is completely dissolved. Simmer for 1 minute, stirring to prevent the flour from scorching. Slowly add the flavored milk, stirring or whisking constantly, until it is incorporated and the flour is dissolved into it. Bring it to a simmer, stirring constantly, and reduce the heat to low. Season with a large pinch of salt and several liberal grindings of white pepper and simmer the sauce, stirring occasionally, until it is fairly thick and the flour has lost its pasty raw taste, about 10 minutes.

three Meanwhile, wash the chicken and pat dry. Lay the cutlets on a flat work surface, between two sheets of wax paper or plastic wrap, and lightly beat them to a uniform thickness of about ¼ inch.

four Melt the 4 tablespoons butter in a sauté pan over medium heat. Add the garlic and curry powder and sauté until fragrant, 30 to 60 seconds. Add the chicken cutlets and sauté, turning them once, until both sides are nicely browned and are about half-cooked, about 5 minutes. Add the lemon juice and let it mostly evaporate. Sprinkle the cutlets with a pinch or so of salt. Add the broth slowly, stirring and scraping the pan to loosen any cooking residue that may have stuck to it. Bring the broth to the boiling point and reduce the heat to low. Simmer, turning once, until the cutlets are cooked through, about 15 minutes.

five Remove the cutlets to a warm platter. Increase the heat under the sauté pan to medium and slowly stir in the béchamel sauce. Bring it to a simmer and simmer for 2 or 3 minutes, or until it is somewhat thickened. Add the cream, taste, and adjust the seasonings, adding a little salt and a pinch or so of sugar if needed to bring up the curry's flavor. Return the cutlets to the sauce and heat them through. Turn off the heat. Transfer the cutlets to a warm serving platter, pour the sauce over them, and serve at once.

Almond Chicken Cutlets

ALMONDS AND CHICKEN marry well, and here the marriage is particularly enhanced by the salty-sweet flavors of the wine-and-soy marinade. The sliced almonds make an elegant and delicious breading that need not be confined to a Chinese menu; it will go well with just about any appetizer and side dish that does not contain nuts.

SERVES 4

2 whole boneless chicken breasts, prepare for cutlets as on page 40

1 tablespoon sweet rice wine or mirin or amontillado sherry

1 tablespoon light (not "lite") soy sauce

1/4 cup all-purpose flour

1 large egg, lightly beaten

3/4 cup Chinese dry bread crumbs

3/4 cup sliced almonds

Salt

Peanut or vegetable oil, for frying

Lettuce Leaves

Sweet-and-Sour Sauce (page 165), Plum Sauce (page 163), or Quick Plum or Apricot Sauce (page 164)

one Wash the chicken breasts and pat dry. Lay them on a flat work surface. Press a breast half flat with your hand and with a very sharp knife, slice it in half horizontally. Repeat with the remaining breast. In a large nonreactive glass or stainless steel bowl, toss the chicken with the wine and soy sauce until the chicken is uniformly coated. Set aside to marinate for 30 minutes in the refrigerator.

two Place the flour on a plate. Beat the egg in a shallow bowl. Combine the bread crumbs, almonds, and a healthy pinch of salt in another shallow bowl and toss until they are well mixed. Lift the chicken cutlets out of their marinade one at a time, letting the excess flow back into the bowl. Roll the cutlet lightly in the flour, dip it into the egg until it is coated, let the excess flow back into the bowl, and then roll the cutlet in the crumb mixture, patting the crumbs and almonds into all sides. Lay the chicken on a clean plate and repeat with the remaining chicken until all of it is breaded. Set aside for 15 minutes. (The cutlets may be made up to this point several hours ahead of time. Cover and refrigerate if they are to sit for more than 30 minutes.)

three Fit a wire cooling rack in a cookie sheet and set aside. Fill a large cast-iron skillet with enough oil to come halfway up the sides. Over medium-high heat, bring the oil to 375°F (hot but not smoking). Add enough cutlets to fill the pan without crowding. Fry until the bottoms are golden brown, 2 to 3 minutes.

48

Turn, and continue frying until the second sides are golden brown, 2 to 3 minutes more. Lift the cutlets from the fat, drain well, and then set on the wire rack. Repeat with the remaining cutlets until all are cooked.

four Slice the cutlets crosswise on the diagonal into 5 or 6 pieces each, arrange them decoratively on each plate or on a platter lined with lettuce leaves, and serve at once with your choice of dipping sauce.

NOTE: Chinese and Japanese bread crumbs are both dry, but they are not as fine as Western bread crumbs usually are, and they have not been toasted, so they are very white. You will find them in Asian markets, but if you cannot get them, trim the crust from several slices of firm white home-style bread and leave them lying on a wire cooling rack overnight, or until they are dry and hard. Don't dry them in the oven, because they should not toast at all. Crush them by putting them into plastic bags or between 2 sheets of wax paper. Lightly crush them with a rolling pin or wooden mallet; don't pulverize them to a powder, however. They should still have plenty of texture.

THE NAKED BIRD

One of the really tasty parts of fried birds has gotten a lot of bad publicity lately—and that is the crackling, crispy skin. Many modern cooks (and eaters) delicately eschew the skin on the advice of the low-fat-food police who would have us believe it is really bad news for our arteries if we come within a mile of the stuff. Historically, the crisp skin of a roasted or fried bird has been prized the world over as one of the tastiest parts of the bird. The Chinese, for example, seem even today to share humorist Roy Blount's assessment that poultry skin is "a major food group." While naturally you do not want to make eating it a daily thing, there is no reason why even people on restricted diets cannot enjoy this tasty treat on occasion. Besides, the skin is already quite high in fat, so it does not absorb any of the frying fat while it cooks, and loses most of its own fat in the process.

The skin best achieves this delicate, golden perfection when there is no breading to get in the way, as cooks from all over the globe have long known. In this chapter are some of those classic bare-backed fried chickens. Whether the chicken is cut up, split down the back, flattened and pan-fried whole, or dipped whole into deep fat, the crispy skin is the star attraction here, so don't virtuously peel it away and leave it lying on the edge of your plate. Remember that virtue is its own reward and doesn't expect birthday presents—and crunch away.

Five Fragrance Chicken

Wu Xiang Ji

IN CHINA, CRISPLY fried or roasted poultry skin is highly prized and may be served as a separate treat from the rest of the bird. When that is the case, the only coating that the chicken will get is a flavoring rub, marinade, or a thin honey glaze. The bird may be steamed first or it may be raw when it goes into the fat; it may be cut up into small morsels, disjointed into 8 pieces, or left whole; it may be stuffed with rice or not stuffed at all—there are literally hundreds of variations on the theme—but all have the same goal in mind—plenty of crispy, flavorful skin.

SERVES 4

one Wash the chicken and pat dry.

two Combine the soy sauce, wine, sugar or molasses, five-spice powder, and egg white in a large, nonreactive glass or stainless steel bowl. Stir until thoroughly mixed. Beat in the cornstarch until it is dissolved and smooth. Add the chicken pieces to the marinade and toss until they are uniformly coated, then set aside to marinate, covered and refrigerated, for at least 1 hour.

three Fill a deep-fryer or Dutch oven with oil at least 2 inches deep, but no more than halfway up the sides. Over medium-high heat, bring the oil to 325°F, well shy of the smoking-hot stage. Thoroughly drain the chicken from the marinade and add the pieces to the oil to fill the pot without crowding. Fry for 3 minutes, then lift the pieces out of the oil, allowing them to drain well. Set aside on a platter and continue until all the chicken has been fried. Turn off the heat. Allow the chicken to rest for 5 minutes or up to 1 hour. (The chicken can be made 1 hour or so ahead up to this point.)

four When you are ready to serve the chicken, reheat the oil to 375°F (hot but not smoking). Fry the chicken for 2 to 3 minutes, until it is deeply colored and the skin is crisp. Lift the pieces from the fat, drain well, then drain briefly on absorbent paper. Transfer the chicken to a serving platter and serve hot or at room temperature.

1 small frying chicken, weighing less than 3 pounds, cut up for frying Chinese-style as on page 11

1/4 cup light (not "lite") soy sauce

2 tablespoons rice wine or extra-dry sherry

1 teaspoon brown sugar or molasses

1 teaspoon Chinese five-spice powder

1 large egg white

2 tablespoons cornstarch

Peanut or vegetable oil, for frying

Chinese Five-Spice Powder This is a spice blend of star anise, Szechwan pepper, fennel, cinnamon, and cloves—or sometimes star anise, Szechwan pepper, cinnamon, nutmeg, and cloves. If you can't find it, you can make a plausible substitution by mixing equal parts powdered star anise and white pepper (or substitute 2 parts powdered allspice for both) with ground fennel seeds, cinnamon, and cloves.

Thai Fried Chicken

THIS RECIPE IS adapted from Jennifer Brennan's *The Original Thai Cookbook,* which, with her cooking classes in California, helped introduce an entire generation of Americans to authentic Thai cooking. It's the traditional Siamese way of frying chicken, but we don't often see it on Thai menus in our country. The chicken is rubbed with a paste of garlic, pepper, and a peculiarly Thai ingredient—the roots of the cilantro plant. If you can't get cilantro with the roots still attached, then try substituting the stem. It won't taste the same, but the stem is closer to the root's flavor than the leaves or seeds are.

SERVES 4

1 frying chicken, weighing no more than 3 pounds, cut up for frying as on page 11, with the skin left intact

1 whole garlic bulb, lightly smashed with the side of a cleaver, separated, and peeled

3 tablespoons black peppercorns, crushed or coarsely ground

3 tablespoons roughly chopped cilantro root

Peanut oil, for frying

Salt

Fresh cilantro sprigs and fine shreds of fresh lemon peel, for garnish

Thai Sweet and Hot Garlic Sauce (recipe follows)

2 cups hot Chinese-Style Rice (page 172)

one Wash the chicken and pat dry. Combine the garlic, peppercorns, and cilantro root in a mortar and crush it to a paste, or put them into a blender or food processor fitted with a steel blade and process to a paste. Rub the garlic paste into all surfaces of the chicken and set it aside to marinate for 1 hour, refrigerated.

two Fit a wire cooling rack in a cookie sheet and set aside. Half fill with oil about 2 inches deep, a Dutch oven, wok, or deep-fat fryer that will hold all the chicken at once. Over medium-high heat, bring the oil to 375°F (hot but not smoking). Add the chicken a few pieces at a time, beginning with the dark meat pieces. Fry, maintaining a temperature of 365°F, turning if necessary, until the chicken is cooked through and golden brown, 20 to 25 minutes. Drain thoroughly on the wire rack.

three Sprinkle with a couple of pinches of salt, scatter the sprigs of cilantro among the chicken pieces, sprinkle the shreds of lemon peel over all, and serve hot, with the sauce and rice passed separately.

Thai Sweet and Hot Garlic Sauce

Nam Jim Gratiem

THIS PUNGENT SWEET sauce is used for dipping just about any fried meat, poultry, fish, or vegetables. It is also traditional with Thai spring rolls.

MAKES 1 CUP

one In a blender or food processor fitted with a steel blade, combine 1/2 cup water, the sugar, vinegar, garlic, chile paste, and a large pinch of salt. Process until smooth.

1/2 cup Demerara, turbinado, or light brown sugar
1/2 cup rice or distilled white vinegar
6 large garlic cloves, lightly crushed
1 teaspoon prepared Thai chile paste
Salt

two Transfer the puree to a saucepan over medium heat. Bring slowly to a boil and simmer until the sauce is reduced by about half and lightly thickened. It will thicken more as it cools; if you find it is too thick when cooled, thin it with a little water. Serve at room temperature, but store unused portions in the refrigerator in a clean, covered container for up to 2 months.

Indonesian Curry Fried Chicken

Ayam Goreng Asam

SIMILAR RECIPES TO this one can be found all over the chain of islands between India and Australia that make up modern Indonesia, Malaysia, and Polynesia. The distinctive flavor of tamarind is what distinguishes the chicken, tenderizing the flesh and giving it its peculiarly tropical character. If it is unavailable to you, substitute fresh lemon or lime juice; it won't taste quite the same, but it will provide the necessary tartness to balance the curry spices.

SERVES 4

one Dissolve the tamarind in 1/3 cup boiling water. If you are using lemon or lime juice instead, set it aside. Wash the chicken and pat dry. Check to make sure that you have removed all small, loose bones and bone shards. Put the chicken in a large nonreactive glass or stainless steel bowl and set aside.

two Grind the coriander and cumin seeds in a spice mill or blender. Mix them with the garlic, a large pinch or two of salt, several liberal grindings of pepper, the sugar, and the turmeric. Stir this into the tamarind or citrus juice until it is dissolved. Add it to the chicken, rubbing it into each piece, and set aside to marinate for 1 hour, refrigerated (or cover and refrigerate overnight).

three Position a wire cooling rack over a cookie sheet. Lift the chicken from the marinade and lay it on the rack. Set aside to drain for at least 15 minutes or until the chicken is fairly dry. Don't wipe it; you'll lose a lot of the flavor.

four Fill a Dutch oven or deep-fat fryer with enough peanut oil to come halfway up the sides. Over medium-high heat, bring the oil to 375°F (hot but not smoking). Add the chicken, a few pieces at a time, beginning with the dark meat, until the pot is full but not crowded. Fry, stirring occasionally, until the chicken skin is golden and crispy and the chicken is cooked through, 10 to 12 minutes.

five Lift the chicken out of the fat, allow it to drain well, and transfer it to a clean wire rack (not the one you let it dry on). Repeat with the remaining chicken if it all will not fit into the pot at once. Serve hot.

1 teaspoon-sized chunk tamarind pulp or $\frac{1}{3}$ cup freshly squeezed lemon or lime juice

1 frying chicken, weighing no more than 3 pounds, cut up for frying Chinese-style as on page 11, skin and all

2 rounded teaspoons whole coriander seeds

1 rounded teaspoon whole cumin seeds

4 garlic cloves, minced

Salt and freshly milled black pepper

1 teaspoon light brown sugar

1 teaspoon ground turmeric

Peanut oil, for frying

Tamarind Paste The tamarind *(Tamarindus indica)* is a tropical tree, the fruit of which is a large brown pod containing highly acidic, dark, fleshy pulp surrounding its seeds. The pulp is used in cooking as lemon juice or other acids are. It is sold in cakes at Asian, Middle Eastern, and Caribbean markets. A lump of the cake is broken off and soaked in water to produce a paste or thin juice.

54

Mexican Fried Chicken with Oregano

Pollo con Oregano

THIS FRIED CHICKEN, a favorite of the food stalls in the open market of Oaxaca, Mexico, is from Zarela Martinez's *The Food of Oaxaca.* Zarela explains that the advantage, both for a street vendor and a busy home cook, is that the chicken can be prepared well ahead of time and sautéed to order at the last minute. It is unusual in that the chicken is first poached, then marinated, and finally fried to golden crispness just before serving.

Its key flavoring is Mexican oregano, the fleshy, pungent leaves of which have a more assertive flavor than Mediterranean oregano. It is sold dried in ethnic markets and live plants can sometimes be found at specialty greenhouses. If you can't find it, however, substitute any other variety that is available to you. It will still be very good.

SERVES 4

1 frying chicken, weighing no more than 3$^{1}/_{2}$ pounds, cut up for frying as on page 11, not skinned

2 bay leaves

1 small onion, unpeeled

5 large garlic cloves unpeeled

Salt

$^{1}/_{2}$ teaspoon whole black peppercorns

1 teaspoon dried Mexican oregano, or 1 tablespoon chopped fresh oregano

$^{1}/_{4}$ cup olive, peanut, or vegetable oil

one Wash the chicken and pat dry. Put it into a pot with the bay leaves, whole onion, 2 garlic cloves (unpeeled), 2 large pinches of salt, and the whole peppercorns. Add enough cold water to cover the chicken by 1 inch. Turn on the heat to medium-high and bring the water to the boiling point, carefully skimming off any scum that rises to the top. Reduce the heat to low and simmer gently until the chicken is just cooked through, about 20 minutes. Turn off the heat.

two Remove the chicken from the cooking liquid. Strain the liquid through a wire sieve and set it aside. Place the chicken in a nonreactive stainless steel or glass bowl that will comfortably hold all the pieces at once. Lightly crush, peel, and mince 1 of the remaining garlic cloves. Scatter it and the oregano over the chicken and sprinkle it with a couple of large pinches of salt. Toss until the seasonings are evenly distributed. When the cooking liquid is cooled, add just enough to barely cover the chicken. Set aside the remaining liquid for soup or another purpose. Cover the chicken and marinate, refrigerated, for 4 hours or overnight.

three Half an hour before you are ready to finish the chicken and serve it, remove it from the refrigerator, lift it from the marinade, and pat it dry. Lightly salt the chicken and set aside. Strain the marinating liquid and add it to the other reserved liquids to be used for another purpose. Lightly crush and peel the 2 remaining garlic cloves. Put them with the oil into a sauté pan that will comfortably hold the entire chicken without crowding it. Turn on the heat to medium-high. Fry the garlic, pressing it with the back of a spoon to release its full flavor into the oil, until it is golden, but not brown. Remove and discard the garlic and add the chicken to the pan. Sauté, turning once or twice, until all sides are golden brown, about 3 minutes per side. Serve at once.

Moroccan Fried Chicken

M'Hammer

TYPICAL OF AFRICAN cooking, this fried chicken from Morocco is a kind of fricassee in reverse. The chicken is cooked like a classic Moroccan *tagine,* a stew without a preliminary browning. However, it departs from a *tagine* on two important points: instead of being cut up into serving pieces, it is generally left whole, and when it is tender and nearly falling off the bone, it is quickly fried to a crispy, rich brown.

The recipe is adapted from *Moroccan Cooking* by Latifa Bennani-Smires.

SERVES 4

one Wash the chicken and pat dry. Put half the onions in a close-fitting lidded stewing pot that will comfortably hold the chicken, broth, and onions with at least 1 inch of headroom

1 small frying chicken, weighing no more than 3 pounds

2 medium onions, thinly sliced

Salt

3 cups Chicken Broth (page 18), Quick Broth (page 17), or water

Freshly milled white (preferred) or black pepper

¼ teaspoon crumbled saffron threads

3 large sprigs parsley or fresh cilantro

Zest from 2 Moroccan-preserved lemons (optional)

Juice of 1 lemon

2 tablespoons chopped parsley

4 tablespoons butter

1 cup olive or peanut oil

to spare. Put the chicken on top of the onion (sprinkle it liberally with salt if you are using water), and liberally grind white or black pepper over the bird. Add the broth and water, if needed, to completely cover the chicken. Add the saffron, sprigs of parsley or cilantro, remaining onion and zest.

two Over medium-high heat, bring the liquid to a boil. As soon as it begins to boil, reduce the heat to a slow simmer. Loosely cover the pan and simmer slowly until the chicken is very tender, about 3/4 hour. Turn off the heat.

three Remove the chicken carefully from the liquid without breaking the skin. Let it drain on a wire rack set over a cookie sheet or on a platter, then return any accumulated liquids to the stew pan. Pat the chicken dry and set aside. Turn up the heat under the stew pan to medium-high and bring the liquid to a boil. Reduce the heat to medium and cook, stirring occasionally, until the sauce is reduced, thick, and somewhat creamy, about 20 minutes. Add the lemon juice and chopped parsley and turn off the heat.

four While the sauce is reducing, combine the butter and oil in a large coated, non-stick skillet or Dutch oven over medium-high heat. When the fat is very hot, but not yet smoking (375°F), add the chicken carefully and fry, turning it frequently, until it is golden brown on all sides and the skin is crisp, 8 to 10 minutes. Turn off the heat, carefully lift the chicken from the fat, drain it thoroughly, and serve hot with the sauce passed separately.

Preserved Lemons An essential ingredient in much North African cookery, preserved lemons are the whole fruit pickled with salt and fresh lemon juice. Though preserved whole, generally only the peel is used. They can be purchased at some Middle Eastern markets, but if you can't find them, they are easy to make. Wash the fruit, pat dry, and cut them lengthwise as if you were cutting them into quarters, but without cutting through the stem end. Rub the inside of the lemons generously with sea or pickling salt—1/4 cup for every pound of fruit (about 1 tablespoon for each lemon). Pack them tightly into a sterilized jar, leaving at least 1 inch of headroom, and cover them with freshly squeezed lemon juice. Tightly cover the jar and keep it in a cool dark place or refrigerator. The lemons will be ready in 3 to 4 weeks.

Nigerian Fried Chicken

IN NIGERIA, THE chickens used for cooking are mature hens. While they are richer and more flavorful than young fryers, they are also tougher. Nigerian cooks therefore use a preliminary slow-stewing with tenderizing *akanwu,* or rock salt. You can use a young fryer and cut the stewing stage to 30 minutes, but it will not be as flavorful. A Nigerian cook would probably use only one pot for this dish; I've adapted the recipe to two pots so that the chicken is done at the same time as the sauce.

The recipe is from my friend Chi Ezek-wueche, a lovely Nigerian artist who is now living and working in Macon, Georgia.

SERVES 6

1 medium stewing hen (about 5 pounds), skinned and cut up for frying as on page 11

1 large yellow onion, thinly sliced in rings

2 large green or red bell peppers, finely chopped

1 large fresh green chile (or 2 to 3 small ones), seeded and ground to a paste in a mortar or blender

Cayenne pepper (optional)

Salt and freshly milled black pepper

4 tablespoons chopped fresh basil leaves (chopped just before using)

2 teaspoons curry powder

1 teaspoon grated fresh ginger

1/2 teaspoon rock salt or commercial meat tenderizer

Peanut oil, for frying

6 medium ripe tomatoes, scalded, peeled, and chopped, or 2 cups canned Italian plum tomatoes, chopped

2 cups hot Carolina-Style Rice (page 171)

one Wash the chicken, pat dry, and place in a Dutch oven. Pour 1 cup cold water over the chicken. Add half of the onion, half of the bell pepper, half of the chile paste, a pinch of cayenne, a large pinch of salt, several liberal grindings of black pepper, 2 tablespoons of basil, 1 teaspoon of curry powder, 1/2 teaspoon grated ginger, and the rock salt or meat tenderizer. Over medium heat, bring the liquid to a boil, uncovered. Cover the pot, reduce the heat to low, and simmer slowly until the chicken is tender but not falling off the bone and most of the liquid has been absorbed, about 1 hour. Turn off the heat, drain, reserving the cooking liquid, and let the chicken drain completely on a sieve.

two Wipe out the pot. Add 2 tablespoons peanut oil over medium heat. When the oil is hot, add the remaining onion and sauté until it is golden brown, 8 to 10 minutes. Add the remaining bell pepper, chile paste, a large pinch of salt, several liberal grindings of pepper, 1 tablespoon chopped basil, 1 teaspoon curry powder, and ½ teaspoon grated ginger. Sauté until very fragrant, about 2 minutes. Add the tomatoes and reserved cooking liquid and bring to a boil. Cook, stirring frequently, until the tomatoes begin to fall apart and their liquid is evaporated, about 15 minutes. (For a more concentrated sauce, you may opt to reduce the heat to low and simmer slowly for 1 hour, if you have the time.)

three Meanwhile, fill a second Dutch oven or deep cast-iron skillet with enough peanut oil to come halfway up the sides, at least 2 inches deep. Over medium-high heat, bring the oil to 325°F (medium frying heat). Add the chicken and fry it, turning once if it is not submerged, until the outside is golden brown on all sides, 5 to 8 minutes.

four Lift the chicken from the oil, drain thoroughly, and place it on a warm serving platter. Surround it with rice and sprinkle the thick sauce over it. Sprinkle the remaining 1 tablespoon basil over all and serve at once.

Armenian Butter-Fried Chicken with Eggplant

Tapaka

THE ARMENIAN WAY of frying a chicken is to split it down the back, flatten it, and fry it whole in clarified butter. It is one of the most delicious of all fried chickens; but in order for it to be successful, the bird must be very young and quite small, weighing no more than 1½ pounds (what used to be called "broilers" in our markets). Nowadays, however, with commercial breeding practices resulting in 4-pound fryers, small birds are very difficult to come by. You can approximate it with large Cornish hens or a 3-pound chicken cut into quarters.

The recipe is adapted from *The Cuisine of Armenia* by Sonia Uvezian.

SERVES 4

one Peel and slice the eggplant into ½-inch rounds. Salt them generously and layer them in a colander. Set aside in the sink to drain for 30 minutes. Scald the tomatoes for 30 seconds in boiling water. Peel, core, cut into quarters, and seed. Set aside.

two Wash the chickens and pat dry. Using a sharp kitchen knife or scissors, cut through the back of each bird on both sides of the backbone. Remove the backbone and set it aside to use in making broth. Spread the birds apart and thoroughly wash them inside and out. Pat dry and lay them skin side up on a work surface. Press flat with your hand, then cover with heavy plastic wrap or wax paper. Lightly pound them with the flat side of a cleaver or a heavy mallet until flattened. Sprinkle generously with salt and liberal grindings of black pepper and set aside.

three Finely chop 2 of the garlic cloves and set them aside. Put the remaining garlic into a mortar with a small pinch of salt and crush it to a paste. Combine the garlic paste and broth in a saucepan and bring it to a simmer over medium heat. Reduce the heat to low and simmer until the broth is reduced by a third. (An alternate way of preparing the garlic broth is to put the garlic

1 pound small eggplant, preferably the Italian or Japanese variety

Salt

4 medium ripe tomatoes or 8 plum tomatoes

2 young very small chickens, weighing no more than 1½ pounds, or 2 large Cornish hens, weighing at least 1¼ pounds each, or one 3-pound chicken

Freshly milled black pepper

4 to 8 garlic cloves, lightly crushed

1½ cups Chicken Broth (page 18) or any homemade broth (canned broth won't work)

½ cup clarified butter (page 14)

1 medium green bell pepper, cut into 1-inch squares

into the broth whole, bring it to a simmer, and cook until the garlic is very soft, and the broth reduced, 10 to 15 minutes. Puree it in a food processor or blender fitted with a steel blade.) Keep the broth warm until you are ready to serve the chicken.

four Heat 6 tablespoons of the butter in a large cast-iron skillet over medium heat. Add the chicken, skin side down, and cover the pan. Cook until the skin is golden brown, about 15 minutes. Reduce the heat to low and continue cooking for 10 minutes more. Turn the chicken, cover, and cook until it is a rich golden brown and cooked through, about 10 minutes more. If you like, remove the lid during the last 5 minutes to crisp the skin.

five Meanwhile, wipe the eggplant dry. Combine the remaining 2 tablespoons butter and the peppers in a large skillet over medium-high heat. Sauté until the peppers are bright green, about 2 minutes. Add the eggplant and sauté until it begins to color, about 4 minutes. Add the chopped garlic and sauté until fragrant. Add the tomatoes and continue sautéing until they are hot through, 3 to 4 minutes more. Turn off the heat, taste and season with salt and several liberal grindings of pepper, and transfer to a serving bowl.

six When the chicken is done, remove it with tongs to a warm platter. Carefully pour off all but a spoonful of the fat, then deglaze the pan with the garlic broth, stirring and scraping to remove any solids that may have stuck to the pan. Pour the broth into a sauce bowl. Serve at once, passing the broth, chicken, and vegetables separately.

DEEP-FRYING A WHOLE BIRD

This method of cooking a whole bird is quick and delicious and has certain distinct advantages, but it involves gallons of boiling grease and must be approached with both common sense and caution. First, this is strictly an outdoors project. It cannot be done in your kitchen. Secondly, it is not a floor show or spectator sport. This is no time for showing off to company or children. Aside from someone to assist you with the bird if you can't handle it alone, you don't need any distractions; this requires all your attention. Keep everyone else at a safe distance, and keep children and pets out of the yard not only while you are heating and cooking, but until the fat in the pot is cooled as well.

For equipment, you will need an outdoor gas burner (this can be rented from restaurant and party-supply rentals outlets), an 8- to 10-gallon pot, preferably with a frying-basket insert, a long tool such as a clean poker or long, very sturdy barbecue fork, tongs, a large wire rack set over a flat pan or cookie sheet (a wire-rack broiling pan is ideal), and heavy-duty oven mitts or welder's gloves. You and anyone who will be helping you should wear heavy, long old trousers and shoes in case of splatters.

The burner stand and the pot must be very stable. Set it up on a level patio or driveway where it won't matter if the grease splatters. Before you start heating the fat, be thoroughly familiar with every step of the recipe. If you are planning to handle the bird with a long tool and not a frying basket, practice using that tool first and be sure you can comfortably handle it with the weight of the bird on it. Also make sure it will hold the bird securely. Use clean, good-quality oil and never ever fill the pot more than a little less than half full. You'll need plenty of headroom for the grease to foam and boil up when the bird is added to the pot.

Crispy Skin Chicken

BEFORE YOU BEGIN, please read the preceding notes on frying a whole bird.

The Chinese actually have many different ways of preparing a whole chicken for frying. Very young, small birds may be marinated or rubbed with seasonings, dried well, and fried without preliminary cooking. Older, larger birds are usually poached or steamed before they are fried. Either way, you will need to begin preparations several hours ahead.

This follows the poach-and-fry method. If the bird is very young and tender (weighing less than 3 pounds), you may omit the poaching and fry it without preliminary cooking. Omit the broth and combine all the ingredients in a large stainless steel or glass bowl. Marinate the chicken for at least 1 hour, lift it out of the marinade, then hang it to dry as directed in step 3. It will need about 30 minutes to fry.

SERVES 4

1 frying chicken, weighing no more than 4 pounds

3 tablespoons soy sauce

3 tablespoons rice wine or extra-dry sherry

3 tablespoons honey

2 large or 4 small scallions or other green onions, thinly sliced

3 quarter-sized fresh ginger slices

3 large garlic cloves, lightly crushed and roughly chopped

1 teaspoon Chinese five-spice powder

1 × 3-inch piece orange zest cut from the fruit with a vegetable peeler

1 quart Chicken Broth (page 18), Quick Broth (page 17), or 2 cups canned broth mixed with 2 cups water

1 tablespoon cornstarch

Peanut oil, for frying

Plum Sauce (page 163), Quick Plum or Apricot Sauce (page 164), Sweet-and-Sour Sauce (page 165), or Hot Chinese Mustard (page 162)

one Wash the chicken and pat dry. Put it in a close-fitting kettle that will comfortably hold it when covered by 1 inch of liquid. Add 2 tablespoons each of the soy sauce, wine, and honey, the scallions, ginger, garlic, five-spice powder, orange zest, and broth. Add enough water to cover the chicken by 1 inch. Lift out the chicken and place the kettle over medium-high heat. Bring to a boil and let it boil for 4 to 5 minutes.

two Carefully lower the chicken into the boiling liquid, cover, and bring the liquid back to a boil. Reduce the heat to a slow simmer and poach the chicken for 15 minutes. Turn off the heat and let the chicken sit in the liquid for about 10 minutes longer. Lift the chicken out of the poaching liquid, drain it thoroughly, and pat it dry.

63

three Combine the remaining 1 tablespoon of soy sauce and wine with the cornstarch and beat until it is dissolved. Add the remaining 1 tablespoon honey and beat until smooth. Paint this mixture over the entire surface of the chicken. If you have a vertical roasting stand for poultry, set it over a plate and stand the bird on it; otherwise, lay the bird on a roasting rack. Refrigerate until completely dry (about 2 hours). Take the chicken from the refrigerator 30 minutes before cooking.

four Though Chinese cooks deep-fry whole chickens indoors in a wok, I recommend that you do the frying outdoors if at all possible. Choose a deep kettle that will hold the chicken with plenty of headroom for the fat to boil up. Add enough peanut oil to come a little less than halfway up the sides of the pot. Over medium-high heat, bring the oil to 375°F (hot but not smoking). Carefully lower the chicken into the fat, using a long tool such as a barbecue fork or poker, or a deep-fryer basket. Don't let it drop into the fat or it will splatter. Fry until the skin is a rich deep brown, 10 to 15 minutes, maintaining the temperature at 365°F. Lift the chicken out of the fat using tongs and a long-handled barbecue fork or clean poker inserted into the cavity, or, if you've used a fry basket, lift it out with the basket. Do not attempt to lift the bird by its wings or legs; they'll tear loose, allowing the bird to fall back into the fat and splatter. Hold the chicken over the pot to let the fat drain, then transfer the chicken to a wire rack set over a cookie sheet. Let it sit for 5 minutes.

five Chop the chicken into serving pieces with a cleaver as they do in China, or present the bird whole and carve it at the table in the Western manner. Serve with any of the suggested dipping sauces.

THIS BIRD IS FULL OF IT

When boneless chicken is stuffed with a savory filling, breaded, and fried, it always makes a spectacular show at the table—both for the eyes and the mouth. The recipes seem complicated and fancy—and, in a way, they are—yet most of them are very simple to put together. Stuffing is an especially happy thing to do with chicken breasts, which can otherwise be dry and not as interesting as other parts of the bird. The showy, crispy breading holds in the moisture and makes an inviting contrast to the succulent filling, which not only keeps the chicken flesh very moist but spills out onto the plate, making its own sauce when the chicken is cut open. As an added advantage, most of the recipes can be made well ahead of time and then quickly fried just before your guests come to the table—or while they are letting a first course settle.

Chicken Cordon Bleu

Suprêmes de Volaille Cordon Bleu

THIS OLD "GOURMET" standby can indeed be spectacular, or it can be exceedingly dull. Everything rests on the quality of the ingredients. With good cheese, first-rate ham, homemade crumbs, and a little care in the cooking, you can't go wrong. If, however, you use indifferent, packaged boiled ham and ordinary cheese, and add insult to injury by overcooking them, you'll find yourself wondering what all the fuss is about.

The ham should not be too thin, only as thin as you can cut it with a knife, so if you are using prosciutto that is sliced to order, don't let them slice it too thin.

SERVES 4

2 whole boneless chicken breasts, prepared for cutlets as on page 40

2 ounces thinly sliced uncooked country ham or prosciutto

4 ounces Gruyère cheese

1 large egg

1½ cups dry bread crumbs

¼ cup all-purpose flour

Dijon mustard

Peanut oil, for frying

one Wash the chicken and pat dry. Place the chicken breasts skinned side up on a sheet of wax paper or plastic wrap. Cover them with a second sheet of paper or wrap and, with a flat (not textured) wooden mallet, lightly beat them until flattened to a uniform thinness of less than ¼ inch. Set aside.

two Cut the ham and cheese into thin slices ½ inch wide and 2 inches long. Break the egg into a shallow bowl and beat until smooth. Spread the crumbs on a second shallow bowl. Spread the flour on a dinner plate.

three Lay the chicken pieces on a flat work surface skinned side down. Lightly spread the inside of each breast with a little mustard (don't use too much or the mustard will overpower the other flavors). Stack 2 slices of cheese and a slice of ham (2 if they are very thin) in the center of each breast. Fold over the small side of the breast, then fold each end up, like an envelope, and finally fold over the large side. Make sure that the filling is completely encased. Roll the chicken first in the flour, shake off the excess, and dip each breast in the egg, allowing the excess to flow back into the bowl. Lay it in the crumbs. Roll it carefully so that it doesn't open up (crumbs should not get inside the folds or they won't stay closed when it cooks), patting the crumbs into all sides. When the piece is coated, lay it on a clean, dry plate and repeat until all the pieces are breaded. Set aside for at least 15 minutes to allow the breading to set. (You may make them several hours or even a day ahead up to this point. Cover and refrigerate, but take them out half an hour before cooking.)

four Fill a deep Dutch oven or a deep-fat fryer with enough peanut oil to come halfway up the sides, at least 2 inches deep. Over medium-high heat, bring the oil to 375°F (hot but not smoking). Add the chicken and fry until golden brown, maintaining a temperature of 365°F, 4 to 5 minutes.

five Drain well and serve at once.

Chicken Kiev

ELEGANT, SHOWY, DELICIOUS, and embarrassingly easy once you know a couple of tricks, good old Chicken Kiev is a great way to give life to the dullest part of the bird and is a sure crowd pleaser whether the crowd is your family or high company.

The triple-dip method here—first flour, then egg, then the crumbs—insures a sturdy coating that helps to seal the breast and hold in the butter for that spectacular burst of golden deliciousness when you cut into it at the table.

SERVES 4

2 whole boneless chicken breasts, prepared for cutlets as on page 40

1/2 cup unsalted butter, slightly softened

1 tablespoon finely minced parsley

1 tablespoon finely minced fresh chives or scallion tops

1 tablespoon freshly squeezed lemon juice

Salt and freshly milled white pepper

1/4 cup all-purpose flour

1 1/2 cups dry bread crumbs

1 large egg

Peanut or vegetable oil, for frying

one Wash the chicken and pat dry. Place the chicken breasts skinned side up on a sheet of wax paper or plastic wrap. Cover them with a second sheet of paper or wrap and, with a flat (not textured) wooden mallet, lightly beat them until flattened to a uniform thinness of less than 1/4 inch. Set aside.

two Put the butter in a bowl with the parsley, chives or scallions, and lemon juice. Add a healthy pinch of salt and a few liberal grindings of white pepper. Knead until the seasonings are evenly mixed. Form the butter into 4 equal logs about 2 inches long. If it is too sticky to shape, chill it until it is firm enough to handle. Lay the butter sticks on a plate lined with wax paper and set them in the freezer until they are cold and hardened, about 15 minutes. (You may make the butter hours or even a day ahead, refrigerate it instead of putting it into the freezer. Just keep it very cold.)

three Spread the flour and crumbs in 2 shallow bowls. Break the egg into a third bowl and beat until it is light and thoroughly mixed. Spread the chicken breasts skinned side down on a flat work surface. Lay one piece of chilled herb butter on each breast a little off center on the larger side of the breast. Fold the smaller side over it, then fold over the top and bottom, then the large side, making sure that the butter is completely encased in meat. Gently roll the breasts in the flour, shake off the excess, then dip them in the egg, allowing the excess to flow back into the bowl. Finally, roll them gently in the crumbs until they are thoroughly coated. Lay them on a clean plate and refrigerate them for at least 1 hour. (You may make them several hours ahead up to this point.)

four Fill a deep Dutch oven or a deep-fat fryer with enough peanut oil to come halfway up the sides, at least 2 inches deep. Over medium-high heat, bring the oil to 375°F (hot but not quite smoking). Slip the chicken into the hot oil and fry until they are golden brown, maintaining a temperature of 365 °F, about 4 minutes. It is critical not to overcook them, or the butter will leak out into the frying fat. Drain thoroughly on a wire rack and serve at once.

NOTE: While you can assemble the chicken breasts well ahead of time, don't be tempted to fry Chicken Kiev ahead and try to hold it in a warm oven. It doesn't work. After all, it only takes a few minutes to fry them. Also, if you double the recipe, don't try to fry more than 4 at a time. As for the herbs: You can substitute finely minced shallots or garlic for the chives and add another minced fresh herb to the butter mix, such as tarragon, thyme, or basil, but don't use dried herbs of any kind.

Chicken with Spinach and Feta

SPANAKOPITA-GREEK SPINACH pie—is actually common all over the eastern Mediterranean. Here the pie's classic filling, savory with garlic, dill, and pine nuts and creamy with feta, is stuffed into a boneless chicken breast. It makes an exceptionally moist and flavorful stuffing, but even with this juicy filling, take care not to overcook the chicken.

SERVES 4

one Wash the chicken and pat dry. Lay the chicken breasts on a work surface. With a very sharp knife, make a horizontal slit down the center of one side. Cut almost all the way through, forming a pocket. Don't cut through the other side or the top and bottom. Repeat until all the breasts are slit. Set aside.

two Wash the spinach in several changes of water, making sure that all the grit and dirt is cleaned from the leaves. Remove the tough parts of stem and discard them. Drain the spinach and put it in a large soup kettle. Don't add water; the liquid clinging to the leaves will be sufficient. Cover the kettle and place it over medium-high heat. Cook until the spinach is wilted, about 4 minutes. (If you are using frozen spinach, put it into a covered pan with 2 tablespoons water and cook for 2 minutes.) Drain thoroughly, squeezing out any excess water; let the spinach cool enough to handle and chop it roughly. Set aside.

three Put the white parts of the scallions and the olive oil into a large skillet. Over medium heat, sauté, tossing frequently, until wilted but not browned, about 4 minutes. Add the garlic and continue sautéing until it is fragrant, about a minute more. Add the green tops of the scallions and turn off the heat. Add the spinach, parsley, dill, feta, and pine nuts to the pan. Toss until thoroughly mixed. Taste and add a pinch or so of salt, if needed, and a few liberal grindings of black pepper. Toss to mix in the seasonings.

2 whole boneless chicken breasts, prepared for cutlets as on page 40

³/₄ pound fresh spinach or one 10-ounce package frozen spinach, thawed

2 large scallions or other green onions, thinly sliced with white and green parts separated

2 tablespoons olive oil

2 teaspoons minced garlic (2 to 3 cloves)

2 tablespoons chopped parsley

¹/₄ cup chopped fresh dill or 1 tablespoon dried

2 ounces feta cheese, crumbled

1 tablespoon pine nuts

Salt and freshly milled black pepper

¹/₄ cup all-purpose flour

1 large egg

2 cups dry bread crumbs

Peanut or vegetable oil, for frying

1 lemon, cut into 8 wedges

four Divide the spinach filling among the breast pieces, completely filling each pocket. Secure the open sides with toothpicks. Spread the flour and crumbs in two shallow bowls. Break the egg into a third bowl and beat until it is light and thoroughly mixed. Lightly roll each breast in the flour, shake off the excess, and dip them into the beaten egg, coating all sides. Let the excess flow back into the bowl, then roll them in the crumbs, patting the crumbs into the entire surface. Place the breasts on a plate and set aside for at least 15 minutes. (The chicken may be prepared up to this point several hours or a day ahead. Cover and refrigerate, but take them out half an hour before cooking them.)

five Fit a wire cooling rack in a cookie sheet and set aside. Fill a Dutch oven or deep-fat fryer with enough oil to come halfway up the sides, at least 2 inches deep. Over medium-high heat, bring the oil to 375°F (hot but not smoking). Add enough of the chicken to the pan to fill it without crowding. Fry until golden brown, maintaining a temperature of 365°F, 5 to 6 minutes, turning once if necessary.

six Drain well, then lay them on the wire cooling rack to finish draining. Transfer to a warm platter and serve hot with lemon wedges scattered among them.

Chicken Breasts with Fresh Mozzarella and Basil

Petti di Pollo alla Margherita

MARGHERITA IS THE name of a classic Neopolitan pizza topped with fresh tomatoes, basil, and mozzarella. I've given it to this recipe because it incorporates those same flavors, only instead of blanketing the top, the classic "topping" goes on the inside. The result is a filling that keeps the chicken very moist, light, and fresh-tasting, and makes a lovely contrast to the crispy fried exterior.

SERVES 4

one Wash the chicken and pat dry. Lay the chicken breasts on a flat work surface. With a very sharp knife, make a horizontal slit down the center of one side. Gently cut almost all the way through, forming a pocket. Don't cut through the other side or the top and bottom. Repeat until all the breasts are slit. Set aside.

two Using a vegetable peeler, peel the tomatoes, core them, and split them lengthwise. Scoop out and discard the seeds, then cut the halves into wide strips, flattening the lobes of the tomato into a single layer. Thinly slice the mozzarella. Fold back the top flap of each breast. Lightly season the inside with salt and a few grindings of pepper. Lay a few slices of mozzarella inside each one, cover with sliced tomato, then sprinkle lightly with salt. Lay the basil leaves over the tomato. Fold the top of the breast over the filling, which should fill the breast without sticking out at any point. Secure the side of the breast with a toothpick.

three Mix together the bread crumbs and Parmigiano in a shallow bowl. Break the egg into another bowl and beat until light. Put the flour into a third bowl. Roll the stuffed breasts lightly in the flour, shake off the excess, then dip them in the egg until they are completely coated. Allow the excess egg to flow back

- 2 whole boneless chicken breasts prepared for cutlets as on page 40
- 2 very ripe plum tomatoes
- 4 ounces fresh mozzarella
- Salt and freshly milled black pepper
- 4 to 8 large basil leaves
- 1/2 cup dry bread crumbs
- 1/2 cup freshly grated Parmigiano-Reggiano
- 1 large egg, beaten
- 1/4 cup all-purpose flour
- Olive, peanut, or vegetable oil, or butter and olive oil mixed, for frying

70

into the bowl, then roll the breasts in the crumb-cheese mixture until thickly coated. Lay the breaded chicken on a clean, dry plate and let the breasts stand for half an hour to set the breading. (You may make them as much as 2 hours ahead. Cover and refrigerate, then let them sit at room temperature for half an hour before cooking them.)

four Pour enough oil, or ¼ pound of butter and enough olive oil, into a deep cast-iron skillet to come halfway up the sides. Over medium-high heat, bring the oil to 375°F (hot but not smoking). Slip the chicken into the oil and fry until golden brown, maintaining a temperature of 365°F, turning them halfway through the cooking, 3 to 4 minutes per side. Drain thoroughly. Serve at once.

NOTE: If you cannot get fresh mozzarella and must be content with a block of the supermarket variety, grate it into a shallow bowl and pour about ¼ cup of heavy cream over the mozzarella. Let it soak for about half an hour, then squeeze out the excess moisture. It will take about 1 heaping table-spoonful to fill each breast. It won't be the same as fresh mozzarella, but it will be infinitely better.

Stuffing Other Parts of the Bird

The breast fillets of the chicken are easy to manage when stuffing. Since most markets sell them boned, skinned, and ready to use, they are very convenient; but they have a drawback: As the largest and leanest of the bird's muscles, they can be tough and dry, especially if you get distracted and let them overcook. That's not a problem with the thigh and leg. You practically have to burn them before they dry out. That isn't to say that you should not be just as careful in cooking them, but they are more forgiving of a slip.

Though thighs and legs are seldom sold boned, boning them yourself is not much trouble, and you can use the bones and scraps for making Quick Broth (page 17). More-over, once they are boned, they are ready to stuff, since the boning creates a ready-made cavity for the filling. See page 11 for detailed instructions.

Chicken Thighs Hunter-Style, with Sweet Potato Stuffing

 SWEET POTATO STUFFING is an old American filling that is favored with game, especially rich animals, such as duck, oppossum, and raccoon. Here, it gives a savory gamy flavor to chicken thighs. Hunters do not fool around in the kitchen: Most of the time they season their catch generously with salt and pepper, roll it in flour, and fry it. But occasionally, they will dress up the catch and sauce it with Madeira, as it is here.

SERVES 4

1 pound sweet potatoes (about 2 medium), baked, still hot

6 tablespoons unsalted butter, or 2 tablespoons butter and 4 tablespoons bacon drippings

1/2 cup soft bread crumbs or crumbled corn bread

2 large scallions or other green onions, minced

1 tablespoon chopped fresh sage or 1 teaspoon crumbled dried

Grated zest of 1 lemon

Salt and freshly milled black pepper

Whole nutmeg in a grater

8 chicken thighs, boned as on page 11, but not skinned

1/4 cup all-purpose flour

1/4 cup minced shallot or yellow onion

1/4 cup Madeira or dry sherry

1 cup Quick Broth (page 17), Chicken Broth (page 18), or 1/2 cup canned broth mixed with 1/2 cup water

one Peel the sweet potatoes while they are still hot and mash the pulp until it is smooth. Mix in 2 tablespoons of the butter until it is melted and incorporated. Add the crumbs, scallions, sage, and lemon zest. Season liberally with salt, a few grindings of black pepper, and a liberal grating of nutmeg.

two Wash the chicken and pat dry. Place the boned thighs on a flat work surface, skin side down. Put a rounded tablespoon of the stuffing on the center of each thigh. Fold the flesh of the thigh over it, and then pull the skin together to form a package. Don't press or you will squeeze out the stuffing. If some of it does ooze out, wipe it away and don't try to put it back; you probably had too much to begin with. Sew up the skin with a trussing needle and kitchen twine, or secure it with toothpicks. Sprinkle with salt and a few grindings of pepper and set aside.

three Put the remaining butter or drippings in a large sauté pan. Over medium-high heat, melt the fat and heat until almost smoking. Quickly roll the thighs in the flour, shake off the excess, and slip them into the pan in a single layer. Fry, turning them frequently, until they are golden brown on all sides, about 4 minutes. Reduce the heat to medium and continue cooking until the thighs are cooked through, the skin crisp, and the stuffing hot (165°F), 25 minutes more. Transfer them to a warm platter.

four Spoon off all but 2 tablespoons of the fat and return the pan to medium-high heat. Add the minced shallot or onion and sauté until it is golden brown but not scorched, about 5 minutes. Pour the Madeira or sherry into the pan, stirring and scraping to release any cooking solids that may be stuck to the pan, and let it come to a good boil. When the wine is slightly reduced, add the broth and bring it back to a boil. Cook until it is reduced and thickened, about 5 minutes more. Turn off the heat, taste, adjust the seasonings of the sauce, and pour it over the chicken. Serve at once.

Chicken Thighs "Saltimbocca"

SALTIMBOCCA MEANS "jump in the mouth," and it is the name given to a traditional Roman dish of sautéed rolls of veal, prosciutto, and sage. No one who has ever tasted these little morsels wonders how they came to have such a name. This is the same idea: The cavities of boned chicken thighs are filled with prosciutto and fresh sage leaves, sautéed in butter and olive oil, and finished off with Marsala or white wine.

SERVES 4

8 chicken thighs, boned as on page 11, but not skinned

8 thin slices of prosciutto, about 2 inches square

8 to 16 fresh sage leaves (do not use dried sage)

Salt and freshly milled black pepper

2 tablespoons unsalted butter

2 tablespoons olive oil

2 large garlic cloves, lightly crushed

¼ cup all-purpose flour

½ cup dry Marsala or white wine

one Wash the chicken and pat dry. Spread the boned thighs on a flat work surface, skin side down. Lay a slice of prosciutto on the center of each and top it with 1 to 2 fresh sage leaves (depending on size). Roll the thighs up over the ham and sage, pulling the skin together to form a package. Sew up the skin with a trussing needle and kitchen twine or secure it with a toothpick. Sprinkle with salt and several liberal grindings of pepper. Set aside.

two Combine the butter and oil in a large sauté pan that will hold all the thighs in one layer without crowding them. Add the garlic. Over medium-high heat, melt the butter. When the foaming has subsided, quickly roll the stuffed thighs in the flour, shake off the excess, and slip them into the pan in a single layer. Fry, turning frequently, until golden brown on all sides, about 4 minutes. When the garlic becomes colored nut-brown, take it out of the pan and discard it.

three Reduce the heat to medium and cook, turning frequently, until the thighs are cooked through and the skin is crispy, 8 to 10 minutes more. Remove them from the pan and transfer them to a warm platter.

four Spoon off all but 2 tablespoons of the fat remaining in the pan and raise the heat to medium-high. Pour in the wine and cook, stirring and scraping to loosen any cooking residue that may be stuck to the pan, until it is reduced and thickened, about 2 minutes more. Turn off the heat, pour the sauce over the chicken, and serve at once.

THE PARTY BIRD: PICK-UP FRIED CHICKEN FOR PARTIES, PICNICS, AND SNACKS

Fried chicken is a perennial favorite party food. With its savory crust, juicy interior, and built-in handle, it may be the most perfect pick-up food around: the one essential item in any picnic basket, the centerpiece on the table at many family reunions, a fixture on the menu of any tavern worth its beer, and the first thing to disappear from a cocktail party buffet. Unless you are cooking for a vegetarians' convention, your popularity as a host is assured when your guests are greeted by a platter of fried chicken. Hot or cold, it is loved by children and adults alike.

Almost any deep- or pan-fried chicken will adapt well to a finger-food menu; in this chapter, however, are recipes that are especially suited to the occasion. The party bird fits no specific classification; it crosses all lines. It may be battered, breaded, or fried without breading; it may be pan-fried, deep-fried, or fried and baked; it may come with a sumptuous dipping sauce or only a wedge of lemon. It may be hot, it may be cold, it may be crackling crisp or meltingly tender. It may be boneless or not. Its only requisite is that it be in small, self-contained portions that one can pick up with the fingers and dispense with in a bite or two.

Nuggets and Fingers

Children in particular love bite-sized morsels of boneless chicken meat, but nuggets are something that very few people ever outgrow. The neat, self-contained, easy to pick up portions have an added advantage at parties of leaving no waste. They can be served on their own, with one or more dipping sauces on the side, or turned into sandwiches, or in any way that suits you and your guests. But they needn't be confined only to party occasions. Any of them make a great lunch or dinner main course, especially when you have children at the table.

Cajun Popcorn Chicken

"CAJUN POPCORN" is a colloquial name for spicy fried crawfish tails. Elsewhere in the South and even in Louisiana, tiny shrimp, catfish fillets, and chicken nuggets are fried the same way and given a similar name. Whether they are so-called because they resemble popcorn in size or because they get gobbled by the handful is moot; both are true. Plan to make a lot more than you think you'll need; they disappear fast and furiously.

SERVES 4 AS A MAIN COURSE, 8 AS AN APPETIZER

FOR THE CAJUN SEASONING MIX:

1/2 teaspoon cayenne pepper (or more, to taste)

1 teaspoon freshly milled black pepper

1 teaspoon paprika

2 teaspoons onion powder

1 teaspoon garlic powder

1 1/2 teaspoons crumbled dried thyme

Salt

1 cup all-purpose flour

1 cup fine white cornmeal

1 pound boneless chicken breast or chicken thighs (or both), skinned

2 eggs, lightly beaten

2 tablespoons milk

Peanut or vegetable oil or lard (or a mixture of oil and lard), for frying

Horseradish Cocktail Sauce (recipe follows), or Tartar Sauce (page 160)

1 lemon, cut into 8 wedges

one Combine the seasoning mix in a large, wide, shallow bowl. Add a healthy pinch of salt, the flour, and cornmeal. Toss until they are evenly mixed.

two Wash the chicken and pat dry. Cut into bite-sized chunks, being careful to remove any fat, tendons, and cartilage from the meat.

three Beat together the egg and milk in a shallow bowl. Add the chicken to the egg mixture and toss until all are coated.

four Preheat the oven to 150° F (or Warm setting). Fit a wire cooling rack into a cookie sheet. Fill a deep Dutch oven or deep-fat fryer with enough oil or lard to come halfway up the sides, at least 2 inches deep. Over medium-high heat, bring the fat to 375°F (hot but not smoking). A few at a time, lift the chicken pieces out of the egg, allowing the excess to flow back into the bowl, and then drop them into the seasoned flour. Roll until they are well coated, gently shake off the excess, and add them to the pan until it is full but not crowded. Fry until golden brown, turning them halfway if they are not completely submerged, about 3 minutes.

five Drain them thoroughly and transfer them to the rack. Put the rack in the oven to keep the chicken warm while the remaining pieces cook. Repeat until all the chicken is fried. Serve piping hot, with Horseradish Cocktail Sauce and lemon wedges passed separately.

Horseradish Cocktail Sauce

USUALLY SERVED WITH fried fish, boiled seafood, and oysters on the half shell, this spicy sauce also melds well with Cajun Popcorn Chicken (page 76), Beer-Battered Chicken Drumettes (page 88), and Spicy Chicken Drumettes (page 90).

MAKES ABOUT 1 CUP

¹/₂ cup tomato ketchup

¹/₄ cup prepared horseradish

1¹/₂ tablespoons freshly squeezed lemon juice

Louisiana hot pepper sauce

Sugar

Combine the ketchup, horseradish, and lemon juice in a bowl. Mix well. Add a few dashes of hot sauce to taste and the smallest pinch of sugar. Mix well, taste, and adjust the seasonings. If you like it really spicy, adjust the horseradish and hot sauce accordingly. If, on the other hand, you prefer a milder sauce, up the amount of catsup. Serve cold.

Coconut Chicken Fingers

COCONUT SHRIMP—DEEP-FRIED shrimp breaded with grated coconut—has become very fashionable on restaurant menus, and no wonder—when properly made, they are spectacular. The coconut breading needn't be confined to seafood, however; it's also great with chicken fingers. The chicken is marinated briefly in bitter orange juice, as for Cuban Fried Chicken (page 31), before being floured, dipped in egg, and coated with grated coconut. You may go far enough afield here to use unsweetened shredded coconut, but do go to the extra step of making coconut milk for the egg dip, and don't use a packaged coconut that is sweetened for confectionary uses.

**SERVES 4 AS A MAIN COURSE,
8 AS AN APPETIZER**

one If you are using boneless breasts or thighs, cut them crosswise (against the grain of the muscle) into ½-inch-wide fingers. If you are using chicken tenders, remove the long tendon that runs down the center as follows: Lay the tender on the work surface with the tendon flat against the work surface. Place the edge of a knife against the tendon at the point that the tendon protrudes from the top end. Grasp the tendon end with your other hand and pull. It should come out as it scrapes against the knife blade. Rinse the meat and pat dry.

2 whole boneless chicken breasts, skinned, split, and trimmed as on page 11, or 1 pound chicken tenders (the finger-shaped "tenderloin"), or boned and skinned thighs, as on page 11

¼ cup fresh bitter (Seville) orange juice, or 2 tablespoons fresh orange juice mixed with 2 tablespoons fresh lime juice

2 tablespoons strained fresh coconut juice or coconut milk (see Note)

2 large eggs

2 cups freshly grated coconut, or unsulfured, unsweetened shredded coconut

Salt and freshly milled black pepper

¼ cup all-purpose flour

Peanut oil, for frying

Sweet-and-Sour Sauce (page 165), Hot Chinese Mustard (page 162), or Fresh Mango Sauce (page 158)

two Put the chicken fingers in a nonreactive glass or stainless steel bowl and add the bitter orange juice (or combined orange and lime juice). Toss well and set aside to marinate for 30 minutes, refrigerated. Meanwhile, combine the coconut juice with the egg in a shallow bowl and beat until uniformly mixed and smooth. Put the grated coconut into another shallow bowl.

three Lift the chicken out of its marinade and pat dry. Discard the marinade. Season the chicken liberally with a sprinkling of salt and several grindings of pepper, then roll them lightly in the flour and shake off the excess. Dip them one at a time into the egg mixture and then roll them in the grated coconut. Lay them on a clean, dry plate.

four Fill a Dutch oven or deep-fat fryer with enough oil to come halfway up the sides, at least 2 inches deep. Over medium-high heat, bring the oil to 375°F (hot but not smoking). Slip in enough chicken fingers to fill the pan without crowding and fry until the coconut is golden brown, 3 to 4 minutes. Serve hot with Sweet-and-Sour Sauce, Hot Chinese Mustard, Fresh Mango Sauce, or your favorite chutney.

NOTE: Unsulfured, unsweetened dried coconut actually makes a fine breading. The flavor isn't as fresh as fresh coconut, but it is more concentrated. If you are using it, you'll need coconut milk to substitute for the fresh juice. To make it, pour ½ cup boiling water over ½ cup of the shredded coconut. Let it steep for at least an hour, then strain it, pressing hard on the solids. Discard the solids. For fresh coconut juice, pierce one of the "eyes" and drain out the juice before cracking the coconut open. Strain the juice through a wire strainer to catch any bits of husk or shell.

Golden Coin Chicken

"GOLDEN COINS" is an apt moniker for these tasty little nuggets. To be authentic, they should be strung onto skewers like the gold coins of China. This is easiest to do if it is done after the first frying. Golden Coin Chicken makes great hot hors d'oeuvres for a cocktail party, but you can also use it as a main course. In either case, serve the chicken piping hot, with pungent, slightly sweet Chinese vinegar, Hot Chinese Mustard, Sweet-and-Sour Sauce, plum sauce, or Fresh Mango Sauce.

SERVES 4 AS A MAIN COURSE,

8 AS AN APPETIZER

2 whole large boneless chicken breasts, skinned, split, and trimmed as on page 11

2 tablespoons rice wine or extra-dry sherry

2 tablespoons soy sauce

1 tablespoon brown sugar

1 medium scallion, minced

1 garlic clove, crushed and minced

1 quarter-sized fresh ginger slice, minced

Peanut oil, for frying

1/2 cup cornstarch

1 large egg, beaten until smooth

Chinese vinegar, Hot Chinese Mustard (page 162), Sweet-and-Sour Sauce (page 165), either plum sauce (pages 163 to 164), or Fresh Mango Sauce (page 158)

one Wash the chicken and pat dry. Slice the breasts across the grain of the muscle into ⅛-inch-thick slices. Cut each slice into a 1-inch round medallion.

two Combine the wine, soy sauce, sugar, scallion, garlic, and ginger in a large nonreactive stainless steel or glass bowl. Add the chicken and let it marinate for half an hour, refrigerated. Soak 12 bamboo skewers in water for 5 minutes. Drain and *thoroughly* dry them. They should be damp but not dripping wet.

three Fit a wire cooling rack into a cookie sheet. Fill a deep cast-iron skillet or deep-fat fryer with enough oil to come halfway up the sides, at least 1 inch of oil. Over medium-high heat, bring the oil to 375°F (hot but not smoking).

four Drain the chicken, discarding the marinade, and pat it dry on absorbent paper. In a shallow bowl, dissolve the cornstarch in water and add the beaten egg. Beat until smooth. Add the chicken to the batter and toss until all the pieces are well coated.

five When the oil is hot (375°F), lift out enough chicken to fill the pan without crowding it, allowing the excess batter to flow back into the bowl, and add the pieces to the pan one at a time. Fry until golden brown, about 2 minutes, and drain well on absorbent paper. Transfer the pieces to the wire rack and repeat with the remaining chicken. Cool slightly.

six Thread the chicken in equal portions onto the skewers, about 5 per skewer, spaced ¼-inch apart. Bring the oil temperature back up to 375°F. Fry the skewers until golden and crisp, about 1 minute. Lift it out of the fat, drain thoroughly, and transfer to the wire rack to finish draining. Serve hot, with Chinese vinegar and dipping sauces passed separately.

Creole Chicken Poor Boy

FRIED CHICKEN BREASTS are an excellent sandwich filling, and any of the breaded chicken cutlets in this book also make a wonderful sandwich. Here, Creole-flavored cutlets are piled onto a buttered and toasted French baguette and garnished with lettuce, thinly sliced sweet onions, and tartar sauce or mayonnaise. You just about can't get a sandwich in the South without some mayonnaise on it, but if you want to lighten this one up, you can omit the spread; the chicken is rich enough by itself. You can use individual rolls instead of a baguette if you would prefer, but do use good, sturdy home-style bread.

SERVES 4

one Wash the chicken and pat dry. Lay the chicken breasts on a flat work surface, press each one flat with your hand and, while holding it, carefully slice it in half horizontally with a very sharp knife. Repeat with the remaining breasts and put the slices into a

2 whole boneless chicken breasts, skinned, split, and trimmed as on page 11

2 garlic cloves, minced

Salt and freshly milled black pepper

Louisiana-style hot sauce

½ cup dry white wine

1 cup all-purpose flour

½ teaspoon cayenne pepper

1 teaspoon crumbled dried thyme

1 teaspoon garlic powder

1 teaspoon onion powder

1 fresh French baguette

Unsalted butter

Lard or peanut or vegetable oil, for frying

1 large egg, beaten

Tartar Sauce (page 160) or Mayonnaise (page 159)

½ sweet onion, such as Vidalia, or medium red onion, thinly sliced

4 large leaves romaine lettuce, cut into fine ribbons

nonreactive glass or stainless steel bowl. Add the garlic, a healthy pinch of salt, a liberal grinding of pepper, and a few shots of hot sauce to taste. Toss to coat the chicken evenly and then pour the wine over it. Cover and marinate for 1 hour, refrigerated, or overnight.

two In a paper or plastic ziplock bag, combine the flour with a heaping teaspoon of salt, several liberal grindings of pepper, the cayenne, thyme, and garlic and onion powders. Close the top and shake until the seasonings are evenly distributed. Set aside.

three When you are ready to make the sandwich, preheat the oven broiler and position a rack about 8 inches below it. Split the baguette lengthwise and lay it open on a cookie sheet. Spread generously with softened butter and toast under the broiler until the surface is golden brown and crisp. Turn off the broiler and set the baguette aside.

four Fill a deep cast-iron skillet with enough fat to come halfway up the sides, at least 1 inch deep. Over medium-high heat, bring the fat to 375°F (hot but not smoking). Drain the marinade from the chicken breasts. Dip them one at a time in the beaten egg, then drop them into the seasoned flour. Close the bag and toss until well coated. Lift out the coated breast, shake off the excess, and slip it into the fat. Repeat until the pan is full. Fry, turning once, until the breast slices are golden brown on both sides and cooked through, about 3 minutes per side. Drain and lay on a wire rack set over a cookie sheet. Repeat with the remaining chicken until all of it is fried.

five Lightly spread the bread with tartar sauce or mayonnaise. Lay the chicken breast pieces, overlapping them if necessary, on the bottom half of the baguette. Scatter the sliced onion over the top and then the lettuce. Cover with the top half of the bread. Divide the sandwich into 4 equal sections and serve at once.

CHICKEN POOR BOY À LA MEDIATRICE: This tasty variation is made in the same way as the famous Creole oyster loaf, *la mediatrice* (the peacemaker). Instead of splitting the baguette in half, cut off the top about a third of the way down. Scoop out the bread from the center of the loaf and set it aside for making crumbs. Generously butter the hollowed-out loaf and underside of the top slice and toast them under the broiler. Make 1 batch of Cajun Popcorn Chicken (page 76). When it is ready, drain it thoroughly and fill the cavity of the loaf with the chicken. Cover it with the top and serve at once, passing lemon wedges and Tartar Sauce (page 160) separately.

Japanese Fried Chicken

JAPANESE DEEP-FRIED CHICKEN, *toriniku tatsuta-age,* is really an adaptive variation of Chinese antecedents: The chicken is cut into manageable bite-sized nuggets, marinated, mixed with starch, and fried quickly in deep fat. The key difference is the kind of starch used in the coating—*katakuri-ko,* a potato starch. The remaining ingredients and the technique are essentially the same. This chicken is good either hot or at room temperature and is therefore a popular lunchbox dish in Japan. That fact also makes it ideal for parties and picnics.

SERVES 4 AS A MAIN COURSE, 8 AS AN APPETIZER

1 pound boneless chicken (preferably from the thighs), skinned

2 tablespoons soy sauce

2 tablespoons sake

1 tablespoon freshly grated fresh ginger

1 teaspoon toasted sesame oil

1 large garlic clove, lightly crushed

1/3 cup *katakuri-ko* (Japanese potato flour or starch) or potato starch

Peanut or vegetable oil, for frying

one Wash the chicken and pat dry. Cut into bite-sized nuggets. Combine the soy, sake, ginger, and sesame oil in a large nonreactive glass or stainless steel bowl. Add the chicken and the garlic and toss until the chicken is evenly coated. Cover and refrigerate at least 1 hour or overnight.

two Sprinkle the potato starch over the chicken and toss until it forms a smooth batter with the marinade.

three Fill a deep-fat fryer or Dutch oven with enough oil to come halfway up the sides, at least 2 inches deep. Over medium-high heat, bring the oil to 375°F (hot but not smoking). Stir the chicken again to coat it evenly and lift it out, one piece at a time, and slip it into the hot fat. Fry until the chicken is light gold, about 2 minutes. Drain well on a wire rack set over a cookie sheet. Let it cool slightly.

four Bring the temperature of the oil back to 375°F. Return the chicken pieces to the pot and fry until they are crisp and golden, about 1 minute. Lift from the fat, allowing it to drain thoroughly, and then drain well on the wire rack. Serve hot or at room temperature.

Sesame Chicken Fingers

THOUGH SESAME SEEDS are a well-known element of Asian and African cooking, few people expect them to figure in the cooking of South Carolina and Georgia. However, West Coast African slaves gradually introduced African ingredients like sesame seeds (called benne seeds around here) into Lowcountry cookery. Consequently, it is difficult to place this crunchy sesame batter coating; it has a suggestion of all these cuisines about it. Well, it really doesn't matter where they came from—what counts is that they're delicious.

**SERVES 4 AS A MAIN COURSE,
8 AS AN APPETIZER**

one If you are using boneless breasts or thighs, cut them crosswise (against the grain of the muscle) into ½-inch-wide fingers. If you are using chicken tenders, remove the long tendon that runs down the center as follows: Lay the tender on the work surface with the tendon flat against the work surface. Place the edge of a knife against the tendon at the point that the tendon protrudes from the top end. Grasp the tendon end with your other hand and pull. It should come out as it scrapes against the knife blade. Rinse the meat and pat dry.

two Combine the flour, baking powder, a large pinch of salt, a small one of cayenne, and a few liberal grindings of black pepper in a bowl. Mix until the seasoning is well distributed and make a well in the center. Add ½ cup water to the yolk and beat until it is smooth. Pour it into the center of the flour and gradually beat the flour into it until it forms a smooth batter. Stir in the sesame seeds. In the separate bowl, beat the egg white until it forms stiff—but not dry—peaks.

2 whole boneless chicken breasts or 1 pound chicken tenders (the finger-shaped "tenderloin") or boned thighs, skinned and trimmed as on pages 11 to 12

½ cup all-purpose flour

½ teaspoon baking powder

Salt, cayenne pepper, and freshly milled black pepper

1 large egg, separated

3 tablespoons untoasted sesame seeds

Peanut or vegetable oil, for frying

Sweet-and-Sour Sauce (page 165), Horseradish Cocktail Sauce (page 77), Honey Mustard (page 161), and/or Fresh Mango Sauce (page 158)

three Fit a wire cooling rack in a cookie sheet. Preheat the oven to 150°F (or Warm setting). Fill a deep-fryer or Dutch oven with enough oil to come halfway up the sides, at least 2 inches. Over medium high heat, bring the oil to 375°F (hot but not smoking).

four When the oil is hot, gently fold the beaten egg white into the batter. Add the chicken fingers, a few at a time, and lift them out of the batter, allowing the excess to flow back into the bowl. Slip enough chicken into the fat to fill the pan without crowding it and fry, maintaining the oil temperature at 365°F, until golden brown, 3 to 4 minutes. Drain thoroughly and transfer to the wire rack and keep them warm in the oven while you fry the remaining fingers.

five Just before serving, fry the fingers a second time at 375°F for 1 minute to crisp them. Serve hot with your choice of dipping sauces.

Fried Wings or Drumettes

There isn't much meat on a chicken wing, but what there is is exceptionally flavorful and succulent. Whether you serve whole wings or just the joint closest to the breast (called drumette because it looks like a miniature drumstick), they'll disappear in a hurry, so be sure that you make more than you think you'll need. Many markets sell drumettes already cut, but they are easy to do yourself if the trimmed ones aren't available.

While strictly speaking, the drumette is only the first, large joint of the wing (at the shoulder), both joints are frequently called for in drumette recipes, and the second joint is especially tasty and succulent, so I always make use of it in a "drumette" recipe. The wing tips make lovely broth.

Wings and drumettes are great with just about any marinade, rub, batter, or breading in this book, but they are particularly successful with any Southern fried breading or batter (pages 99 to 114), or the batter used in Florentine Fried Chicken (page 20). You may also bread them with coconut (as in Coconut Chicken Fingers, page 78). Allow 8 to 10 minutes cooking time.

Buffalo Wings

THE ANCHOR BAR in Buffalo, New York, claims to have served the first and original Buffalo wings, but the chicken recipe with arguably the world's most confusing and amusing name is now a national bar-food classic. The wings are, of course, named for their hometown; they aren't bovine, but in many places, they are so hot that they kick like one. Deep-fried and traditionally served with mayo-based blue cheese dressing and celery sticks, they are messy to eat, fattening as the dickens, and absolutely delicious.

The only beverage to serve with Buffalo wings is very cold beer, and plenty of it.

SERVES 6 TO 8

24 whole chicken wings (4 to 4¹/₂ pounds)

Salt and freshly milled black pepper

4 celery ribs

¹/₂ cup clarified butter (page 14)

¹/₂ cup or more Louisiana hot sauce

1 tablespoon wine vinegar

3 to 4 large garlic cloves, crushed but left in one piece (optional)

Peanut or vegetable oil, for frying

Garlicky-Green Blue Cheese Dressing (recipe follows)

one Disjoint the wings, setting aside the tips for the broth pot, wash them under cold running water, and pat dry. Spread them on a platter, sprinkle lightly with salt and freshly ground pepper, and set aside. Wash the celery, remove the tough strings, and cut it into thin 2-inch sticks. Put them in a bowl with several cubes of ice and cover with cold water. Set aside.

two Put the clarified butter, hot sauce, vinegar, and garlic, if using, in a large skillet that will comfortably hold all the wings in no more than 2 layers. Place it over medium heat and bring to a simmer. Turn off the heat and set it aside.

three Fit a wire cooling rack over a cookie sheet and preheat the oven to 150°F (or Warm setting). Fill a Dutch oven or deep-fat fryer with enough oil to come halfway up the sides, at least 2 inches deep. Over medium-high heat, bring the oil to 375°F (hot but not smoking). Put enough wings into the pot to fill it without crowding (beginning with the drumettes, which take a little longer to cook), adding a few at a time so that the fat temperature never dips below 365°F. Fry, maintaining the oil at 365°F, until the wings are cooked through and crispy, 8 to 10 minutes (they will float and the foaming will subside when they are done). Lift them out a few at a time, allowing the fat to drain from them thoroughly. Transfer to the wire rack and keep them in the warm oven while you fry the remaining wings.

four When all the wings are cooked, drain the celery, pat dry, and put in a serving bowl. Bring the sauce to a simmer over medium-low heat, turn off the heat, and add the wings to the pan. Toss until they are uniformly coated and lift them out of the sauce with tongs. Spread the wings in one layer on a warm serving platter and serve hot with the celery sticks and blue cheese dressing passed separately.

NOTE: You can crisp the wings in the oven after they are sauced, or even make them ahead and reheat them in the oven. Arrange the wings on a rimmed cookie sheet in one layer. Position a rack in the upper third of the oven and preheat it to 375°F. Bake until they are hot and crispy, about 10 minutes.

The original hot sauce used for Buffalo wings on their home turf was Frank's Louisiana Hot Sauce (now a Durkee's brand: "Frank's Original Red Hot Cayenne Pepper Sauce"—whew; what a mouthful). It's thicker and not as hot as some pepper sauces.

Garlicky-Green Blue Cheese Dressing

MAKES ABOUT 2½ CUPS

one Combine the scallion, garlic, parsley, mustard, and egg in a food processor fitted with a steel blade or a blender. Pulse until mixed. Add 1 tablespoon of the lemon juice or vinegar, a healthy pinch of salt, and 1 tablespoon of the oil. Process for 1 minute.

two With the motor running, slowly add the remaining oil in a very thin drizzle, the slowest you can manage. (If you have a food processor with a small hole in the feed tube "pusher," add ¼ cup of the oil to this first and let it trickle through, then add the remaining oil by hand.) The dressing will be the consistency and color of green mayonnaise.

three Turn the dressing out into a mixing bowl. Fold in the blue cheese and remaining 1 tablespoon lemon juice, then thin it to a dipping consistency with heavy cream or buttermilk. Cover and chill for at least 1 hour before serving.

2 small or 1 large scallion or other green onion, white and green parts, roughly chopped

1 large garlic clove, crushed

1 tablespoon minced parsley

1 tablespoon Dijon mustard

1 large egg

2 tablespoons lemon juice or wine vinegar

Salt

1¼ cups peanut or vegetable oil

¾ cup crumbled blue cheese

2 to 4 tablespoons heavy cream or buttermilk

Beer-Battered Chicken Drumettes

THIS YEASTY BATTER is great not only for wings but for all parts of the bird—especially the livers—and for vegetables, shrimp, and fish fillets as well. It's delicious on its own, but you can vary the batter by adding sesame seeds or other flavorings. Note that the batter must be made ahead—the optimum is the day or morning before you are planning to use it. It must rest in the refrigerator for at least 3 hours to allow the yeast in the beer to become active.

SERVES 4 AS A MAIN COURSE, 8 AS AN APPETIZER

1¹/₂ cups all-purpose flour
Salt and freshly milled white pepper
¹/₂ teaspoon cayenne pepper
1¹/₄ cups flat beer
2 large egg yolks
24 whole wings (4 to 4¹/₂ pounds)
Peanut or vegetable oil, for frying
Honey Mustard (page 161), Sweet-and-Sour Sauce (page 165), or Thai Sweet and Hot Garlic Sauce (page 53)

one Sift together the flour, a healthy pinch or two of salt, a few liberal grindings of white pepper, and the cayenne into a nonreactive glass or stainless steel mixing bowl. Make a well in the center and pour in the beer. Gradually beat it into the flour until it forms a smooth batter. Beat in the egg yolks one at a time. Cover and refrigerate for at least 3 hours or overnight.

two Wash the chicken and pat dry. Cut through the joint between the large bone, separating the drumette. Cut off the tip at the joint and set it aside to use in broth. Put the wings in a nonreactive glass or stainless steel bowl. Sprinkle generously with salt and several liberal grindings of pepper. Set aside for 30 minutes, refrigerated, or for several hours or overnight.

three Set a wire cooling rack in a cookie sheet and preheat the oven to 150°F (or Warm setting). Fill a Dutch oven or deep-fat fryer with enough oil to come halfway up the sides, at least 2 inches deep. Over medium-high heat, bring the oil to 375°F (hot but not smoking).

four When the oil is hot, dip the wing pieces one at a time into the batter. Allow the excess to flow back into the bowl, and slip it into the fat. The fat will foam up a lot, so wait a few seconds for it to subside some before adding another piece. Repeat until the pan is full but not crowded. Fry for 8 to 10 minutes, until the drumettes are golden brown and cooked through, maintaining a temperature of 365°F (they will float to the top when they are done). Take them up one at a time, letting them drain well, then transfer them to the wire rack and keep them in the oven while you fry the remaining pieces. Serve hot with your choice of dipping sauces.

NOTE: This batter can be varied by adding 3 minced garlic cloves and ¼ cup of untoasted sesame seeds or chopped peanuts. Serve with Thai Sweet and Hot Garlic Sauce (page 53). You can also make the batter even more fluffy by folding in 2 stiffly beaten large egg whites just before dipping the chicken into it. The batter can be used for other chicken parts, boneless chicken fingers, or livers. Whole legs, thighs, and breasts will take about 20 minutes to cook; boneless fingers or livers, 3 to 4 minutes.

Sesame Chicken Wings

THIS IS A variation of classic Cantonese sesame chicken.

**SERVES 4 AS A MAIN COURSE,
8 AS AN APPETIZER**

one Disjoint the wings and set the tips aside to use in broth. Rinse the wing halves under cold running water and pat dry. Combine the wine, soy, garlic, a tiny pinch of cayenne, and the sesame oil in a large bowl. Add the egg to the wine-soy mixture and beat until it is incorporated. Put the wings into the mixture and toss until they are coated. Let them marinate, refrigerated, for at least 30 minutes.

two Combine the flour and sesame seeds in a shallow bowl and toss until they are evenly mixed. One at a time, lift the wings out of their marinade, allowing the excess to flow back into the bowl. Roll them in the sesame-flour mixture until they are well coated, shake off the excess, and lay them on a clean, dry plate in one layer.

24 chicken wings (4 to 4¹/₂ pounds)
1 tablespoon rice wine
1 tablespoon soy sauce
1 large garlic clove, minced
Cayenne pepper
¹/₂ teaspoon toasted sesame oil
1 large egg, lightly beaten
²/₃ cup all-purpose flour
²/₃ cup untoasted sesame seeds
Peanut or vegetable oil, for frying
Sweet-and-Sour Sauce (page 165), Hot Chinese Mustard (page 162), and/or either of the plum sauces (pages 163 to 164)

three Position a rack in the center of the oven and preheat the oven to 150°F (or Warm setting). Fit a wire cooling rack into a cookie sheet. Fill a Dutch oven or deep-fat fryer with enough oil to come halfway up the sides, at least 2 inches deep. Over medium-high heat, bring the oil to 375°F (hot but not smoking). One at a time, slip enough of the wings into the fat to fill the pan without crowding it, and fry, maintaining a steady heat of 365°F, until the wings are golden brown and cooked through, 8 to 10 minutes. Drain thoroughly, transfer to the rack, and keep them in the warm oven while you fry the remaining wings. Serve hot with any of the dipping sauces suggested.

Spicy Chicken Drumettes

THESE SPICY DRUMETTES are perfect party pick-up food: They are tasty, self-contained, and come with their own handle built in. You can make them ahead and reheat them with a second frying or baking in a 300°F oven, but they are best made when you are ready to serve them.

SERVES 8 TO 12

one Wash the chicken and pat dry. If you are using whole wings, cut through the joint between the large bone, separating the drumette. You may leave the second joint and tip in one piece, or cut off the tip and use it in broth. Put all the chicken in a large nonreactive glass or stainless steel bowl. Combine the buttermilk or yogurt, garlic, and onion and pour it over the chicken. Toss to coat the chicken evenly and set aside for 30 minutes to 1 hour, covered and refrigerated, or for several hours or overnight.

48 chicken drumettes or 24 whole wings (4 to 4¹/₂ pounds)

2 cups buttermilk or plain, all-natural yogurt

3 large garlic cloves, minced

3 tablespoons grated onion

3 cups all-purpose flour

1 cup fine stone-ground cornmeal

Salt and freshly milled black pepper

1 teaspoon cayenne pepper or more to taste

1 tablespoon sweet paprika

1 tablespoon crumbled dried thyme

1 tablespoon crumbled dried sage

Peanut or vegetable oil, for frying

Honey Mustard (page 161), Sweet-and-Sour Sauce (page 165), Horseradish Cocktail Sauce (page 77), or Thai Sweet and Hot Garlic Sauce (page 53)

two In a paper or large plastic ziplock bag, combine the flour, cornmeal, 2 healthy pinches of salt, several liberal grindings of pepper, the cayenne, paprika, thyme, and sage. Close the top and shake until the seasonings are evenly distributed.

three Fit a wire cooling rack over a cookie sheet and preheat the oven to 150°F (or Warm setting). Fill a Dutch oven or deep-fat fryer with enough oil to come halfway up the sides. Over medium-high heat, bring the oil to 375°F (hot but not smoking).

four When the oil is hot, lift the drumettes one at a time out of the marinade, allow the excess to flow back into the bowl, and drop it into the bag of flour. When several drumettes are in the bag, close the top and shake until they are well coated. Lift them out one at a time, shake off the excess flour, and slip them into the fat. Repeat until the pan is full but not crowded. Fry until golden brown and cooked through, 8 to 10 minutes. They will float when they are done. Lift them out of the fat one at a time, allowing the fat to completely drain from them, and transfer them to the wire rack. Keep them warm in the oven while you fry the remaining pieces. Serve hot with your choice of dipping sauces.

Croquettes and Fritters

Making something palatable of leftovers has been a daunting task ever since man began cooking. But "Leftovers again?!" is one groaning complaint that you will never hear when the leftovers are these crisply fried little morsels. When made into marble-sized balls, they make a superlative hot hors d'oeuvres for cocktails. In larger portions, they make an elegant and satisfying main course for a company luncheon or family dinner.

Chicken and Green Tomato Fritters

GREEN TOMATOES ARE a traditional Southern-fried favorite that is a great accompaniment for chicken, though they are not usually served with fried chicken. Here, the two Southern-fried favorites are combined in a savory fritter that makes a fine hot hors d'oeuvres with drinks before dinner, or it can serve as either a first or a main course at dinner. It also gives an interesting twist to any luncheon menu.

SERVES 6 AS A MAIN COURSE, 12 TO 14 AS AN APPETIZER

2 large green tomatoes, diced

Salt

2 tablespoons unsalted butter or olive oil

1 medium onion, diced

2 large garlic cloves, minced

2 cups cooked diced chicken

1 tablespoon chopped fresh sage or 1 teaspoon crumbled dried

1 tablespoon chopped fresh thyme or 1 teaspoon dried

1 tablespoon chopped parsley

2 cups fine cornmeal, preferably stone-ground

2 teaspoons baking powder

Freshly milled black pepper

Ground cayenne pepper

2 large eggs, beaten

2 cups all-natural plain yogurt or buttermilk

Lard or peanut or vegetable oil for frying

Horseradish Cocktail Sauce (page 77), Honey Mustard (page 161), or Hot Chinese Mustard (page 162)

one Place the tomatoes in a colander or wire mesh sieve and sprinkle generously with salt. Toss to distribute the salt evenly and set aside in the sink or over a plate for 30 minutes.

two Over medium-high heat, combine the butter or oil and onion in a sauté pan. Sauté, tossing frequently, until the onion is softened and translucent but not browned, about 5 minutes. Add the garlic and continue sautéing until fragrant, about 1 minute. Turn off the heat. Add the chicken and herbs and toss until they are evenly mixed. Set aside.

three Sift the cornmeal, 1 teaspoon salt, the baking powder, several liberal grindings of black pepper, and a pinch or so of cayenne into a large mixing bowl. In a separate bowl, combine the egg and yogurt or buttermilk and beat until it is smooth. Set aside.

four Fill a Dutch oven or deep-fat fryer with enough lard or oil to come halfway up the sides of the pan, at least 2 inches deep. Over medium-high heat, bring the oil to 375°F (hot but not smoking).

five Press the excess moisture from the tomatoes and pat them dry. Make a well in the center of the meal and pour in the egg mixture. Using as few strokes as possible, quickly stir until it is fairly smooth. Add the tomatoes and chicken and fold them in until uniformly mixed.

six Fit a wire rack in a cookie sheet and set aside. Drop the batter by rounded tablespoonfuls into the hot fat and fry until golden brown, turning midway if necessary, 4 to 5 minutes. Drain thoroughly on the wire rack. Serve with Horseradish Cocktail Sauce, Honey Mustard, or Hot Chinese Mustard passed separately.

NOTE: For smaller hors d'oeuvres portions, fry the batter in rounded teaspoonfuls. They will require less time to cook, 2 to 3 minutes. The fritters can be made entirely ahead: Remove them from the fat before they are completely done (golden brown and set but still a little soft). Drain completely, and let them cool on a wire rack. When you are ready to serve them, reheat the oil to 375°F and fry them until they are hot and crisp, 1 to 2 minutes.

Pepper Vinegar A common condiment for fried green tomatoes is pepper vinegar—which is the vinegar in which hot peppers have been pickled. It's great on these fritters, too. Pepper vinegar is widely available in the South, but you can also make your own: Wash 1½ cups small fresh hot peppers (left whole—they can be either red or green—your choice) and dry them. Pack them into a sterilized pint jar, leaving ½ inch of space at the top of the jar. Bring 1 cup of cider vinegar to a rolling boil and pour it over the peppers, completely covering them by about ¼ inch. If it doesn't cover them, boil a little more vinegar and add it. Cover with a sterilized lid and let cool, then put it away in a cool, dark place for 2 weeks before using. This pickle has not been processed; after the initial steeping, store it in the refrigerator.

Egyptian Chicken Fritters

Koftit Ferakh

THESE SPICY MIDDLE Eastern croquettes make wonderful hot hors d'oeuvres. Variations of them are legion and can be found throughout the Middle East. This version is adapted from Claudia Roden's wonderful *A Book of Middle Eastern Food*.

**SERVES 4 AS A MAIN COURSE,
8 AS AN APPETIZER**

2 slices firm white bread

Whole milk

2 cups cooked coarsely chopped chicken meat

1/2 cup pistachios, roughly chopped

1 large egg, lightly beaten

Juice of 1/2 lemon

1 tablespoon olive oil

1/2 teaspoon powdered turmeric

Salt and freshly milled black pepper

Peanut or vegetable oil, for frying

1/4 cup all-purpose flour

1 lemon, cut into 8 wedges

one Put the bread into a bowl and pour enough milk over it to saturate it and set it aside for about 10 minutes. Put the chicken meat through a meat grinder or mince it very fine with a sharp knife or in the food processor (don't overprocess) and transfer it to a large mixing bowl. Drain the bread and squeeze it dry, discarding the milk.

two Add the bread, pistachios, and the beaten egg to the chicken and season with the lemon juice, olive oil, turmeric, a generous pinch of salt, and a few liberal grindings of pepper. Knead all the ingredients together until the seasoning is well distributed and the mixture is a smooth paste. Roll it into marble-sized balls between your hands and set them on a clean, dry plate.

three Fit a wire cooling rack into a cookie sheet. Fill a Dutch oven or deep-fat fryer with enough peanut oil to come halfway up the sides, at least 2 inches deep. Over medium-high heat, bring the oil to 375°F (hot but not smoking). Roll the chicken balls lightly in the flour, shake off the excess, and slip them into the hot fat until the pan is full but not crowded. Fry until golden brown, about 2 minutes. Drain, blot briefly on absorbent paper, and transfer to the wire rack. Transfer them to a serving dish, scatter the lemon wedges among them, and serve hot.

94

Indonesian Chicken and Coconut Croquettes

Rempah Ayam

THESE SPICY COCONUT-LACED croquettes are typical of the flavors of the Indonesian and Malaysian islands, which stretch south from the tip of Thailand and the South China Sea to the northern coast of Australia. Be careful not to overcook the croquettes, especially if you are using only breast meat, or they will be dry and tough.

SERVES 4 AS A MAIN COURSE, 8 AS AN APPETIZER

1 small frying chicken, weighing no more than 3 pounds, skinned and boned as on page 11, or 2 whole boneless chicken breasts, skinned

1 rounded tablespoon coriander seeds

1 rounded teaspoon cumin seeds

1 teaspoon Indonesian or Thai chile paste (*sambal ulek* in Indonesian; see Note)

1 tablespoon finely minced ginger

Peanut oil, for frying

1 small yellow onion, minced

4 large garlic cloves, minced

1 teaspoon crushed dried shrimp paste (sometimes labeled as *blachan* or *trassi*)

1 tablespoon Demerara or turbinado sugar, or light brown sugar

2 large egg yolks

1 cup freshly grated coconut

Salt

1 lemon, cut into 8 wedges

one Put the chicken through a meat grinder or finely chop it with a chef's knife. Set aside. Grind the coriander and cumin to a powder in a mortar or spice mill. Combine it with the chile paste (*sambal ulek*) and ginger and mix well.

two Put 2 tablespoons of peanut oil in a sauté pan and add the spice mixture. Over medium heat, cook the spices until they are very fragrant and beginning to toast. Add the onion, garlic, dried shrimp paste, and sugar. Sauté, stirring constantly, until the onion is softened and golden, 2 to 4 minutes. Turn off the heat.

three Combine the onion-spice mixture, ground chicken, egg yolks, and ½ cup of the coconut in a nonreactive glass or stainless steel bowl. Add a large pinch or so of salt and mix well. Form the mixture into 2-inch round cakes and press them into the remaining ½ cup coconut until they are uniformly coated. Set aside on a dry plate.

four Preheat the oven to 150°F (or Warm setting) and fit a wire cooling rack over a cookie sheet. Fill a skillet with enough oil to cover the bottom by ½ inch.

95

Over medium-high heat, bring the oil to 375°F (hot but not smoking). Put in enough of the croquettes to fill the pan without crowding and fry, turning halfway, until they are nicely browned on both sides, about 2 minutes per side. Drain briefly on absorbent paper, then transfer to the wire rack. Keep them in the warm oven while you fry the remaining croquettes. When all the croquettes are fried and drained, transfer them to a warm platter, scatter the lemon around them, and serve hot.

NOTE: Market ground turkey also works very well in this recipe. Use 1 pound of uncooked ground turkey. To serve them as a cocktail hors d'oeuvres for 6 to 8 people, roll the mixture into 1-inch round balls. If you can't find dried shrimp paste, prepared paste is sometimes available in jars at Asian markets, or substitute 2 or 3 dried shrimp, readily available at Asian markets, and grind them.

Chile Paste Throughout Southeast Asia, a common seasoning is a paste made of chiles, garlic, salt, and vinegar. It goes by various names, *sous prik* in Thailand, *toung ot* in Vietnam, and *sambal ulek* (or *oelek*) in Indonesia. Both Vietnamese and Indonesian versions of this sauce are manufactured in the United States and are available at specialty markets and even some supermarkets. Thai, Vietnamese, and Indonesian brands are available in Asian markets. Thai versions can be sweeter than the other varieties and vary in potency. If you cannot find them, making your own is not difficult: Process 6 to 8 fresh red chiles (split and seeded) and 6 garlic cloves (crushed and peeled) in a blender with a teaspoon of salt and enough rice vinegar to make a paste. You can also substitute hot sauce mixed with a few drops of garlic juice.

It is axiomatic that the results of any given recipe will vary subtly from cook to cook. This is because all cooks, no matter how faithfully they might follow a recipe, will bring to the pot their individual taste and experience. The Chinese call it "wok presence," and nowhere is this better illustrated than in what can arguably be called the South's national dish—fried chicken. The core ingredients are fairly static: chicken, flour, salt, pepper, and frying fat. Yet, you could give those same ingredients to a roomful of Southern cooks, and you will have as many variations, each tasting completely different from the others, as you will have cooks. This book easily could have been filled with nothing else but variations on Southern fried chicken and still it would only have scratched the surface.

However, as many variations as there are, all of them fall within two basic either/or categories, or schools of thought: marinated/not marinated, crispy crust/soft, tender crust. Within these simple categories lie all the infinite, subtle variations that make each cook's chicken unique. Within the marinade school, there are three basic types: the buttermilk faction, the sweet-milk faction, and the salt-water faction. In New Orleans, we can add a fourth—the French-style wine-marinade faction. The not-marinated school is divided, too. There is the season-the-chicken-first faction, and the season-the-breading-only faction. The crispy-crust school includes both deep-frying and pan-frying; the soft crust school consists of only one basic double-fry method: The chicken is partially fried, then steamed until tender, and refried to set and only partially crisp the crust. Within each of these schools, cooks go their own ways, adding to or subtracting from the marinade, varying the seasonings, changing the breading, adding to or subtracting from the breading, blending several kinds of fat for a more complex flavor—the list is endless.

With the recipes that follow, I have tried to give you a representative collection that covers most of the basic variations, but rest assured: I will still get letters from fellow Southerners telling me that I have missed the boat altogether.

Basic Southern Fried Chicken with Cream Gravy

 THIS RECIPE HAS appeared, with very little variation, in almost every cookbook printed in the South, from Mary Randolph's *The Virginia House-Wife* (1824) right through to Mrs. Dull's *Southern Cooking* (1928). If any recipe can be said to be the one, true Southern fried chicken, this would be it. Even the oldest included cream gravy as an integral part of the recipe.

Though a cast-iron skillet seems to make the best Southern fried chicken, you can deep-fry the chicken if you prefer; either way will taste authentic. The only "must" is the fat—pure lard. You must use lard; don't argue. Though many Southern cooks have bowed to the times and nowadays use vegetable oils and shortenings, lard is still the only fat that will give you the traditional crispness and flavor.

SERVES 8

2 frying chickens, weighing no more than 3 pounds each, cut up for frying as on page 11

Salt and freshly milled black pepper

3 cups all-purpose flour

Lard, for frying

Cream Gravy (page 154)

one Put the chicken pieces in a basin of cold water and soak them for a few minutes. Drain well and pat dry with a clean towel or paper towels. Season generously with salt and a liberal grinding of black pepper. Put the flour in a paper or large ziplock plastic bag, close the top, and give it a quick shake to loosely dust the inside of the bag with the flour.

two Put enough lard in a large cast-iron skillet that will hold both chickens without crowding (or use 2 pans, or plan to fry in batches) to come at least ½ inch up the sides. Over medium-high heat, melt the lard and bring to 350°F (hot but not smoking).

three Beginning with the dark meat, drop the chicken a few pieces at a time into the bag, close the top, and shake until they are thoroughly coated. Take them out of the bag, shaking off the excess flour, and slip them into the hot fat. Repeat until all the chicken pieces are coated and in the pan. (If you don't have a large enough pan, use 2 pans or cook the chicken in batches. If you fry in batches, preheat the oven to 150°F (or Warm setting) to hold the cooked chicken. Don't flour the chicken until you are ready to cook it.)

four Reduce the heat to medium. Fry the chickens slowly, maintaining the temperature at about 325°F, until the bottom side of each piece is a rich golden brown, 12 to 15 minutes. Carefully turn them and continue cooking until each piece is golden brown on all sides and just cooked through, about 12 minutes more. Though some recipes indicate that the chicken is done when it no longer sizzles as you turn it over, that isn't a good guide. If it doesn't sizzle, it means the chicken is dried out and overcooked.

five Pour off all but 2 tablespoons of the cooking fat. Put the skillet back over the heat and make the gravy (see page 154). Serve hot or at room temperature.

NOTE: If you are frying in batches and holding cooked chicken in the oven, don't hold it for more than half an hour. Any longer and the chicken will dry out.

Southern Batter-Fried Chicken

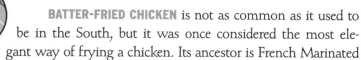

BATTER-FRIED CHICKEN is not as common as it used to be in the South, but it was once considered the most elegant way of frying a chicken. Its ancestor is French Marinated Batter-Fried Chicken (page 22), but the marinating stage is not as complex. Traditionally, this chicken is pan-fried, but I find it easier to deep-fry batter-coated food.

SERVES 4

1 cup all-purpose flour

1 teaspoon baking powder

Salt, freshly milled white pepper, and whole nutmeg in a grater

1 large egg

1¼ cups whole milk

1 frying chicken, weighing no more than 3 pounds, skinned and cut up for frying as on page 11

Lard or peanut or vegetable oil, for frying

one Sift the flour, baking powder, 1 teaspoon salt, several liberal grindings of white pepper, and a few generous gratings of nutmeg into a mixing bowl. In a separate bowl, beat the egg until it is fluffy, then beat in the milk. Make a well in the center of the flour and pour in the egg-milk mixture. Gradually whisk the flour into the liquid until it forms a smooth batter. Cover and refrigerate for at least 30 minutes.

two Wash the chicken under cold running water and put it in a large nonreactive glass or stainless steel bowl. Add a very small handful of salt and enough cold water to cover the chicken completely. Toss until the salt is dissolved and set aside to soak for 30 minutes, refrigerated.

three Preheat the oven to 150°F (or Warm setting). Fit a wire cooling rack over a cookie sheet. Fill a Dutch oven or deep-fat fryer with enough lard or oil to come halfway up the sides. Over medium-high heat, bring the fat to 375°F (hot but not smoking). Meanwhile, drain the chicken and pat it dry. Lightly stir the batter.

four Add the chicken to the batter, coating it completely. Beginning with the dark meat, lift the chicken out one piece at a time, letting the excess batter flow back into the bowl. Then slip the battered pieces into the fat. Repeat until the pot is full but not crowded. Fry until lightly, until browned and well sealed, about 5 minutes.

five Reduce the heat to medium (325°F). Fry the chicken, turning only once, until it is cooked through and golden brown, about 20 minutes longer.

six Lift the chicken from the fat, let the fat drain from it completely, and transfer it to the wire rack. If you are frying a second batch, place the cooked chicken in the warm oven until all of it is fried. Serve hot or at room temperature.

Buttermilk Fried Chicken

BATHING CHICKEN IN buttermilk is an old Southern trick that harkens back to the early French and English practice of marinating chicken in a tenderizing acid. It accomplishes several things at once. Not only does it tenderize the bird, it enhances the flavor and reacts with the flour coating to make an exceptionally crispy breading. This is an ideal chicken for picnics or family gatherings where you will be serving everything cold, because the outer skin stays crisp long after the bird cools to room temperature.

Unless it is served at a picnic, this chicken is usually accompanied (depending on where you are in the South and at which meal you are eating it) with Cream Gravy made from the drippings and Carolina-Style Rice (page 171), grits (page 173), or Creamed Potatoes (page 174), and/or biscuits (page 170).

SERVES 4

1 frying chicken, weighing no more than 3 pounds, cut up for frying as on page 11

2 cups buttermilk or plain all-natural yogurt, stirred until creamy

3 cups all-purpose flour

1 tablespoon salt

1 tablespoon freshly milled black pepper

$^{1}/_{2}$ teaspoon cayenne pepper (optional)

Lard or peanut or vegetable oil, for frying

Cream Gravy (page 154)

one Wash the chicken and pat dry. Put the chicken pieces in a large nonreactive glass or stainless steel bowl. Pour the buttermilk or yogurt over the chicken and turn the pieces until all are coated and submerged in the liquid. Let marinate for 1 hour, refrigerated.

two Combine the flour, salt, pepper, and cayenne, if using, in a paper or large zip-lock plastic bag. Close the top and shake until the seasoning is well distributed.

three If you plan to serve the chicken hot, preheat the oven to 150°F (or Warm setting). Fit a wire cooling rack on a cookie sheet and set aside. Fill a 14-inch diameter, deep cast-iron skillet with enough lard or oil to come halfway up the sides. Over medium-high heat, bring the fat to 375°F (hot but not smoking).

four Beginning with the dark meat, lift the chicken out of the marinade, allowing the excess to flow back into the bowl and drop them into the bag with the seasoned flour. Close the top and shake until the chicken is well coated. Lift them out of the flour, shake off the excess, and slip them into the pan. Repeat until all the pieces are coated and in the pan. Fry until the outside is well sealed and beginning to brown, turning the chicken once, 3 to 4 minutes. Reduce the heat to medium and continue frying, maintaining the fat temperature at 325°F, until the chicken is just cooked through and golden brown, 20 to 25 minutes for the thighs and drumsticks, 15 to 20 minutes for the breast meat and wings, turning it halfway.

five Remove the pieces as they are done, drain them well, and transfer to the wire rack. If you want to serve it hot, keep the finished chicken in the warm oven.

six Pour off all but 2 tablespoons of the fat and make Cream Gravy (see page 154). Pass the gravy separately, along with any of the accompaniments mentioned above.

NOTE: You can deep-fry buttermilk chicken if you prefer. Heat the fat to 375°F, and maintain a steady temperature at around 365°F. It will take a little less time to cook—15 to 20 minutes. Again, white meat will be ready before dark meat. To make pan gravy, take up 2 tablespoons of the fat and use it to make the gravy in a separate pan.

Many Southern cooks season the buttermilk marinade with salt, pepper, and a few dashes of hot sauce. You can also vary the seasonings in the flour, adding a tablespoon of dried herbs of your choice, and spices such as paprika, cayenne, or curry powder to taste.

You may opt to sprinkle the seasonings over the chicken after you take it out of the marinade, but before coating it with flour, which assures a more even seasoning.

Herb-and-Spice Southern Fried Chicken

A CERTAIN WELL-KNOWN take-out chicken with eleven herbs and spices is not the only Southern fried chicken that is seasoned with a complex blend of herbs and spices; it is just one of many. You can experiment with the combination until you have your own unique blend. If you don't have a couple of the spices on hand, feel free to omit them. When deep-fried, which is the way I prefer to cook this one, the chicken makes great picnic fare because it stays crispy long after it's cold, and the spice and herb seasoning stands up well to other highly seasoned picnic food.

SERVES 8

one Wash the chicken and pat dry. Put the chicken pieces in a large nonreactive glass or stainless steel bowl. Stir the garlic into the buttermilk or yogurt. Pour it over the chicken and turn until coated and submerged in the liquid. Marinate for up to 1 hour, refrigerated. Meanwhile, combine the spices, herbs, salt, and flour in a paper or large ziplock plastic bag. Close the bag and shake until the seasoning is well distributed.

two If you plan to serve the chicken hot, preheat the oven to 150°F (or Warm setting). Fit a wire cooling rack on a cookie sheet and set aside. Fill a Dutch oven or deep-fat fryer with enough lard or oil to come halfway up the sides. Over medium-high heat, bring the fat to 375°F (hot but not smoking).

three Beginning with the dark meat, lift the chicken pieces out of the marinade one at a time, allowing the excess to flow back into the bowl, and drop them

2 frying chickens, weighing no more than 3 pounds each, cut up for frying as on page 11

2 tablespoons chopped garlic (about 8 large cloves)

4 cups buttermilk or plain all-natural yogurt, stirred until smooth

3 cups unbleached all-purpose flour

Lard or peanut oil, for frying

FOR THE HERB AND SPICE MIX:

½ teaspoon ground cayenne pepper

1 teaspoon freshly ground cumin

½ teaspoon ground mace

1 teaspoon freshly grated nutmeg

1 teaspoon paprika

1 teaspoon freshly milled black pepper

1 teaspoon ground ginger

2 teaspoons crumbled dried basil

2 teaspoons bay leaves ground to a powder (use a spice mill or blender)

2 teaspoons crumbled dried oregano

2 teaspoons crumbled dried sage

2 teaspoons crumbled dried thyme

1 tablespoon salt

into the bag with the seasoned flour. Close the bag and shake until the chicken is well coated. Lift out of the flour, shake off the excess, and slip enough of the pieces into the fat to fill the pan or fryer without crowding it. Deep-fry until the outside is a rich brown and the chicken is tender, maintaining the temperature at 365°F, for 15 to 20 minutes, turning the chicken once, if necessary.

four Remove the pieces as they are done, drain well, and place on the wire rack set in a cookie sheet. If you want to serve it hot, keep the finished chicken in the warm oven while you fry the second batch.

Southern Fried Chicken Livers

DEEP-FRYING CHICKEN LIVERS is one of the most satisfying of all ways to cook them: The outside is crisp and golden, while the inside remains creamy, slightly sweet, and meltingly tender. The important thing is not to overcook the livers, or they will be dry, mealy, and bitter.

Traditional Southern cooks frequently marinate frying chickens in buttermilk. The acid helps tenderize the meat and reacts with the flour to form an especially crisp outer crust. Here, it also mellows the flavor of the livers and makes them especially rich and creamy.

Though unorthodox by both Southern and Italian standards, these livers make a fine "sauce" for pasta, especially linguine or short, tubular pastas such as rigatoni. Pasta sauce needn't be a liquid, per se; Italians frequently use such ingredients as deep-fried eggplants to dress pasta, so using the livers as a pasta sauce is not inconsistent with an Italian sensibility.

SERVES 4 TO 6

one Drain the livers well and rinse under cold running water. Remove any fat and cut out any greenish spots. Cut the livers into individual lobes if they are large and whole, leave smaller livers in one piece.

two Put the livers in a large nonreactive glass or stainless steel bowl and pour the buttermilk or yogurt over them. Stir until they are all coated and let them marinate for half an hour (or longer), covered and refrigerated.

three Put the flour, herbs, paprika, pepper, and salt in a paper or large ziplock plastic bag. Close the top and shake until the seasonings are evenly mixed into the flour. Set aside.

four Fit a wire cooling rack on a cookie sheet and preheat the oven to 150°F (or Warm setting). Fill a Dutch oven or deep-fat fryer with enough peanut oil to come halfway up the sides of the pan, at least 2 inches deep. Over medium-high heat, bring the oil to 375°F (hot but not smoking). Drain the livers thoroughly, discarding the marinade, and put them in the bag with the flour. Close the top and shake vigorously until the livers are all well coated with flour. Lift out the livers a few at a time, shaking off the excess flour as you do, and slip them into the hot fat. When the pan is full, but not crowded, fry the livers until they are golden brown, 3 to 4 minutes. Lift them out, drain well, transfer them to the wire rack, and keep them in the warm oven while you fry the remaining livers. Serve hot, passing the lemon wedges separately.

2 pounds chicken livers

2 cups buttermilk or plain all-natural yogurt, stirred until creamy

3 cups all-purpose flour

1 tablespoon crumbled dried sage

1 tablespoon crumbled dried thyme

2 teaspoons paprika

2 teaspoons freshly milled black pepper

2 teaspoons salt

Peanut or vegetable oil, for frying

1 lemon, cut into 8 wedges

DEEP-FRIED LIVERS CAJUN-STYLE: Put several generous shots of Louisiana hot sauce in the marinade before adding the livers. Omit the herbs, paprika, and black pepper and season the flour with 2 tablespoons Cajun Seasoning Mix (see Cajun Popcorn Chicken, page 76).

Fried Chicken à la Creole

HERE'S ANOTHER TRADITIONAL Southern fried chicken that is spicier and more aromatic than the usual, but is nonetheless not much different below its showy surface. The method does not deviate from tradition: The chicken is marinated in acid, rolled in seasoned flour, and pan-fried in lard. The marinade is wine instead of buttermilk and is spiked with hot sauce and garlic; the flour is highly seasoned with herbs and spices. As a rule, I am fond of neither onion nor garlic powder—they tend to be pushy and harsh-tasting. However, here they are an important part of the flavors of the coating, and the frying blunts their sharpness. Just don't overdo them.

SERVES 8

2 frying chickens, weighing no more than 3 pounds each, cut up for frying as on page 11

2 cups dry white wine

Louisiana hot sauce (such as Tabasco)

2 large garlic cloves, minced

Lard or peanut oil, for frying

3 cups all-purpose flour

1 tablespoon dried thyme

1 tablespoon salt

1 teaspoon freshly milled black pepper

1/2 teaspoon cayenne pepper

1/2 teaspoon garlic powder

1/2 teaspoon onion powder

2 large eggs, beaten

one Wash the chicken and pat dry. Put the chicken pieces in a large nonreactive glass or stainless steel bowl. Combine the wine, a few shots of hot sauce (to taste, but don't overdo it), and the garlic. Pour over the chicken and turn until all the pieces are submerged in the wine bath. Marinate, covered and refrigerated, for at least 1 hour or overnight. Let the chicken sit at room temperature for 30 minutes before cooking it.

two Fill a deep cast-iron skillet with enough lard or oil to come halfway up the sides. Fit a wire cooling rack into a cookie sheet. Preheat the oven to 150°F (or Warm setting). Over medium-high heat, bring the fat to 375°F (hot but not smoking)

three Combine the flour, thyme, salt, peppers, and garlic and onion powders in a paper or large plastic ziplock bag. Close the top and shake until the seasoning is evenly distributed.

four Beginning with the dark meat, lift the chicken a few pieces at a time out of the marinade. Let the excess flow back into the bowl, then dip them in the egg until all sides are coated. Lift them out, allowing the excess egg to flow back into the bowl, then drop the pieces into the bag of seasoned flour. Close the top and shake until the chicken is well coated. Lift the chicken out a few pieces at a time, and slip it into the fat. Repeat until the pan is full without crowding. Fry, turning the chicken once, until the outside is sealed and golden, about 10 minutes. Reduce the heat to medium and continue frying at about 375°F until cooked through, about 10 minutes more for white meat and 15 minutes for dark meat. Drain well on the wire rack and hold it in the oven while you fry the remaining chicken. Serve hot.

Granny Fowler's Sunday Fried Chicken

WHEN SHE MARRIED my grandfather, a widower with many children, Granny was herself a widow with several children of her own. Their marriage added two more to the brood—my father and his sister, Ruth. With his children, her children, and their children crowding their four-room house and the Great Depression at their door, Granny always had too many mouths to feed and never enough food. But no one ever seemed to mind the daily pot of dried beans, so long as they could look forward to her fried chicken on Sunday. Portions were small and there were always plenty of biscuits, rice or potatoes, and gravy to stretch the meal as far as it would go. But Granny's singular gift for making the most meager of meals taste really good made even biscuits and gravy seem like a feast.

Granny kept right on cooking those big Sunday dinners until shortly before she died. She was not a very demonstrative woman, but as we sat around her kitchen table on those Sunday afternoons, she didn't have to tell us that she loved us; we could taste it.

108

SERVES 4

one Put 2 cups cold water in a large bowl and add a very small handful of salt. Stir until the salt dissolves and add the chicken. Set aside for 30 minutes. Meanwhile, spread the flour in a shallow bowl or large plate and fit a wire cooling rack over a cookie sheet. Set aside.

two Drain the chicken and pat dry. Season liberally with a sprinkling of salt and several liberal grindings of pepper. Put ½ inch of fat into a large, deep, lidded skillet that will hold the chicken without crowding in one layer. Turn on the heat to medium-high. When the fat is very hot but not smoking (375°F), lightly roll the chicken in the flour one piece at a time, beginning with the dark meat, shake off the excess, and slip it into the fat. Brown it lightly on the bottom, about 4 minutes, then turn it and brown the other side.

1 frying chicken weighing no more than 3 pounds, cut up for frying as on page 11
Salt
Freshly milled black pepper
1¾ cups all-purpose flour
Lard or vegetable oil, for frying
Cream Gravy (page 154)

three Reduce the heat to medium-low (325°F) and carefully spoon off all but about ⅛ inch of the fat into a heatproof container. Slowly pour in ¼ cup of water into the center of the pan, let it boil up, then cover the pan. Cook, turning the chicken once, until it is just cooked through, about 20 minutes.

four Remove the lid, raise the heat to medium-high, allowing any remaining moisture to evaporate, fry until the chicken is crisp, about 5 minutes more. Remove the chicken to the wire rack, drain well, and transfer it to a serving platter.

five Pour off all but 2 tablespoons of the remaining fat into a heatproof container. Return the skillet to the heat and make Cream Gravy. Serve the chicken with the gravy and Granny's Hot Potato Salad (page 176) passed separately.

Jewish Georgia Fried Chicken

BOTH COLONIAL PORT cities of Charleston and Savannah have long been home to active and substantial Jewish communities. Most families have long since adapted their cooking to a Southern mode, but even in reformed congregations, the cooking retains traces of older traditions, particularly on holidays. This recipe is an example of that blending of traditions. Lemon juice and bourbon replace the buttermilk marinade, vegetable oil replaces the lard, and, for Passover, the chicken is coated in seasoned matzoh meal. However, though there is no pork fat or milk, the chicken isn't "kosher" unless it's been slaughtered according to kosher law, and cooked following kosher regulations.

The recipe is adapted from Joan Nathan's *Jewish Cooking in America*.

SERVES 4 TO 6

1 frying chicken, weighing no more than 3 pounds, skinned and cut up for frying as on page 11

Salt

2 large garlic cloves, minced

2 teaspoons sweet paprika

2 tablespoons freshly squeezed lemon juice

1 tablespoon bourbon

1 teaspoon aromatic bitters

2 cups matzoh meal

Freshly milled black pepper

Peanut or vegetable oil, for frying

2 large eggs, beaten

one Wash the chicken under cold running water and pat dry. Place it in a large nonreactive glass or stainless steel bowl. Sprinkle a pinch of salt, the garlic, and paprika over it and toss until uniformly coated. In a separate bowl, combine the lemon juice with the bourbon, bitters, and ¼ cup water. Pour this over the chicken and toss it once again to coat. Cover, refrigerate, and marinate for at least 1 hour or overnight. Let the chicken sit at room temperature for 30 minutes before cooking it.

two Put the matzoh meal in a paper or large plastic ziplock bag and add 2 large pinches of salt and several liberal grindings of pepper. Close the bag and shake until the seasoning is well mixed with the meal. Set aside.

three Fit a wire cooling rack on a cookie sheet. Preheat the oven to 150°F (or Warm setting). Fill a deep cast-iron skillet with enough oil to come halfway up the sides, at least ½-inch deep. Over medium-high heat, bring the oil to 375°F (hot but not smoking).

FRIED CHICKEN

four Beginning with the dark meat, lift the chicken one piece at a time out of the marinade, dip it into the egg until coated, let the excess flow back into the bowl, and drop them into the bag of matzoh meal. Close the top and shake until they are coated with the meal. Lift them out one at a time, shaking off any excess meal, and slip them into the pan. Repeat until the pan is full but not crowded. Fry the chicken, turning once, until the outside is sealed and golden, about 10 minutes.

five Reduce the heat to medium and fry at 325°F, turning only once more, until the chicken is completely cooked through, 10 to 15 minutes longer. Remember that white meat will be done before dark meat. Drain well, and if you are frying in batches or are doing a double recipe, put the cooked chicken on the rack in the oven, and keep it warm while you fry the second batch.

NOTE: This chicken can be deep-fried instead of pan-fried. Use a large Dutch oven or electric deep-fryer. Begin the frying at 375°F, then maintain an oil temperature of 365°F. The chicken will be done in 15 to 20 minutes.

Maryland Fried Chicken

THOUGH MARYLAND DID not secede with the South during the War Between the States, its northern border is the famed Mason-Dixon Line which divides the South from the rest of the country, making the state—at least geographically—a part of the region. But Marylanders are Southern in ways other than geography, one of the most distinctive of which is their almost passionate love of fried chicken. As is true of the rest of the region, Maryland has as many ways of chicken frying as it has cooks. This is just one of them.

The crust of this chicken will not be crisp, but it shouldn't be soggy, either. The chicken is usually accompanied by Cream Gravy (page 154), which is often made with butter instead of the residual cooking fat. You may also serve it, as Marylanders sometimes do, with fried mush (which is similar to fried polenta) or with hot waffles.

SERVES 4

1 frying chicken, weighing no more than 3 pounds, cut up for frying as on page 11

Salt and freshly milled black pepper

Lard or vegetable oil, for frying

1 cup all-purpose flour

Cream Gravy (page 154), not made ahead but at the point indicated in the recipe

one Wash the chicken, pat dry, and sprinkle liberally with salt and a few grindings of pepper. Set aside.

two Choose a deep, lidded cast-iron skillet that will hold all the chicken in one layer without crowding it. Fill with enough lard or oil to come about ½ inch up the sides. Over medium-high heat, bring the fat to 365° to 375°F (hot but not smoking).

three Beginning with the dark meat, roll the chicken in the flour, shake off the excess, and slip the pieces into the fat. When the chicken is all in the pan, cover it and fry until the bottoms are nicely browned, about 3 minutes. Turn, cover, and brown the second side.

four Reduce the heat to medium (325°F.) Carefully spoon off most of the fat into a heatproof container leaving about ⅛-inch of fat in the pan. Add ¼ cup water to the pan, cover, and cook, turning the chicken once, until tender and all the liquid is evaporated, 20 to 25 minutes.

five Line a platter or cookie sheet with absorbent paper. Remove the chicken and drain it briefly on the paper, then transfer it to a warm serving platter. Pour off all but 2 tablespoons of fat and make the gravy as on page 154. Serve hot with the gravy passed separately.

Chicken Kentuckian

THIS IS KENTUCKY fried chicken like you have never had before. Rich and elegant, yet earthy and forthright, it sold my first book, *Classical Southern Cooking.* Everyone thought it was the most marvelous thing they had ever tasted—and no wonder: There is something magic that happens when bourbon and mushrooms are put together. I wish I could take credit for it, but it's an old family recipe from my friend and pastor, the Reverend William H. Ralston. The recipe first appeared in print in *Heritage Receipts,* a collection prepared by the Episcopal Church Women of Saint John's Church that is a treasury of traditional Savannah cooking.

You do not, of course, want to waste a premium single-barrel sipping whiskey by cooking with it, but the better the bourbon you use, the better the chicken will taste. My personal preference is W. L. Weller's.

SERVES 6

one Wash the chicken and pat dry. Spread on a platter or large plate and lightly dust with salt and flour. Wipe the fresh mushrooms with a dry cloth and slice them thickly. If they are especially large, cut them up into bite-sized pieces. Set aside.

two In a large, heavy skillet or sauté pan, heat the butter and olive oil over medium-low heat. Add the chicken pieces and scallion and sauté, turning the

2 small frying chickens, no more than 2 1/2 to 3 pounds each, skinned and cut up for frying as on page 11

Salt

1/2 cup all-purpose flour

8 to 10 large wild mushrooms, sliced thick (or 1/2 pound domestic crimini mushrooms and 1/2 ounce dried boletus reconstituted by soaking them in 1 cup boiling water for 30 minutes)

4 tablespoons unsalted butter

1 1/2 tablespoons extra virgin olive oil

2 teaspoons chopped scallion

1/2 cup bourbon

1 cup heavy cream

chicken frequently, until golden and tender, about half an hour. While the chicken cooks, baste it with spoonfuls of bourbon every few minutes, being careful to add it in small amounts so there is never any liquid accumulated in the pan.

three When the chickens are cooked through and golden and all the bourbon has been added, transfer the chicken from the skillet to a warm platter. If you are using only fresh mushrooms, turn up the heat and add them to the skillet. Sauté, tossing and stirring them constantly, for about 3 minutes. If you are using reconstituted dried mushrooms, lift them out of their soaking water, dipping them to loosen any sand that is clinging to them, and put them in the pan. Filter the soaking water through a paper towel or coffee filter and pour it into the pan. Bring it to a boil, stirring frequently, and evaporate all the liquid. Add the sliced fresh mushrooms and sauté as above.

four Add the cream and scrape loose any residue that may be stuck to the skillet. Simmer until it is just heated through and starting to thicken. Taste and correct the seasonings, then pour it over the chicken. Serve at once with Spoon Bread (page 169).

Chicken Country Captain

COUNTRY CAPTAIN is a spicy tomato-based curry that came into the South by way of England's East Indian trade. Contrary to mythical tales of its origins in America, it's really an English adaptation of Indian cookery. Since the early nineteenth century, it has been popular all along the Atlantic seaboard, with every Southern port from Baltimore to Savannah laying claim to its origin. Actually, none of them can really claim it—but it isn't wise to try to tell them so.

The recipe differs from most of the previous ones in that the fried chicken is simmered in its sauce after the frying step.

SERVES 4

one Wash the chicken and pat dry. Put the butter or oil in a large lidded cast-iron skillet and place it over medium-high heat. When the fat is melted and hot, but not smoking or browning, add the chicken pieces and fry until they are well browned on all sides. Spoon off all but 3 tablespoons of the fat. Add the curry powder and sauté until fragrant, about 1 minute. Add the onions and peppers. Sauté, tossing frequently, until softened, but not browned, about 5 minutes. Add the garlic and continue sautéing until fragrant, about a minute more.

1 frying chicken, weighing no more than 3 pounds, skinned (optional) and cut up for frying as on page 11

4 tablespoons butter or olive oil

1 tablespoon curry powder

1 large onion, chopped

1 large green bell pepper, chopped

2 large garlic cloves, minced

1 tart apple (such as Granny Smith), peeled and diced

2 pounds ripe tomatoes, scalded, peeled, seeded, and chopped as described on page 155 or 2 cups seeded and chopped canned Italian tomatoes with their juices

1 teaspoon sugar

Salt

1 cup currants or raisins

1 tablespoon chopped parsley

4 cups hot Carolina-Style Rice (page 171)

1/2 cup grated unsweetened coconut

1/2 cup toasted peanuts or pine nuts

two Add the apple and toss until the pieces are uniformly coated with the curry mixture. Add the tomatoes, sugar, and currants or raisins and bring to a boil. Reduce the heat to a gentle simmer, cover, and simmer, stirring and turning the chicken occasionally, until it is cooked through and tender, about 30 minutes.

115

three When the chicken is tender, if there is too much liquid in the pan and the sauce seems watery, remove the chicken from the pan and raise the heat to medium-high. Let it boil until the sauce is thick, stirring frequently to keep it from scorching. Turn off the heat and stir in the parsley. Serve hot over rice, with the coconut and peanuts or pine nuts passed separately.

NOTE: You can add condiments to suit your own palate, passing chutney, peeled tangerine sections, freshly grated lemon or orange zest, or chunks of fresh pineapple separately.

The Shallow End: Sautés and Stir-Fries

The words "fried chicken" for most of us conjure an image of a bird with a rich, golden brown coating that results from deep-fat or pan-frying. But that is not the only way to fry a chicken. When we recognize sautéing and stir-frying as a form of frying in shallow fat, it opens up a whole world of marvelous fried chicken dishes to us, fried either in shallow fat or almost no fat at all.

There are two basic types of shallow frying: sautéing, in which frying is the only activity, and stir-frying, the Far Eastern method of sautéing in a wok. These methods may seem to have little to do with each other, but they are closely interrelated. A more detailed description of each is included in the introduction to the individual sections, and in The Chicken Fryer's Kitchen (pages 5 to 6).

SAUTÉING

For our purposes, the type of sautéing employed for most of these recipes is a light pan-frying in very shallow fat. Liquid may be introduced to the pan, but usually it is allowed to evaporate fairly quickly, since it is intended as a flavoring agent more than as a medium for cooking. Sautéing a chicken is possible only with a very young, very tender bird. In cultures where the eggs are more prized than the flesh of the chicken, only the older, more mature hens that have stopped laying are the ones used for cooking. Since these tough old birds must be cooked slowly with moist heat (either stewing or baking) sautés are rare in the cook's repertory of those areas. But where tender young chickens are plentiful, the variations on sautéing are legion. What follows barely scratches the surface.

Fried Chicken Malabar

AS ENGLAND'S INVOLVEMENT in India increased during the nineteenth century, the spicy cookery of that ancient land migrated west and had a distinct influence on the cookery of Englishmen who never crossed the English Channel. This dish is one such migration; it is an adaptation, from Eliza Acton's *Modern Cookery for Private Families,* published in 1845. Miss Acton was very careful: The recipe is authentic and actually typical of Malabar cookery.

SERVES 4

1 frying chicken, weighing no more than 3 pounds, cut up for frying as on page 11, but not skinned

Salt

1½ to 2 tablespoons mild curry powder

8 tablespoons clarified butter (see page 14)

2 medium yellow onions, thinly sliced

1 lemon, cut into 8 wedges

one Wash the chicken pieces and pat dry. Sprinkle lightly with salt, and rub all surfaces well with the curry powder. Gently lift the skin and rub some of the curry under it. Set aside on a platter for at least 20 minutes or up to 1 hour refrigerated.

two Heat 4 tablespoons of the clarified butter in a large sauté pan over medium heat. When the butter is melted and hot, add the chicken and fry slowly, turning it frequently, until the chicken is golden brown and cooked through, 25 to 30 minutes.

three While the chicken is cooking, heat the remaining butter over medium heat in another wide skillet. Add the onions and cook, stirring frequently, until golden brown, dry, and crisp, about 20 minutes. Be careful not to let them scorch or blacken; they should be crisp and brown, but not burned. Drain well on absorbent paper, season with a pinch or so of salt, and set aside.

four When the chicken is tender, lift it out of the fat and drain it thoroughly by holding it over the pan until all the fat is drained away and transfer it to a platter. Scatter the onions over it and the lemon wedges among it and serve at once.

Indian Chicken Sauté with Yogurt Sauce

ACCORDING TO LEGEND and many historians, chickens are supposed to have originated in the jungles of India. It may well be true, for Indian chicken cookery is certainly an ancient and highly developed art. This sauté, with its heady perfume of garlic and ginger and its velvety yogurt sauce, is a classic example of Northern Indian cookery. It differs from the other sautés in that it finishes in its sauce. This recipe is adapted from Madhur Jaffrey's lovely book, *An Invitation to Indian Cooking.*

For the best flavor and texture, choose an all-natural yogurt without added thickeners for this recipe, preferably one from an organic dairy. Look for organic dairy products in natural food stores and specialty groceries.

SERVES 4 TO 6

1 frying chicken, weighing no more than 3 pounds, skinned and cut up for frying Chinese-style as on page 11

¹/₂ cup plus 2 tablespoons plain all-natural yogurt

5 large yellow onions, thinly sliced

2 large garlic cloves, lightly crushed

3 quarter-sized slices fresh ginger, peeled and coarsely chopped

7 tablespoons peanut oil

Salt

Ground cayenne pepper

2 tablespoons chopped fresh cilantro or parsley

one Wash the chicken and pat dry. Put ½ cup of the yogurt into a mixing bowl and gradually beat ½ cup cold water into it until it is smooth. Set aside. Combine ½ cup of the onion slices, the garlic, and the ginger in a blender or food processor fitted with a steel blade. Add ⅓ cup cold water and process on high until the mixture forms a smooth paste, stopping the machine to scrape down the sides if necessary. Set aside.

two Put 5 tablespoons of the oil and the remaining sliced onions into a heavy-bottomed skillet or Dutch oven and turn on the heat to medium. Sauté, tossing frequently, until they are well browned, but still limp, 8 to 10 minutes. Using a skimmer or slotted spoon, lift out the onions, leaving as much fat as possible in the pan. Set aside.

three Add the remaining 2 tablespoons oil to the pan and raise the heat to medium-high. Let it get hot, then pat the chicken pieces dry and add as many of them to the pan as will fit without crowding. Fry, turning frequently, until the chicken is well browned on all sides and about half cooked, 7 to 10 minutes. Lift out with tongs and repeat with the remaining chicken. Spoon off all but 2 tablespoons of the fat.

four Reduce the heat to medium-low. Pour the seasoning paste from the blender into the pan. (Avert your face when adding the paste, especially if you are sensitive to onion fumes). Stir the paste constantly, scraping to loosen any solids that may have stuck to the pan while the chicken was frying, until is is fragrant and somewhat thick, about 4 minutes. Stir in 1 tablespoon of the reserved undiluted yogurt, and cook until thickened, about 1 minute. Add the remaining 1 tablespoon undiluted yogurt and cook for another minute. Stir the diluted yogurt mixture and add it to the pan. Return the chicken to the pan and season with a liberal pinch or so of salt and a pinch or two of cayenne to taste. Bring the liquids to a boil, reduce to a bare simmer, cover, and simmer until the chicken is cooked through and tender, about 20 minutes more.

five Remove the lid and transfer the chicken to a warm platter. Raise the heat to medium-high and cook rapidly, stirring frequently, until the sauce is cooked down and thick, 5 to 7 minutes more. Pour the sauce over the chicken, scatter the browned onions over it, and sprinkle generously with cilantro or parsley. Serve hot.

Chicken Sauté with Onions

Poulet Sauté à la Lyonnaise

Á LA LYONNAISE means "in the style of Lyons," and that usually means smothered in sautéed onions. Such is the case here: The onions and chicken undergo a preliminary cooking in two separate pans, then they are combined when the chicken is half cooked, which makes it much easier to control things.

SERVES 4

one Wash the chicken and pat dry. Place the chicken pieces on a platter and sprinkle lightly with a healthy pinch of salt, a few liberal grindings of pepper, and then dust them with the flour, turning to lightly coat all sides. Put 3 tablespoons of the butter and the onions in a sauté pan. Over medium-high heat, sauté, tossing frequently, until the onion is wilted and just beginning to color, about 5 minutes. Stir in 2 tablespoons of the parsley and turn off the heat.

two Put 4 tablespoons of butter in a large lidded cast-iron skillet or heavy-bottomed sauté pan. Over medium-high heat, melt the butter. When the foaming has subsided, pick up the chicken, one piece at a time, shake off the excess flour, and slip it into the pan. Sauté, turning frequently, until the chicken is well browned on all sides, about 10 minutes. Reduce the heat to medium and spread the onions over the chicken. Continue sautéing, turning frequently, until the chicken is cooked through, about 15 minutes more. (You can make the sauté an hour or so ahead up to this point. Reheat it gently over medium-low heat before proceeding.)

three Raise the heat to medium-high and pour the wine into the pan. Bring it to a boil, stirring and scraping to loosen any cooking residue that may be stuck to the pan, and let it simmer for a minute or so.

four Remove the chicken to a platter and continue cooking until the wine is completely evaporated. Pour in the broth, bring it to a boil, and cook until the broth is reduced and thick, about 5 minutes more. Turn off the heat. Add the lemon juice or vinegar and swirl in the remaining 1 tablespoon of butter. Pour the sauce over the chicken, sprinkle with the remaining tablespoon of parsley, and serve at once.

1 small frying chicken, weighing under 3 pounds, skinned and cut up for frying as on page 11

Salt and freshly milled black pepper

1/4 cup all-purpose flour

8 tablespoons unsalted butter

2 large yellow onions, thinly sliced

3 tablespoons chopped parsley

1/2 cup dry white wine

1 cup Chicken Broth (page 18) or 1/2 cup canned broth and 1/2 cup water

1 tablespoon lemon juice or white wine vinegar

Chicken Sauté with Olives

Pollo alla Franceschiello

CHICKEN WITH OLIVES can be found in various forms all around the Mediterranean basin and even turns up in South America, having migrated there with the Spanish colonists. This version is from Sicily and is named for Francesco II, the last king of Sicily before the unification of Italy, supposedly because he was especially partial to it.

SERVES 4

1 frying chicken, weighing no more than 3 pounds, cut up for frying as on page 11, but not skinned

Salt and freshly milled black pepper

2 tablespoons chopped fresh rosemary or 2 teaspoons crumbled dried

3 tablespoons extra virgin olive oil

6 large garlic cloves, lightly crushed, but left whole

²⁄₃ cup whole green brine-cured olives (15 to 20, depending on size)

²⁄₃ cup *giardiniera* or *sottaceti* (Italian mixed vegetable pickles), well drained

¹⁄₂ cup dry white wine

5 or 6 healthy sprigs fresh rosemary, for garnish (optional)

one Wash the chicken pieces and pat dry. Sprinkle salt and then liberally grind black pepper over them. Sprinkle the rosemary over the chicken and pat it into the surface.

two Combine the olive oil and garlic in a large sauté pan or heavy-bottomed skillet. Over medium-high heat sauté, tossing frequently, until the garlic is golden brown. Remove and discard it. Add the chicken, a few pieces at a time so that the pan does not lose too much heat, and sauté, turning frequently, until lightly browned on all sides, 5 to 8 minutes. Reduce the heat to medium-low and sauté, turning occasionally, until the chicken is almost cooked through, about 15 minutes longer. Add the olives and giardiniera and let them heat through and start to sizzle.

three Pour in the wine and cook until it is evaporated, about 5 minutes longer. Transfer the chicken, olives, and giardiniera to a warm platter with a slotted spoon, pour some of the oil over it, and garnish with fresh sprigs of rosemary. Serve at once.

123

Chicken Sauté with Morels and White Wine

Poulet Sauté à la Forestière

HERE IS ANOTHER classic French sauté with mushrooms. Ideally, it should be made with fresh morels. I've used dried morels here, since they are more readily available to most of us. However, if you can get fresh morels (in season in the spring), by all means use them. You'll need ½ pound. Thoroughly clean them and sauté over medium heat in 2 tablespoons butter for 3 to 5 minutes before adding them to the chicken in step 3.

SERVES 4

2 ounces dried morels

1 frying chicken, weighing no more than 3 pounds, cut up for frying as on page 11

Salt and freshly milled black pepper

6 tablespoons unsalted butter

4 ounces fat country ham or prosciutto, julienned

¹⁄₂ cup dry white wine

1 recipe Butter-Browned New Potatoes (recipe follows)

2 tablespoons chopped parsley

one Place the morels in a heatproof bowl. Bring 1 cup water to a boil and pour it over them. Let them stand for 30 minutes. Meanwhile, wash the chicken, pat dry, and spread it on a platter. Sprinkle lightly with salt and a few liberal grindings of pepper. Set aside.

two Lift the morels out of their liquid, dipping to loosen any dirt that may be clinging to them, and put them in a small sauté pan with 2 tablespoons of butter. Strain their soaking water through a coffee filter or undyed paper towel and add it to the pan. Cook over medium-high heat, stirring occasionally at first and more frequently as the liquid evaporates, until the liquid has completely evaporated and been absorbed into the mushrooms. Turn off the heat and set aside.

three Put the remaining 4 tablespoons butter in a large lidded sauté pan or skillet. Over medium-high heat, melt the butter. When it is bubbly, add the chicken and sauté, turning it once, until it is browned on all sides. Reduce the heat to medium-low and add the reconstituted morels and the ham or prosciutto. Cover and cook slowly until the chicken is very tender, turning it occasionally, about 30 minutes more.

four Transfer the chicken and morels to a warm serving platter. Raise the heat beneath the pan to medium-high, and boil down the accumulated liquid by half, scraping to remove any cooking residue that may be stuck to the pan. Add the wine, bring to a boil, and cook briskly until the liquid is reduced by half, about 5 minutes. Turn off the heat, taste and adjust the seasoning, and pour the sauce over the chicken. Surround with the potatoes, sprinkle with the parsley, and serve at once.

Butter-Browned New Potatoes

Pommes des Terre à la Noisette

TRUE POTATOES *NOISETTE* are cut into uniform ovals, but small new potatoes adapt well to the recipe without the time-consuming trimming.

SERVES 4

one Scrub the potatoes under cold running water but don't skin them. Steam them in a vegetable steamer basket over boiling water (medium heat) until barely tender, about 10 minutes. Let them cool enough to handle and peel them by hand.

2 pounds red-skinned new potatoes, as small as possible

2 tablespoons unsalted butter

Salt

two Put the butter in a skillet that will hold all the potatoes in one layer and turn on the heat to medium-high. When the butter is melted and beginning to brown, add the potatoes, reduce the heat to medium, and sauté, tossing frequently, until uniformly golden. Sprinkle lightly with salt, toss, and serve hot.

Chicken Breasts in Brown Butter

Suprêmes de Volaille à Brun or à la Meunière, or Petti di Pollo alla Fiorentina

À LA MEUNIÈRE literally means "in the manner of the miller's wife." What it describes is something pan-fried in browned butter, hence the other French name, *à brun*. However, this is actually not an exclusively French dish. In Italy, it is known as *alla fiorentina,* Florentine style. Well, whatever you call it, it's an especially lovely and quick way to cook chicken fillets. As the name implies, the butter caramelizes to a lovely nut-brown, making one of the simplest and yet most delicious of sauces.

With an appetizer and a couple of side dishes, this recipe will amply feed four, but for heartier appetites in a simpler meal, allow a whole breast per person.

SERVES 2 TO 4

2 large whole boneless chicken breasts, skinned and split as on page 11
1/4 cup all-purpose flour
8 tablespoons unsalted butter
Salt

one Rinse the breasts and pat dry. Lay them on a clean, dry plate and lightly dust them with flour on both sides.

two Put the butter in a large lidded sauté pan or skillet over medium-high heat. When the butter is melted and the foaming subsides, pick up one of the pieces of breast, shake off the excess flour, and slip it into the pan. Repeat with the remaining pieces, shaking off the excess flour each time. Fry until the bottoms are golden brown, about 4 minutes. Turn the breasts, sprinkle the cooked side with a liberal pinch of salt, and continue cooking until the second side is nicely browned and the breasts are just cooked through, about 3 minutes more. If, after you turn the breasts, the butter appears to be getting too brown, turn down the heat to medium. When the breasts are just cooked through, remove the pan from the heat, put a lid on it, and set aside for 1 minute.

three Transfer the breasts to individual serving plates. Shake the pan to mix the butter and any pan juices that have accumulated and pour it evenly over each portion. Serve at once.

VARIATIONS: This really is so good that it doesn't need another thing added to it, but if you want to vary it, try swirling 2 tablespoons of chopped parsley or tarragon into the butter at the end. Or add 2 tablespoons of capers when you turn the breasts in step 2.

Chicken Breasts with Pesto

Petti di Pollo con Pesto

THOUGH THE GENOESE occasionally put pesto, their classic sauce of basil, garlic, and mild Ligurian olive oil on things other than pasta, it is never in the careless catch-all way that we use it in our country. This dish, though it is not Genoese, puts pesto to work in a way that is consistent with Ligurian sensibilities. The secret is that the pesto doesn't cook, but gently melts into the warm sautéed chicken breasts as it would into cooked pasta, beneath a light blanket of fresh mozzarella. The recipe is from Italian cooking authority Michele Scicolone, whose lovely book on Italian cooking, *A Fresh Taste of Italy,* is aptly named.

SERVES 4

2 large whole boneless chicken breasts, skinned and split as directed on page 11

¼ cup all-purpose flour

3 tablespoons extra virgin olive oil

¼ cup Pesto alla Genovese (recipe follows)

4 ounces fresh mozzarella, cut into thin slices

one Lay the chicken breasts on a sheet of wax paper or plastic wrap on a flat work surface. Put a second sheet of paper or wrap over them and lightly pound them flat with the flat side of a mallet until they are of uniform thinness. Spread the flour on a plate.

two Put the olive oil in a large lidded skillet over medium-high heat. When the oil is hot and fragrant, but not smoking, lightly roll the breast cutlets in the flour and shake off the excess. Slip them into the hot oil and sauté quickly until the bottom is golden, about 2 minutes. Turn them and sauté until they are nearly cooked through, 1 to 2 minutes more. Remove from the heat. Spread 1 tablespoon of pesto onto each piece of chicken and lay the mozzarella slices over it, completely covering the pesto. Cover the pan and let it sit until the mozzarella is melted, about 2 minutes longer. Transfer the chicken to a serving platter and pour any cooking juices that have accumulated over it. Serve at once.

Pesto alla Genovese

LIGURIANS CLAIM THAT authentic *pesto alla Genovese*—the fragrant fresh basil sauce of the Italian Riviera—can only be made on its home turf, with Genoese-grown basil, Ligurian olive oil, and genuine sardo cheese. That may be true, but it is still awfully good made with our large-leaved minty basil and a heftier oil.

Classic pesto is made with a mortar and pestle—that's where it gets the name—but the blender and food processor both make pesto that, while not as flavorful as that made with a mortar, is still respectable. Use care and all your judgment when making this sauce. Italian author Anna Del Conte rightly says that pesto is at once one of the simplest of Italian sauces to make and yet the most difficult to make well.

MAKES ABOUT 2 CUPS

3 cups firmly packed basil leaves

2 large garlic cloves, crushed

Salt

3 tablespoons pine nuts (pignoli)

2/3 cup extra virgin olive oil

1/2 cup freshly grated Parmigiano-Reggiano

3 tablespoons freshly grated pecorino

one Combine the basil, garlic, and a healthy pinch of salt in a blender or food processor fitted with a steel blade. Pulse until the basil is roughly chopped.

two Add the pine nuts and oil and process until the nuts and the basil are finely chopped, but not too smooth. It should still have plenty of texture. Add the cheeses and pulse until blended. If the sauce seems too thick, stir in a little more olive oil. Taste and adjust the seasonings.

NOTE: To store pesto, transfer it to a glass bowl and float a ¼-inch-thick layer of olive oil on top. This will help keep it from discoloring. It will keep for up to a week refrigerated. You can also freeze pesto successfully. Omit the cheese and spoon the pesto into small freezable containers in individual portions, float a thin layer of olive oil on top, cover tightly, and freeze. To use frozen pesto, let it thaw and then fold the cheese into the sauce. Frozen pesto turns dark when you use it. There's nothing you can do about it, so don't fret over it.

STIR-FRYING

With a name like Fowler, I'm not about to pretend to be an authority on East Asian cookery and its techniques. However, stir-frying, the most commonplace technique in the Asian repertory, is nothing complicated, and even this Southern Bubba has been able to master it without much difficulty. Basically, if you can pay attention to the pan and keep the food moving, you can stir-fry.

The proverb to keep in mind is that "time waits for no man"—and neither does a stir-fry. You must be completely ready both to cook and to eat; not only will it not wait for you to fumble around while it is cooking, it won't wait for you once it is done, either. Stir-fries do not take kindly to sitting around once they are finished and should go from the wok to the plate to your mouth in short order. Trying to keep stir-fried food warm will overcook it, reheating will only make it flabby and indifferent.

The primary principle behind stir-frying is conservation—that is, of getting the most out of very little. Fuel was in short supply, so the shape and material of the wok, the way each food is cut up, the order in which it is added to the pan, the quick tossing to keep everything in constant direct contact with the heated surface of the pan, all these factors are specifically engineered to make a little fire accomplish a lot. Though it requires quick reflexes and good timing, the comforting thing about stir-frying is that it is extremely logical. Foods that require more time and/or heat go in first, more delicate foods are added later. Seasoning is added to the pan first, flavoring the oil which coats the food and more evenly distributes it in the dish.

The general order follows this logic: 1. Everything—and I mean everything—is prepared ahead and ready for the pan. 2. The pan is preheated. 3. The oil is added and heated. 4. The dry seasonings—garlic, ginger, spices, and the like are added and warmed in the hot oil. 5. The meat is added and partly or completely cooked. 6. The vegetables are added. 7. Finally, the liquid seasonings are added, often with a little stock for a brief steaming to finish off the dish and meld the flavors. The meat may be removed before this stage or even before the vegetables are added, and returned to the pan at the very end. The stir-fry may then be finished with cornstarch paste to thicken and bind it, but often it is not. Though we Westerners are accustomed to thickened sauces, there are many Eastern cooks who seldom make it that way.

There are occasions when certain steps are reversed; for example, sometimes a vegetable is partly precooked, then removed before the meat is added. Sometimes a liquid seasoning (soy, wine, or vinegar) is added before the vegetables. However, those steps are the general order of things. Timing is of the essence. Sometimes the space between these steps is as little as 5 seconds and is never more than a minute or two. After a few times, you'll know by feel and by the look of things when it's time to move on.

Here are a few things to look out for in those steps.

1 Preparing the ingredients. The labor of a stir-fry is stacked at the front. Most of your time is spent preparing; but, fortunately, most of it can be done ahead at your convenience. All the solid ingredients are cut into bite-sized, and often decorative, pieces. Seasonings, thickening agents, and liquids should be premeasured and close at hand. Sometimes they have to be grabbed and added quickly; you won't be able to stop and measure or chop something you've forgotten. Remove all fat, skin, bones, and tendons from chicken meat and cut it across the grain. Cut hard vegetables, such as carrots, into thin slices; softer, high-moisture ones, such as onions, should be cut into larger pieces so that everything cooks evenly.

2 Heating the wok. The wok goes on the heat dry and empty. This way, any moisture that may be in the pan will evaporate before you add the fat. Steel has a low conductivity, but heats up quickly. If your wok is well seasoned, you'll know when it's ready because it will be fragrant and will "fog"—that is, lightly smoke—when it is hot.

3 Adding the oil. The oil must be hot when the food is added, so it is poured into the wok first. This is done by drizzling the oil around the outer edges of the wok so that it slides down the sides, heating up before it hits the bottom. If, at any point after you have started stir-frying, you find that you need more oil in the pan, it is added in exactly the same way so that it warms before it touches the cooking food.

4 Adding the dry seasonings. The chopped ginger and garlic and sometimes spices, such as hot peppers or curry, are added next. This gives them a chance to heat up and begin browning, intensifying the flavor and seasoning the oil before the food is added.

5 Adding the chicken. The chicken must be dry when it goes in. If it has been marinated, the marinade is drained off and the meat is sometimes patted dry (unless the marinade contains cornstarch or egg white, which makes a kind of batter). All meat must be stir-fried in small batches. If you add too much at once, the meat will cool down the wok and will also crowd itself, causing it to steam instead of sear. A good rule of thumb is never to stir-fry more meat than the equivalent of a whole chicken breast at one time.

6 Adding the vegetables. These may be added to the meat, or the meat may be removed, and the wok wiped out before fresh oil and then the vegetables are put in. In either case, add them a few at a time, so that the temperature inside the pan is not lowered too much.

7 Adding the liquids. All liquid is added in the same way as the oil—by drizzling it around the edges of the wok so that it heats before it touches the food. The liquid seasonings, such as soy sauce and rice wine, may be added first and allowed to mostly

evaporate before the stock is added, or they may be the only liquid added. The wok is sometimes covered to let steam build for a minute or two, which finishes off the vegetables. In any case, the amount of liquid is always sparing. A stir-fry is never swimming in sauce.

Ingredients In selecting recipes for this section, I have tried not only to choose with an eye toward the most characteristic dishes, but to the ones that can be made with ingredients readily available to us Western cooks. However, some of the characteristic flavor of the East can be had only by certain spices, prepared sauces, and vegetables that are unfamiliar to Westerners, and which can be found only in Asian or specialty markets. Throughout this section is scattered a series of boxed notes explaining these ingredients.

CHINESE STIR-FRIED CHICKEN

The cooking of China is usually divided into four general regions or schools: northern (or Mandarin) cooking, including the capital of Beijing (what we used to call Peking), eastern cooking from the provinces of the Pacific north, southern (or Cantonese) cooking, and western cooking, particularly the province of Szechwan. The northern regions can be subdivided even further. Cantonese cookery is the best known to Western palates, in part because Canton was originally Europe's gateway to China and in part because most Western Chinese restaurants have been run by Cantonese immigrants. The far north, where traditionally small nomadic tribes wandered the barren plains, is known for hearty lamb and mutton dishes—the food of so many nomads—whereas the region around Beijing (once the gourmet as well as the Imperial capital of China) was much influenced by the sumptuous cookery of the Imperial court and is known for the delicacy and elegance of its cookery. The cookery of the northeastern coast is known, predictably, for its seafood cookery and for light, delicate soups. The Szechwanese kitchen is where stir-frying is most highly developed and is marked by its use of fresh ginger, garlic, hot pepper, and spices, especially Szechwan pepper.

Cashew Chicken

Yao Go Ji-ding

 HIGHLY WESTERNIZED AND possibly the most popular of all Chinese chicken stir-fries, the variations on the chicken with cashews theme are dizzying. One of the best known is the Szechwanese version, *Gong-bao Ji-ding,* which legend attributes to an ambitious politico who first served it to celebrate an imperial appointment. Western adaptations of *Gong-bao Ji-ding* often are not very authentic; the original is made with charred hot peppers—and lots of them. Most of us are more familiar with less volatile versions.

SERVES 2 TO 4

one Wash the chicken and pat dry. Thinly slice across the grain no more than ¼ inch thick. Cut the slices into flat pieces about 1 inch wide and set aside. Combine 2 teaspoons of the cornstarch and 1 tablespoon each of the soy sauce and wine in a medium-sized nonreactive glass or stainless steel bowl. Beat until the cornstarch is dissolved, then beat in the egg white and a small pinch of salt. Add the chicken, toss until coated, and set aside to marinate for 30 minutes, refrigerated.

two Meanwhile, stem and seed the dried pepper and slice it as thinly as possible. Wipe the mushrooms clean, trim off and discard the stems if they are tough, and thinly slice. Cut the scallions into 1-inch lengths. Combine the remaining 2 teaspoons cornstarch, 1 tablespoon soy sauce, and 1 tablespoon wine with the sugar and sesame oil in a small bowl.

1 pound boneless chicken (about 2 whole breasts or 4 boned thighs), skinned

4 teaspoons cornstarch

2 tablespoons light (not "lite") soy sauce

2 tablespoons rice wine or extra-dry sherry

1 large egg white

Salt

1 small dried hot pepper

½ pound fresh shiitake mushrooms

2 scallions or other green onions, trimmed

2 teaspoons light brown sugar

2 teaspoons toasted sesame oil

4 tablespoons peanut or vegetable oil

2 quarter-sized fresh ginger slices, minced

2 large garlic cloves, minced

½ cup toasted cashews, preferably unsalted

2 cups hot Chinese-Style Rice (page 172)

three Place the wok over medium-high heat. When it is very hot, drizzle in 2 tablespoons of the peanut oil and put in the hot pepper. When the pepper is beginning to blacken, lift the chicken out of its marinade and quickly add it to the wok, a few pieces at a time, with the minced ginger and garlic. Stir-fry, scraping away any solids that stick to the wok, until the chicken is white and opaque, about 2 minutes, then remove the wok from the heat and put the chicken in a warm plate or bowl. Cover and set aside.

four Wipe out the wok and return it to medium-high heat. Drizzle in the remaining 2 tablespoons peanut oil and add the mushrooms. Stir-fry until they are wilted, about 1 minute. Add the scallions and toss until they are hot. Return the chicken to the wok and toss until it is hot again, about 1 minute. Stir the liquid seasoning mixture and drizzle it around the edges of the wok. Continue stir-frying until the sauce is thick and coats the chicken, about 1 minute more.

five Stir in the cashews and turn off the heat. Taste and adjust the salt and serve hot with the rice passed separately.

NOTE: You may substitute dried shiitake for fresh ones; you'll need 1 ounce. Put them in a heatproof bowl. Bring 1 cup of water to a boil and pour it over the mushrooms. Soak until they are reconstituted, about 30 minutes. Squeeze out the excess moisture. Strain the soaking liquid through a coffee filter, cover, and set aside to flavor a soup or sauce.

If you like things hot, you can add more peppers to suit your taste. In Szechwan, the mushrooms are omitted and the dish may have as many as a dozen peppers. The peppers are left whole and blackened in very hot oil. The blackening blunts a lot of the impact of the volatile oils and sweetens their flavor, but they're still hot. Don't try it unless you have a really good ventilation system over your cooktop, and keep your face averted from the wok; the smoke from this process is full of the volatile oils that produce the stinging heat and reacts on your throat, eyes, and sinuses like tear gas.

Soy Sauce If you are not familiar with Asian cooking, you probably think soy sauce is soy sauce is soy sauce. If that's the case, the first time you step into an Asian market, you will be dizzied by the variety of soys available. There are Chinese, Japanese, and Korean soys; dark soy, with a smoky, molasses-like undertone, light (not to be confused with "lite") soy, lighter in flavor and color, thick and thin soys, mushroom soys—the list goes on. I have given the specific soy sauce required for each of the stir-fried and Asian deep-fried chicken recipes in this book, with acceptable substitutions where applicable.

Mongolian Chicken with Bean Sauce

Mong Ku Gai Pan

MONGOLIAN COOKERY WAS thought by the ancient Chinese to be rather coarse and crude; however, the Mongols dominated China for a time, and some of their foodways inevitably crept into the cooking and stuck. Notice the flavorings here are a little different from the other stir-fries—stronger, and more direct. There is no ginger—rare for an Asian chicken dish. Instead, the flavorings are bean paste and dark soy sauce, which makes a robust, smoky-sweet sauce with an aftertaste of molasses. If you can't find it, substitute a light soy or Japanese soy sauce with a teaspoon of molasses stirred into it.

SERVES 2 TO 4

one Wash the chicken and pat dry. Thinly slice across the grain into ¼-inch-wide flat strips. Combine 1 tablespoon soy sauce, 1 tablespoon rice wine, 1 teaspoon cornstarch, and 1 teaspoon of the sugar in a medium-sized nonreactive glass or stainless steel bowl. Beat until it is smooth and add the chicken. Toss until all the pieces are uniformly coated and set aside to marinate, refrigerated, for at least 30 minutes or up to 1 hour.

two Meanwhile, if you are using fresh mushrooms, remove the stems and thickly slice them. If you are using dried mushrooms, bring 1 cup water to a boil. Place the mushrooms in a heatproof bowl and pour the water over them. Soak for 30 minutes, drain (you may save the liquid for another use), and squeeze out the excess moisture. Thickly slice them and set them aside.

2 whole boneless chicken breasts, skinned

2 tablespoons dark soy sauce

2 tablespoons rice wine or extra-dry sherry

2 teaspoons cornstarch

4½ teaspoons Demerara, turbinado, or light brown sugar

1 ounce dried Chinese black or shiitake mushrooms, or ½ pound fresh shiitake

4 large garlic cloves, lightly crushed

4 small fresh red chile peppers, split lengthwise and seeded

1 medium yellow onion, cut lengthwise into thin strips

Salt

2 tablespoons Chinese yellow bean paste

4 tablespoons peanut or vegetable oil

1 red bell pepper, cut into 1-inch dice

½ cup Chicken Broth (page 18) or ¼ cup canned broth and ¼ cup water

4 small scallions or other green onions, cut into 1-inch lengths

1 teaspoon toasted sesame oil

2 cups hot Chinese-Style Rice (page 172)

134

FRIED CHICKEN

three Mince the garlic, chiles, and 1 tablespoon of the onion with a very sharp knife until it forms a paste. Add a pinch of salt and set aside. In a separate bowl, gradually stir 2 tablespoons water into the bean paste until it is smooth. Stir in the remaining 3½ teaspoons sugar and set aside. In a separate bowl, dissolve the remaining cornstarch in the remaining 1 tablespoon soy sauce and wine. Set aside.

four Place a wok over high heat. When it is quite hot, drizzle in 2 tablespoons of the oil. Drain the chicken from the marinade and add the chicken to the wok. Stir-fry until it has lost its raw pink color, about 1 minute. Remove the chicken from the wok with a slotted spoon.

five Drizzle in the remaining 2 tablespoons oil, then add the sliced onion, mushrooms, and pepper and stir-fry until the onion is translucent, about 2 minutes. Add the garlic-chile-onion paste and stir-fry until it is very fragrant, about 30 seconds. Return the chicken to the wok, drizzle in the broth, give everything a good toss, and cover. Steam until the vegetables are crisp-tender, about 2 minutes or less. Remove the lid and add the scallions. Toss well and add the diluted bean paste and the soy sauce and wine mixture, and stir-fry until the sauce is thick and has coated all the vegetables and chicken.

six Turn off the heat. Stir in the sesame oil and turn the chicken out into a warm serving bowl or platter. Serve at once with the hot rice passed separately.

Sesame Oil The extracted oil of toasted and raw sesame seeds, frequently used as a seasoning in most Asian cuisines, may also turn up in African and Caribbean cookery. Sesame oil is dribbled into soup, tossed in a stir-fry, or drizzled over fried food to add extra flavor. Both toasted and untoasted sesame oil are available at Asian markets, most natural food stores, and many specialty groceries. Toasted sesame oil has a deep, rich amber color and is much more complex in flavor than untoasted sesame oil. If you cannot find it, untoasted sesame oil can be substituted for it.

Cantonese Chicken Curry

Yea tsup Ga Li Gai

CURRY SPICES, ACCORDING to Martin Yan, are recent comers to the Chinese kitchen and do not figure in the older, more traditional cuisines. However, as he notes, they are popular in southern China, particularly Canton, Hong Kong, and the island of Hainan. Since Cantonese cooking is the one that is most familiar to Westerners, curries are often found on the menu in Chinese-American restaurants.

In selecting the curry for this dish, make sure that you buy Chinese curry paste, and not Thai, Vietnamese, or Indonesian curry pastes, which are very hot and pungent. If you can't locate Chinese curry, use a mild commercial curry mix. Curry paste is more flavorful and has better keeping qualities than powder.

SERVES 2 TO 4

one Wash the chicken, pat dry, and cut across the grain into thin, flat strips. In a small bowl, stir together the soy sauce, wine, and cornstarch. Set aside.

two Place a wok over high heat. When it is hot, drizzle in the oil. Add the garlic, ginger, and hot peppers. Stir-fry until fragrant and beginning to color, 5 to 10 seconds. Add the curry paste (or powder) and stir-fry until fragrant and dissolved, 5 seconds more. Add the chicken and stir-fry until it is opaque and has lost its raw pink color, about 2 minutes.

1 pound boneless chicken (about 2 whole breasts, 4 thighs, or 1 whole breast and 2 thighs), skinned

1 tablespoon light (not "lite") soy sauce

1 tablespoon rice wine or extra-dry sherry

2 teaspoons cornstarch

3 tablespoons peanut or vegetable oil

2 large garlic cloves, minced

2 quarter-sized fresh ginger slices, minced

2 small dried hot red chiles, seeded and cut into thin strips

2 teaspoons Chinese curry paste or 1 tablespoon mild curry powder

1 medium onion, cut lengthwise in thin strips

1 medium red bell pepper, cut into thin strips

1/2 cup Chicken Broth (page 18) or 1/4 cup canned broth and 1/4 cup water

1/2 cup Rich Coconut Milk (page 151) or canned coconut milk

1/2 cup freshly grated coconut or unsweetened frozen coconut

2 cups hot Chinese-Style Rice (page 172)

three Remove the chicken from the wok and add the onion and red pepper. Stir-fry until they are glossy and hot, about 1 minute. Return the chicken to the wok, add the broth, and bring to a boil, stirring and tossing constantly. Add the coconut milk, bring to a boil, and reduce the heat to medium. Simmer until the chicken is cooked through and the onion and pepper are crisp-tender, 3 to 5 minutes.

four Quickly stir the soy sauce-and-wine mixture to redistribute the cornstarch and pour into the wok. Simmer until the sauce is thickened.

five Turn off the heat. Turn the curry into a warm serving bowl. Sprinkle with the grated coconut and serve at once with the hot rice passed separately.

Szechwan Chicken with Red Pepper Shreds

La-jiao Zi Ji

THIS LOVELY DISH with its snowy chunks of chicken and fine bright threads of red pepper is, aside from Cashew Chicken, perhaps the best known of Szechwan's chicken dishes. Variations are popular in Western Chinese restaurants and throughout the countries of Southeast Asia. The Vietnamese version, flavored with fish sauce instead of sesame oil, is picturesquely known as *ga kho,* "singing chicken." Though the dose of hot pepper here looks lethal, the flavor is actually rather delicate. It is hot, yes, but not so hot that you cannot taste anything else.

SERVES 2 TO 4

one Wash the chicken, pat dry, and cut into 1-inch cubes. In a medium-sized bowl, combine 2 teaspoons of the cornstarch with 2 teaspoons of the soy sauce, stirring until the cornstarch is dissolved. Add a large pinch of salt and stir until it dissolves. In a separate bowl, lightly beat the egg white. Add the chicken to the marinade and toss, then add the egg white and toss to coat the chicken well. Set aside to marinate for 30 minutes, refrigerated.

two Particularly if you are sensitive to the acid, wear rubber gloves when handling fresh hot peppers. Stem the peppers and cut them in half lengthwise. Remove all the seeds and white membranes and discard them. Cut the peppers lengthwise into very thin strips. Set them aside. (Clean your hands thoroughly before you touch anything else.)

three Combine the remaining 2 teaspoons cornstarch and 3 teaspoons soy sauce in a small bowl and mix until smooth. Stir in the wine, vinegar, and sesame oil. Set aside.

four Place a wok over high heat. When it is hot, drizzle in the oil. Lift the chicken out of the marinade, allowing the excess to flow back into the bowl. Slip it into the hot oil and stir-fry until it is opaque and white on the outside, about 1 minute. Remove it with a slotted spoon and, off the heat, remove and discard all but 2 tablespoons of the oil from the wok.

five Return the wok to the heat. When the oil is hot again, add the ginger, garlic, and hot pepper shreds. When it is fragrant (this will be only a matter of seconds—less than half a minute), return the chicken to the wok and give it a good toss. Quickly stir the soy sauce-and-wine mixture to redistribute the cornstarch and pour it into the wok. Stir vigorously until all the chicken is coated and cooked through, about 2 minutes or less. Serve hot, with the hot rice passed separately.

NOTE: You can up the heat, if you must, by adding a couple of extra peppers, or tone it down by using a milder pepper that is not very hot, but don't use less pepper: You'll need at least the amount called for to give the chicken the proper flavor.

1 whole boneless chicken breast, skinned

4 teaspoons cornstarch

5 teaspoons light (not "lite") soy sauce

Salt

1 large egg white

4 small fresh red cayenne, serrano, or jalapeño peppers

1 tablespoon rice wine or extra dry sherry

2 teaspoons rice vinegar

2 teaspoons toasted sesame oil

½ cup peanut or vegetable oil

2 quarter-sized fresh ginger slices, minced

2 large garlic cloves, minced

2 cups hot Chinese-Style Rice (page 172)

Chicken with Ginger and Mint

Gai Khing

THIS STIR-FRY IS very characteristic of Thai cuisine: garlicky, spicy, hot, and very aromatic—as exquisite to the nose as it is to the eyes and tongue. The basic principles of stir-frying remain intact here; what varies is the way the dish is flavored and finished. Note that there is very little sauce; the liquid seasonings act only as a flavoring agent, and most of their moisture is allowed to evaporate.

In Thailand, a particular dish is more of an idea than a specific recipe. Each cook goes in his own direction from the basic core. While I was researching this book, I came across a dozen recipes for *gai khing* (also spelled *kai khing, gai king,* and *gai pad khing*); no two were the same.

SERVES 2 TO 4

one If you are using fresh mushrooms, wipe them with a dry cloth, cut off the stems, and thinly slice them. If you are using dried ones, put them in a heatproof bowl. Bring 1 cup water to a boil and pour it over the mushrooms. Set aside for 30 minutes, then drain (reserve the liquid to flavor a stock or sauce) and squeeze out the excess moisture. Cut off and discard any stems and slice the mushrooms into thin strips. Set aside.

two Wash the chicken, pat dry, and cut into 1-inch dice.

three Place a wok over high heat. When it is hot, drizzle in the oil. Add the onion and stir-fry until wilted, about 2 minutes. Add the garlic and ginger and continue stir-frying until it is fragrant, about 30 seconds. Add the chicken and stir-fry until it is opaque, about 2 minutes more. Add the soy sauce and half

8 medium-sized fresh or dried shiitake mushrooms

1½ pounds boneless chicken (preferably both dark and light meat, but all breast meat is acceptable)

¼ cup peanut oil

1 medium yellow onion, thinly sliced

5 large garlic cloves, finely chopped

3 tablespoons finely minced fresh ginger

1 tablespoon light (not "lite") or Japanese soy sauce

3 tablespoons chopped fresh mint (or fresh basil, which is also lovely)

6 small scallions or other green onions, cut on the diagonal into 1-inch pieces (including most of the green tops)

2 to 4 fresh red serrano or jalapeño peppers, seeded and cut into fine shreds

1½ tablespoons rice vinegar or dark Chinese vinegar

1 tablespoon light brown sugar

2 tablespoons *nam pla* (Thai fish sauce)

2 cups hot Chinese-Style Rice (page 172)

the mint. Toss and add the mushrooms, scallions, and peppers and stir-fry until the onions are crisp-tender and the chicken is cooked through, 1 to 2 minutes more. Add the vinegar, sugar, and fish sauce and toss until thick.

four Turn off the heat. Add half the remaining mint and toss well. Turn out into a warm serving dish, sprinkle with the remaining mint, and serve at once with the hot rice passed separately.

NOTE: Throughout Southeast Asia, one of the most characteristic seasonings is fermented fish brine sauce. It has a complex, salty-smoky flavor somewhat reminiscent of country ham with a nutty, pleasantly fishy aftertaste. It also thickens slightly when heated. Unfortunately, it has no equivalent in Western ingredients, but is readily available at most Asian markets in larger communities. In Thailand, it is *nam pla;* in Vietnam, *nuoc mam. Nuoc mam* is supposed to be the darkest and most complex tasting. However, they can be used interchangeably in any of these recipes.

This dish is traditionally spicy-hot, and often contains even more pepper than I have included here. However, if you aren't accustomed to hot peppers, there's no need to suffer for authenticity's sake. Use as many or as few as your palate can handle, but don't omit them altogether and don't blow the roof off with them, either. They are an important part of the flavor, but should not overwhelm it. If you are at all sensitive to the acid in hot peppers, wear gloves to handle them. Even if you aren't sensitive, always scrub your hands well before you touch anything else.

Fried Chicken with Mushroom and Cilantro

Moan Chua Noeung Phset Kream

LIKE THAILAND TO its west, Vietnam to its east, and Malaysia to its south, the cookery of Cambodia is a mélange of the cuisines of India, China, Java, and Sumatra. In Cambodia and Vietnam, however, there is also a distinct French influence from the days of the French colonization. All these cross-influences make a contribution to this characteristic dish. The chicken is cooked with the bones still in it, so the cooking time is naturally longer, but the method is still a straightforward stir-fry. If, for ease of serving, you prefer to bone the chicken, refer to the notes at the end of the recipe.

SERVES 4

one If you are using fresh mushrooms, cut off and discard the stems, thickly slice the caps, and set aside. If you are using dried ones, put them in a heatproof bowl. Bring 1 cup water to a boil and pour it over the mushrooms. Let them soak for 30 minutes, then squeeze them dry, cut off and discard the stems, and thickly slice the caps. Set aside.

two Wash the chicken and pat dry. Combine the sugar, vinegar, and fish sauce and stir until the sugar is dissolved. Set aside.

three Place a wok over medium-high heat. When it is quite hot, drizzle in the oil. When the oil is hot, add the chicken and fry, tossing it frequently, until it is well browned, about 5 minutes. Add the garlic and ginger and stir-fry until it is fragrant and golden brown, about 10 seconds. Add the mushrooms and stir-fry until wilted (if fresh) or hot through (if dried).

8 fresh or dried shiitake mushrooms (or Chinese mushrooms)

1 chicken, weighing no more than 3 pounds, cut up for frying Chinese-style as on page 11

1 tablespoon Demerara, turbinado, or light brown sugar

2 tablespoons rice vinegar or Chinese dark vinegar

4 tablespoons Thai *(nam pla)* or Vietnamese *(nuoc mam)* fish sauce

3 tablespoons peanut oil

4 large garlic cloves, minced

3 tablespoons peeled, minced fresh ginger

1/2 cup Chicken Broth (page 18) or 1/4 cup canned broth and 1/4 cup water

3 tablespoons chopped fresh cilantro

2 cups hot Chinese-Style Rice (page 172)

four Drizzle the broth into the wok around the edges. Add the vinegar-and-fish-sauce mixture and toss well. Reduce the heat to medium, cover the wok, and cook until the chicken is just cooked through, about 8 minutes more.

five Remove the lid, raise the heat to medium-high, and stir fry until the sauce is reduced and thick.

six Turn off the heat, transfer the chicken to a warm serving platter, sprinkle with cilantro, and serve at once, with the hot rice passed separately.

NOTE: If you would prefer to use boneless chicken, do not skin the chicken, since the skin is an important part of the flavor and texture of this dish. Chop the boned meat, skin and all, into rather large (2-inch) pieces. Add the ginger and garlic to the wok before the chicken in step 3, stir frying until it is fragrant and golden, about 10 seconds, then add the chicken and stir-fry as indicated. Omit the simmering stage in step 4; add the broth and vinegar mixture and continue stir-frying at medium-high heat until the sauce is reduced and thick, about 5 minutes more.

141

Chicken with Asparagus and Long Onions

MUCH LIKE IN Italy, everything under the rising red sun of Japan is touched by art. It is not enough for the food to taste good at a Japanese table, it must satisfy all the senses, and the aesthetics of the eye become as important as the aesthetics of the palate. Notice that there is a careful balance here in color, texture, and flavor.

Japanese culture has been much influenced by their ancient neighbor to the east, and this is especially true of the cooking. The technique here is Chinese, but the results are distinctly Japanese, with the unique flavors of dashi, Japanese soy, and burdock root.

SERVES 2 TO 4

one Wash the chicken, pat dry, and cut across the grain into thin strips. Combine the ginger, soy sauce, mirin, 1 tablespoon water, and 2 teaspoons of the potato starch in a medium-sized bowl. Beat until smooth. Add the chicken and toss until it is uniformly coated. Cover and marinate for 1 hour, or overnight, refrigerated.

two Scrub the burdock root with a brush under cold running water. Slice thinly and set aside in cold water to cover. Dissolve the remaining 1 teaspoon potato starch in the dashi or diluted fish sauce. Set aside.

three Place a wok over high heat. When it is very hot, drizzle in 2 tablespoons of the oil. When the oil is very hot, add the garlic and stir-fry until it is fragrant, 20 to 30 seconds. Add the chicken and its marinade to the wok. Stir-fry

1 pound boneless chicken (preferably from the thigh), skinned

2 tablespoons grated fresh ginger

2 tablespoons Japanese soy sauce (such as Kikkoman's)

1 tablespoon mirin, sweet sake, or 1 tablespoon sake and 1 teaspoon sugar

3 teaspoons potato starch (*katakuri-ko;* see Note) or cornstarch

1 medium burdock root (about 3/4 inch in diameter by 10 inches long)

1/2 cup dashi (seaweed-bonito broth, page 166) or 1 tablespoon fish sauce diluted with enough water to make 1/2 cup

4 tablespoons peanut oil

2 large garlic cloves, minced

2 Japanese long onions (see Note) or 2 fairly thin leeks, trimmed of any tough dark leaves, or 4 large scallions or other green onions, cut into 1-inch lengths

1 pound asparagus (18 to 24 spears, depending on size), peeled and cut into 1-inch lengths

1 medium carrot, cut decoratively into thin rounds

1 teaspoon sesame oil

2 cups hot Chinese-Style Rice (page 172)

until the chicken loses its raw pink color, about 1 minute. Remove it from the heat and lift the chicken out of the wok using a slotted spoon.

four Return the wok to the heat and add the remaining 2 tablespoons oil. When it is very hot, add the onions or leeks and stir-fry until bright green, about 30 seconds. Add the asparagus and continue stir-frying until bright green, 30 seconds more. Add the burdock root and carrot and toss well. Return the chicken to the wok and stir-fry until the chicken is nearly cooked through, about 1 minute more. Stir the dashi or diluted fish sauce to redistribute the starch and add it to the wok. Simmer quickly until the sauce is reduced and thick, the chicken is done, and the vegetables are crisp-tender, about 2 minutes.

five Turn off the heat, drizzle the sesame oil over all, and toss until it is incorporated. Turn into a warm serving bowl. Serve at once, with the hot rice passed separately.

NOTE: Japanese long onions (also known as "Japanese leeks") are just that: long, slender, and delicate. They can sometimes be found in markets that cater to Asian communities. If you can't get them, substitute leeks that are as thin as you can get, or use 4 medium scallions. Potato starch is also sold as potato flour. Look for it in ethnic groceries and in natural food stores. Its texture is very different from cornstarch, but you can substitute the latter if you prefer.

Chicken Shreds with Coconut-Shrimp Sauce

Ayam Pecel

SUMPTUOUS COCONUT MILK sauces of this sort are common throughout Southeast Asia and figure prominently in many curried stews and fricassees. They point to a strong Indian influence on the region's cookery. This particular version of the sauce is enriched with nuts and dried shrimp paste and is also used as a sauce for roasted fowl.

SERVES 2 TO 4

one Wash the chicken, pat dry, and cut it crosswise into thin slices. Cut each slice into thin strips lengthwise. Set aside. Combine the nuts, chile paste, vinegar, salt, shrimp paste or sauce or shrimp, ginger, garlic, and coconut milk in a blender. Process on high until it forms a smooth paste. Set aside.

two Place a wok over medium-high heat. When it is hot, drizzle in the oil. Add half the chicken. Stir-fry until it has lost its raw pink color, about 1 minute. Lift it out with a skimmer or slotted spoon and stir-fry the remaining chicken. Remove it from the wok.

three If there aren't 2 tablespoons of oil left in the wok, add enough to make 2 tablespoons. Add onion and celery and stir-fry until translucent, about 2 minutes. Pour in the coconut milk mixture, stirring vigorously. Bring it to the boiling point, and return the chicken shreds to the wok. Let it come back to the boiling point, then reduce the heat to medium-low. Simmer slowly until the chicken is cooked through and the sauce thick. Stir in the lemon juice and turn off the heat.

1 pound boneless chicken, preferably both light and dark meat (about 2 whole breasts and 4 boned thighs), skinned

1/2 cup candlenuts (see Note) or macadamia nuts

1 teaspoon Thai, Indonesian, or Vietnamese chile paste (*sambal ulek*, page 96)

1 teaspoon rice vinegar

1 teaspoon salt

2 teaspoons crushed dried shrimp paste (trassi) or 1 tablespoon Chinese shrimp sauce or 4 small cooked shrimp, peeled and chopped

2 quarter-sized fresh ginger slices

4 garlic cloves, lightly crushed

1 cup coconut milk (page 151)

3 tablespoons peanut or coconut oil

1 medium yellow onion, chopped

2 medium celery ribs, strung and chopped

1 tablespoon freshly squeezed lemon juice

2 cups hot Chinese-Style Rice (page 172)

1 small cucumber, peeled and sliced into thin rounds

1 tablespoon chopped cilantro or celery leaves

four Taste and adjust the seasonings. Arrange the rice around the edges of a warm platter. Pour the chicken into the center, garnish with the sliced cucumber and cilantro or celery leaves, and serve at once.

NOTE: Shrimp paste, both dried (trassi) and in a thick, gray paste form (petis), is a common seasoning in Indonesian cookery. It is very pungent with a powerful aroma; a little does big things in the pot. If you cannot get it, peeled fresh shrimp can be substituted, though they will not have nearly as much flavor.

> **Candlenuts** In Southeast Asia, a long, oily nut known colloquially as "candlenuts" are used in dishes like this one. They were once actually rolled in leaves and burned for light, hence the name. They are not available in Western markets, but shelled Brazil or macadamia nuts are reasonable substitutes.

Chicken with Lemongrass

Ga Xao Xa Ot

LEMONGRASS, WITH ITS bright herbal-citrus flavor, is common to most of the cuisines of Southeast Asia. It is available at Asian markets and some specialty produce markets. If you can't find it fresh, some markets sell sliced dried lemongrass. Unfortunately, while it is fine for stews, slow-baked dishes, and other high-moisture cooking methods, it is not an acceptable substitute for this recipe. The dried grass will not soften enough and remains too woody and tough. The finely julienned zest of 2 lemons will come closer to approximating the flavor of fresh lemongrass.

SERVES 2 TO 4

one Wash the chicken, pat dry, cut into small, bite-sized pieces, and set aside. Beginning at the bulb end of the lemongrass, slice about 6 inches of each stalk crosswise as thinly as possible, using only the bottom and some of the tender green part of the leaves. Discard the dried, tough top. You should have about

⅔ cup of sliced grass. Put it into a medium-sized bowl and add about a third of the garlic, the ginger, sugar, 1 tablespoon of fish sauce, and the chiles. Stir until well mixed, add the chicken, and toss until it is well coated. Cover and marinate, refrigerated, for at least 1 hour or overnight.

two Place a wok over high heat. When it is hot, drizzle in the oil. Add the remaining garlic and stir-fry until it is fragrant, 20 to 30 seconds. Add the chicken and its marinade, tossing vigorously. Stir-fry until it is opaque and nearly cooked through, about 4 minutes.

three Add the scallions. Stir-fry until they are crisp-tender but still bright green, and the chicken is done, about 1 minute more. Add the remaining 1 tablespoon fish sauce and toss.

four Turn off the heat. Turn out into a warm serving bowl, garnish with chopped peanuts, and serve at once with the rice passed separately.

1 pound boneless chicken (preferably both dark and white meat), skinned

2 stalks lemongrass, including the bulb

4 large garlic cloves, minced

1 tablespoon grated fresh ginger

1 tablespoon Demerara, turbinado, or light brown sugar

2 tablespoons Vietnamese (_nuoc mam_) or Thai (_nam pla_) fish sauce

2 small fresh or dried red chiles, seeded and cut into fine strips

3 tablespoons peanut oil

4 scallions or other green onions, cut on the diagonal into 1-inch lengths

½ cup unsalted toasted peanuts, roughly chopped

2 cups hot Chinese-Style Rice (page 172)

STIR-FRIED PIECES AND PARTS

We're accustomed in the West to having mostly white-meat chicken in stir-fries. However, the choice breast meat is not all that finds its way into the wok in Asia. Nothing gets wasted; all parts of the chicken are used, including the intestines. The tasty organ meats are often neglected in our part of the world, and some of them, the hearts and intestines, for example, are all but impossible to come by. But gizzards and livers are sold in bulk in most markets and are very inexpensive. No other part of the chicken yields as much flavor for the money.

Chicken Livers in Oyster Sauce

Ho-yu Feng-gan

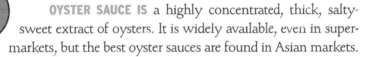

OYSTER SAUCE IS a highly concentrated, thick, salty-sweet extract of oysters. It is widely available, even in supermarkets, but the best oyster sauces are found in Asian markets.

This piquant sauce marries well with chicken livers; though it has a distinctive flavor, it complements their natural sweetness without overpowering them. Because the oyster sauce is most of the seasoning, this stir-fry is also a quick dish to put together.

SERVES 4

one Pick over the livers and cut out any green parts and fat. Wash them under cold running water and pat dry. Divide them into lobes and cut large lobes in half. Place them in a nonreactive glass or stainless steel bowl. Sprinkle them with five-spice powder and set aside. Separate the mushrooms, or, if using shiitakes, discard the stems and slice the caps thickly. In a small bowl, combine the oyster sauce with 2 tablespoons water and stir until smooth.

1 pound (1-pint container) chicken livers

1 teaspoon Chinese five-spice powder

1/2 pound fresh straw mushrooms (or shiitake mushrooms)

2 tablespoons oyster sauce

4 tablespoons peanut oil

2 quarter-sized fresh ginger slices, minced

2 large garlic cloves, minced

2 scallions or other green onions, cut on the diagonal into 1-inch lengths

1 carrot, cut decoratively into 1/4-inch rounds

1/4 pound snow peas, trimmed

1 cup sliced bamboo shoots (well-drained if canned; peeled and blanched if fresh; see Note)

Salt

2 cups hot Chinese-Style Rice (page 172)

two Place a wok over medium-high heat. When it is very hot, drizzle in 2 tablespoons of the oil. Add the ginger and garlic. Stir-fry until fragrant, about 30 seconds. Add the livers and stir-fry until they are firm and have lost their raw red color, about 2 minutes. Remove them from the wok.

three Add the remaining 2 tablespoons oil to the wok. Add the scallions and carrot. Toss and add the mushrooms. Immediately return the livers to the wok with a slotted spoon. Toss and stir-fry until the livers are almost done, about 2 minutes more. Add the snow peas and bamboo shoot if it is fresh. Toss until the peas are bright green and glossy, about 1 minute. Add the accumulated liquid from the livers, the diluted oyster sauce, and the bamboo shoots, if using canned ones. Stir-fry until the sauce is thick, the livers done, and the peas are crisp-tender, about 1 minute more. Taste for salt and add a pinch or so, if needed. Turn out into a warm serving bowl and serve at once with hot rice passed separately.

Bamboo Shoots Until recently, fresh bamboo shoots were not available in the United States. Canned shoots were our only choice and were hardly worth the trouble. However, fresh shoots are becoming more widely vailable at Asian markets and natural food stores and even some supermarkets. Winter shoots are more slender and delicate and will be labeled as such. Fresh bamboo shoots must be peeled and blanched before using them.

Curried Chicken Livers

Murgh Kaleja Kari

THIS IS A classic Indian stir-fry and can be served with any of the usual accompaniments and garnishes that might accompany other similar curried dishes: grated coconut, toasted peanuts or other nuts, chutney, mango pickles, sectioned tangerines, chopped cucumber, or golden raisins.

SERVES 4

one Pick over the livers and cut out any green parts and fat. Wash them under cold running water and pat dry. Divide them into lobes and cut large lobes in half. Place them in a nonreactive glass or stainless steel bowl. Set aside.

two Combine the coriander and cumin in a mortar, spice mill, or blender and grind them to a powder. Add the turmeric and cayenne and mix well. Set aside.

three Place a wok or large skillet over medium-high heat. When it is hot, add the butter or oil and heat. Add the onion and stir-fry until it begins to color, about 3 minutes. Add the garlic and ginger and stir-fry until fragrant, about 30 seconds. Add the spice mix and garam masala and stir-fry until the spices are toasted and very fragrant, about 30 seconds. Add the livers and stir-fry until they lose their raw, red color, about 2 minutes.

four Add the tomatoes, a large pinch of salt, and several liberal grindings of pepper. Bring to a boil, then cover and reduce the heat to medium-low. Simmer until the tomato is pulpy and the livers are cooked through and tender, about 15 minutes. Transfer to a warm serving bowl and serve at once with hot rice passed separately. Or, if you prefer, put the rice around the edges of a warm serving platter, pour the livers into the center, and serve at once.

1 pound (1-pint container) chicken livers

3 rounded teaspoons coriander seeds

2 rounded teaspoons cumin seeds

1/2 teaspoon ground turmeric

1/2 teaspoon ground cayenne pepper

2 tablespoons clarified butter (page 14) or peanut oil

1 large onion, trimmed, split lengthwise, peeled, and cut lengthwise into thin strips

2 large garlic cloves, lightly crushed, peeled, and minced

2 tablespoons grated fresh ginger

1 teaspoon garam masala

4 large ripe tomatoes, scalded with boiling water, peeled, seeded, and chopped, or 1 1/2 cups canned Italian plum tomatoes, seeded and chopped

Salt and freshly milled black pepper

2 cups hot Carolina-Style Rice (page 171)

149

Hot Curried Chicken Livers, Nepali Style

IN NEPAL, all the entrails of the chicken would be used in this dish, including the intestines and the loose skin around the craw. This is an adaptation using only the livers. If you like them, you can substitute half a pound of gizzards and hearts for half the livers. They will need to poach longer than the livers, so put them on first and cook until they are tender, about 30 minutes, then add the livers. This is a "dry" curry—that is, one without a sauce.

SERVES 4

1 rounded teaspoon coriander seeds

1 rounded teaspoon cumin seeds

1 rounded teaspoon yellow mustard seeds

4 large garlic cloves, roughly chopped

1 tablespoon grated fresh ginger

4 green chiles, seeded and chopped

1 teaspoon turmeric

Salt

3 medium onions, chopped

½ to 1 cup Chicken Broth (page 18) or ¼ to ½ cup canned broth and ¼ to ½ cup water mixed

1 pound (1-pint container) chicken livers

2 tablespoons clarified butter (page 14) or peanut oil

2 cups hot Carolina-Style Rice (page 171)

one Combine the coriander, cumin, and mustard seeds in a blender or spice mill and grind them to a powder. Put the ground seeds, garlic, ginger, chiles, turmeric, a large pinch of salt, and 1 tablespoon of the chopped onion in a blender with 2 tablespoons water. Process at high speed until it forms a smooth paste. Since the moisture content of the peppers and onion can vary, add a little more water, if needed, to form a smooth paste.

two Put half the curry paste and a third of the onions in a heavy-bottomed saucepan with just enough broth to barely cover the livers. Over medium-high heat, bring it to a boil. Reduce the heat to medium and simmer for 5 minutes. Add the livers and a healthy pinch of salt and raise the heat to medium-high long enough for the liquid to begin simmering, but don't let it boil. Reduce the heat again to low, cover, and poach the livers until they are cooked through, about 10 minutes. Turn off the heat. Drain the livers thoroughly and set them aside.

three Put a wok or heavy sauté pan over medium-high heat. When it is hot, add the butter or peanut oil and the remaining onions. Stir-fry until golden, about 5 minutes. Add the remaining curry paste and stir-fry until fragrant, about 30 seconds. Add the livers and stir-fry for 3 minutes. Season liberally with a healthy pinch or so of salt to taste, and turn off the heat.

four Transfer to a warm serving dish and serve hot with the rice passed separately. Or, make a ring of rice on a warm serving platter and pour the curried livers into the center.

Rich Coconut Milk

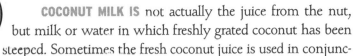

COCONUT MILK IS not actually the juice from the nut, but milk or water in which freshly grated coconut has been steeped. Sometimes the fresh coconut juice is used in conjunction with the other liquid, sometimes not. The amount of "cream" it yields depends in part on the richness of the liquid, but principally on whether the nut meat has been steeped more than once. A second soaking results in a thinner, less fatty "milk."

Canned coconut milk is available in Asian, ethnic, and natural food markets, and in some supermarkets, and can be used in the above recipe or any other recipe calling for coconut milk, but it is better if you take the trouble to make your own.

MAKES ABOUT 2½ CUPS

one Pierce the "eyes" of the coconut (where the stem was attached to the nut) and drain the juice from it through a strainer. Set the juice aside for another use or use it as part of the liquid for manufacturing the milk. On a hard, unbreakable surface, firmly tap the equator of the nut with a hammer, turning it constantly, until it splits in half. Turn each half up like a dome and tap until it shatters. Pry the nut meat loose from the shell, peel the brown skin from it, and grate it with a box grater, cheese grater, or in a food processor.

> 1 coconut
>
> 2 cups whole milk or the coconut juice and enough whole milk to make 2 cups

two Put the coconut into a heatproof bowl. Bring the milk or coconut juice and milk combination almost to a boil over medium heat, stirring constantly. Then pour it over the coconut. Let it steep for 1 hour.

three Line a wire sieve with a triple layer of cheesecloth or clean muslin. Pour the milk through the sieve into another bowl or pitcher. Carefully gather the coconut solids together in the cloth and twist it shut. Squeeze all the liquid from it into the bowl or pitcher of milk. This will result in more "cream."

four For coconut cream, allow the milk to stand until the thick paste of solids rises to the top and skim it off. For very rich milk, however, don't skim it, but stir the cream into the liquid before using.

NOTE: For thinner, less rich coconut milk, substitute water for the milk and skim off the cream before using.

My younger brother could happily make an entire meal of nothing but fried chicken—and not infrequently has. We never had leftovers when he was at the table. But most of us prefer to have something along with the bird—rice, creamy mashed potatoes, a salad, or perhaps a bowl of grits—and many fried chicken dishes are not complete without an accompanying dipping sauce or gravy. This chapter is a sampling of classic "go-withs" for fried chicken—traditional Southern pan gravies, sweet and savory mayonnaises, salsas, and dips, traditional breads and side dishes, and refreshing salads.

SAUCING THE BIRD

Fried chicken is one food that is practically perfect all on its own. Seldom does it need an accompanying sauce. But for many places in the world, the chicken is never served without an accompanying gravy or dipping sauce. Rare is the Southern table without cream gravy, and most Asians would never serve fried chicken without a savory, sweet, or hot dipping sauce. In all cases, the sauce or gravy is not served on top of the chicken—indeed, cream gravy never actually goes on the chicken at all, but on the accompanying bread or starch. With rare exception, they are presented separately, so that each person can dip, ladle, or smear to suit his own tastes.

Cream Gravy (Milk Pan Gravy)

THOUGH CALLED "CREAM GRAVY," this doesn't actually have any cream in it, but the original gravy that accompanied the earliest of the Southern fried chicken recipes was just that—cream lightly reduced in the pan in which the chicken had been fried. For families who could not afford prodigal amounts of cream, flour-thickened milk became the norm, but the old name stuck. Though this gravy is too often indifferently prepared and comes to the table thick and lumpy and wholly unappetizing, it can be a very good sauce so long as the cook uses care and doesn't allow the proportion of flour to milk to get out of hand.

MAKES 2 CUPS

2 tablespoons pan drippings from frying a chicken, left in the skillet along with the solid cooking residue

1 tablespoon all-purpose flour

2 cups whole milk, at room temperature

Salt and freshly milled black pepper

one Place the skillet in which you fried the chicken and left 2 tablespoons pan drippings over medium heat. Sprinkle the flour over the fat and blend it into the fat with a wooden spoon or whisk until it is smooth. Whisking or stirring constantly, slowly pour in the milk. Continue stirring, scraping loose the cooking residue that may be stuck to the skillet, until the gravy begins to boil and thicken. Season the gravy with a pinch or so of salt and a few liberal grindings of black pepper.

two Reduce the heat to low and simmer, stirring occasionally, until the gravy is as thick as you like it and the flour has lost its raw, pasty taste, 5 to 8 minutes longer. Serve hot.

Southern Tomato Gravy

CREAM GRAVY is the usual accompaniment for fried chicken in most of the South. But in the summer, when fresh tomatoes are plentiful, this savory tomato sauce sometimes makes an appearance, especially on country tables.

MAKES 2 CUPS

2 pounds fresh tomatoes

2 tablespoons pan drippings from frying a chicken, left in the skillet along with the solid cooking residue

1 small yellow onion, finely chopped

1 tablespoon all-purpose flour (preferably the seasoned flour from frying a chicken)

Salt and freshly milled black pepper

Bouquet garni made from 1 bay leaf, a sprig of parsley, and 2 to 3 large sprigs fresh thyme tied together with cotton kitchen twine

Chicken Broth (page 18) or water, if needed

one Put the tomatoes in a heatproof bowl and pour boiling water over them until they are completely submerged. Let them stand for 30 seconds, drain off all the water, then core and peel the tomatoes; the skins will slip right off. Split the tomatoes in half crosswise, and squeeze the seeds out into a wire sieve fitted over a bowl. Chop the pulp and add it to the collected juice. Set aside.

two Place the skillet in which you fried the chicken and left 2 tablespoons pan drippings over medium heat. Sauté the onion in the leftover fat, stirring and scraping the pan to loosen any cooking residue that may be stuck to the pan, until the onion is golden brown, 5 to 8 minutes. Sprinkle the flour over the onion and continue sautéing until the flour is browned, 3 to 4 minutes more. Stir in the tomatoes and their juices and let them come to a boil. Season with a liberal pinch of salt, a few grindings of black pepper, and the bouquet garni. If the tomatoes aren't very juicy, thin the gravy with the broth or water. Reduce the heat to a simmer, and simmer slowly for half an hour, stirring occasionally.

three If, at the end of the cooking time, the gravy has thickened too much, thin it with more broth or water, taste and adjust the seasonings, and simmer for a minute or so longer to allow the flavors to blend. Remove the bouquet garni and serve hot.

Raw Creole Sauce

SALSA CRUDA is ubiquitous throughout the Caribbean, Latin America, and around the Gulf Coast of the Deep South. A close cousin to the spicy salsas of the Southwest, it is a fine sauce for dipping fried chicken fingers or nuggets, or for serving alongside South American Fried Chicken (page 33) or Cuban Fried Chicken, Creole Style (page 31). It is also great with broiled or fried fish or seafood.

MAKES ABOUT 2 CUPS

1 or 2 large medium ripe tomatoes

1 medium yellow onion, finely chopped (about ¾ cup)

2 large garlic cloves, minced

1 fresh green banana, jalapeño, or serrano chile, seeded and minced

1 tablespoon chopped fresh cilantro or parsley

¼ cup freshly squeezed lime juice or red wine vinegar

½ cup extra virgin olive oil

Salt

one Peel the tomato with a vegetable peeler, core it, then split it in half crosswise. Remove and discard the seeds and chop the pulp. You should have ¾ cup of pulp. Put the chopped tomato into a serving bowl along with the onion, garlic, and chile. Add the cilantro or parsley, the lime juice or vinegar, and the olive oil and toss until well mixed.

two Let the sauce stand at room temperature for at least 15 minutes (up to 1 hour, if possible). After the flavors have melded, taste the sauce and add a pinch of salt—not too much—just enough to bring up the flavor. Serve at room temperature.

Curry Sauce

BASED ON AN old antebellum Georgia recipe, this is an ideal accompaniment for any breaded cutlet, and is a nice change from pan gravy with Southern fried chicken, but if you want to do a little fusion cooking (or *confusion* as I call it), it is also a good condiment for almost any deep-fried chicken in this book.

MAKES ABOUT 2½ TO 3 CUPS

one Combine the onion, apple, and butter in a medium saucepan over medium heat. Sauté, tossing frequently, until golden and softened, 5 to 8 minutes.

two Meanwhile, combine the flour, curry powder, and a large pinch of salt. When the onion and apple are golden, sprinkle in the curry/flour mixture, stir well, and sauté until it is fragrant. Add the currants or raisins and gradually stir in the Madeira, then the half-and-half. Bring it to a simmer, stirring constantly, then reduce the heat to low and simmer until it is thick and the flour has lost its raw taste, about 5 minutes more. Taste and adjust the seasoning and serve hot.

1 medium onion, diced

1 large tart apple (York, Winesap, Granny Smith, or similar variety), peeled, cored, and diced

2 tablespoons unsalted butter

2 teaspoons all-purpose flour

2 teaspoons curry powder

Salt

½ cup currants or raisins

½ cup Madeira or dry sherry

1½ cups half-and-half

157

Fresh Mango Sauce

THIS TANGY-SWEET, MILDLY hot chunky sauce is just one Latin American variation on the *salsa fresca* (uncooked sauce) theme. It is not only great with almost any fried chicken in this book, it is slap wonderful on grilled chicken, fish steaks, shrimp kabobs, and grilled or roast pork.

You can heat up things by substituting another chile pepper for the green bell pepper, but don't overdo it; the object here is a subtle, peppery undertone.

MAKES ABOUT 3½ TO 4 CUPS

2 large ripe mangoes, peeled, pitted, and cut into large dice

1 large sweet onion or red onion, diced small

½ red bell pepper, diced small

½ green bell pepper, diced small

1 small green chile (such as jalapeño), minced

1 tablespoon minced fresh ginger

1 garlic clove, minced

¼ cup freshly squeezed lime juice

2 heaping tablespoons chopped fresh mint

Salt and sugar

Combine the mangoes, onion, peppers, chile, ginger, garlic, lime juice, and mint in a medium-size nonreactive glass or stainless steel bowl. Season with a large pinch each of salt and sugar and toss until well mixed. Let stand at room temperature for at least 30 minutes before serving, or overnight in the refrigerator. If you refrigerate the salsa, take it out and let it stand at room temperature for 30 minutes before serving. Taste and adjust the seasonings, stir well, and serve at room temperature.

The Mayo Family

Though most mayonnaise in America ends up either in the potato salad bowl or between two slices of bread, it has long been one of the world's favorite sauces for fried food. In France, they even dip their fried potatoes in it. Once you start making your own, you'll see why—and you will never be satisfied with store-bought mayonnaise again. Making this sauce by hand is a painstaking undertaking (though for the fitness conscious, it's a great forearm workout), but if you have a food processor or blender, making mayonnaise is almost as easy as lifting a jar off the grocer's shelf. I've given both the hand method and the machine method here. If you don't have a food processor, and still don't want to make it by hand, the blender also makes very good mayonnaise, but you will have to periodically stop the machine and scrape down the sides of the bowl.

If you are cooking for someone whose immune system may be impaired, do not use homemade mayonnaise, since exposing such persons to possible salmonella contamination is very risky.

Keep all mayonnaises in a tightly covered container in the refrigerator.

Mayonnaise

THIS IS THE basic recipe. It can be spiced up with garlic (see Aïoli below), made piquant with pickles and capers (see Tartar Sauce), or dressed up with herbs (see Herb Mayonnaise). All of these sauces follow the same basic method.

Keep the sauce cold until you are ready to serve it.

MAKES 1½ CUPS

2 large egg yolks or 1 whole large egg

1 teaspoon dry mustard or 1 tablespoon Dijon mustard

Salt and cayenne pepper

1 cup olive oil

Juice of 1 lemon or 2 tablespoons wine vinegar

one To make mayonnaise by the traditional hand method, combine the egg yolks or egg in a mixing bowl with the mustard, a healthy pinch of salt, and a tiny pinch of cayenne. With a wire whisk or hand-held electric mixer, beat until the mixture is smooth.

two Have the oil ready in a container that has a good pouring spout. Pour a teaspoon of oil into the yolk mixture and beat until it is incorporated. Begin adding the remaining oil a few drops at a time, beating until each addition is thoroughly incorporated before adding more. Keep at it until you have used about half the oil.

three Add a little of the lemon juice or vinegar and beat it in, then alternate between the acid and oil until both are completely incorporated. Taste and adjust the seasonings.

FOOD PROCESSOR MAYONNAISE The sauce is less likely to break in this method if you use a whole egg instead of yolks. Put the egg, mustard, a healthy pinch of salt, a tiny one of cayenne, and lemon juice or vinegar in the bowl of a food processor fitted with a steel blade. Process for 1 minute.

159

With the motor running, add the oil in a thin, steady stream. (Add the first ¼ cup through the pin hole of the pusher if your machine has one.) This should take about 2 minutes (or you are pouring in the oil too fast). When the oil is incorporated, let the machine run for a few seconds more. Stop the machine, taste and adjust the seasonings, and pulse it a couple of times to mix them in.

AÏOLI Garlic mayonnaise is another fine dipping sauce for just about any fried food. To make it, simply crush and peel 2 garlic cloves and add them to the food processor with the egg in step 1. If you are making it by hand, put the garlic and salt in the bowl first and crush the garlic to a paste before adding the egg and other ingredients.

TARTAR SAUCE Into one batch of mayonnaise or aïoli, blend 1½ tablespoons each chopped sweet or sour dill cucumber pickles, well-drained capers, minced yellow onion, and parsley or dill. Let stand at least 1 hour before serving.

Herb Mayonnaise

THIS IS A superb dipping mayonnaise—great with any of the chicken finger and nugget recipes in this book, and fine with any fried or raw vegetables or with fried or steamed fish and seafood.

MAKES ABOUT 2 CUPS

one Combine the egg, lemon juice, mustard, garlic, salt, herbs, and 1 tablespoon of the olive oil in the bowl of a food processor fitted with a steel blade. Process for 1 minute. If your processor has a small feed-tube pusher with a pin hole, put the olive oil in it and, with the machine running, let the oil dribble into the egg mixture. If you don't have such a contraption, add the olive oil in a slow, very thin stream through the feed tube. Add the vegetable oil in a thin stream until it is all emulsified. Process for about 15 seconds more, until the mayonnaise is quite stiff. Transfer the mayonnaise to a storage bowl, cover, and refrigerate it overnight, if possible, to allow the flavors to blend before using.

1 large egg

1½ tablespoons freshly squeezed lemon juice

1 tablespoon Dijon mustard

1 garlic clove, crushed

1 teaspoon salt

1 large sprig fresh parsley, rosemary, and basil (do not use dried herbs), with tough stems removed and discarded

¼ cup extra virgin olive oil

1 cup vegetable oil

Mustard

Prepared mustard is a classic condiment for fried chicken, whether it is our own vibrant neon-yellow variety, flavored and colored with turmeric, suave Dijon mustard, or the fiery hot ones from England, China, and Creole Louisiana. Mustard is actually a spice, the small round seeds of a plant in the Brassica cruciferae family—which is related to cabbage, broccoli, and cauliflower. Indeed, in some areas, including my native South, mustard is cultivated more for its properties as a green leafy vegetable than for the spice. There are four primary types of mustard seeds—black, brown, yellow, and white (named for their color). Each has its own nuance of flavor and level of pungency.

Prepared mustard is made from dry mustard powder (or "flour"), the hulled seeds ground to a fine powder. Oddly enough, this powder has almost no smell. Only when it is mixed with liquids does it begin to develop its characteristically pungent aroma. How much aroma and spicy heat it has depends as much on what the mustard is mixed with as it does on the variety of the seeds. Coarse-grained prepared mustards are made with a combination of mustard flour and whole seeds. Excellent commercially prepared mustards are widely available, but here are a couple of homemade sauces that are classic with fried food.

Honey Mustard

THE CONDIMENT FOR any of the party chicken recipes, this spicy sweet mustard is also delicious on ham or turkey sandwiches, burgers, and Creole Chicken Poor Boy (page 81). Though bottled honey mustard is available, it always seems to taste better when you make it yourself.

MAKES ABOUT ³/₄ CUP

½ cup prepared spicy brown mustard (preferred) or Dijon mustard

4 tablespoons honey

Salt and freshly milled white pepper

one Whisk together the mustard and honey in a nonreactive glass or stainless steel bowl. Taste and add a pinch or so of salt, as needed, and several liberal grindings of white pepper. Cover and set aside for 10 to 30 minutes.

two Just before serving, whisk the sauce again. Taste and adjust the seasonings (the flavor will develop). This mustard will keep indefinitely if stored tightly covered and refrigerated.

NOTE: You can also use homemade mustard, such as the Hot Chinese Mustard that follows. For 1 recipe of Hot Chinese Mustard (⅓ cup) use only 3 tablespoons of honey.

Hot Chinese Mustard

THIS IS ONE hot, hot condiment. It is meant to be used sparingly, as a light dipping sauce for spring rolls, fried wontons, and the like. It is also a good condiment for Golden Coin Chicken (page 80) or for any of the chicken finger recipes. Make it at least 1 hour or, better, the day before you plan to serve it.

MAKES ABOUT ⅓ CUP

¼ cup dry English mustard powder
Salt
1 tablespoon rice vinegar
2 tablespoons boiling water (not hot tap water)

one Put the mustard and a good pinch of salt in a mixing bowl and stir well. Gradually beat in the vinegar and then the boiling water, a few drops at a time, until it is a smooth paste.

two Let it cool completely, cover, and let stand for at least an hour or refrigerate overnight. If you refrigerate the mustard, let it sit at room temperature for 30 minutes before serving.

Plum Sauce

FOR DIPPING ANY fried chicken tidbits, spring rolls, fried wontons, or just about any savory fried food you can think of. This sauce not only can be made well ahead, it seems to benefit from it. Plan to make it the day before you will be serving it. Plum sauce will keep for at least 2 weeks if stored tightly covered in the refrigerator.

MAKES ABOUT 2 CUPS

2 pounds dark blue, purple, or black plums, pitted and coarsely chopped (about 4 cups)

1/3 cup Demerara, turbinado, or firmly packed light brown sugar

1/3 cup rice vinegar

1/3 cup Chinese rice wine or extra-dry sherry

2 ounces thinly sliced fresh ginger (about 15 quarter-sized slices)

1 large garlic clove, crushed but left in 1 piece

4 teaspoons soy sauce

2 teaspoons toasted sesame oil

one Combine the plums, sugar, vinegar, wine, ginger, garlic, and soy sauce in a large nonreactive saucepan. Over medium heat, bring the mixture to a boil, stirring frequently. Cook until the juices are lightly thickened, 10 to 12 minutes (this can vary a minute or two one way or the other, depending on the ripeness of the fruit, the thickness of the pan, and the intensity of the heat source).

two Reduce the heat to low and simmer gently until it is the consistency of a jam, 10 to 15 minutes more; the exact time will depend on the amount of moisture in the fruit.

three Place a medium-weave wire sieve over a bowl that will hold all the sauce. Remove and discard the garlic and ginger and pour the sauce into the sieve. Force it through with a whisk, spatula, or wooden spoon. Discard the peels that remain in the sieve. Stir in the sesame oil and let it cool completely, uncovered. Then cover and store in the refrigerator.

Quick Plum or Apricot Sauce

THIS IS A quick version of the previous sauce for when you are short on time or when plums are out of season. It should still be made well ahead and allowed to sit for several hours (a day is even better) before you serve it so that the flavors develop.

MAKES ABOUT 1 CUP

²/₃ cup plum or apricot preserves, preferably without high-fructose sweetener

1 tablespoon grated fresh ginger

1 tablespoon soy sauce

1 tablespoon Demerara, turbinado, or light brown sugar

1 tablespoon rice vinegar

1 garlic clove, crushed (optional; omit if using apricot preserves)

2 teaspoons toasted sesame oil

one Put the preserves in a small nonreactive saucepan and stir until smooth. Over low heat, bring to a simmer. Add the ginger, soy sauce, sugar, vinegar, and garlic (only if using plum preserves). Stir until well blended, bring it back to a simmer, and turn off the heat.

two Let the sauce cool to room temperature, then stir in the sesame oil. Cover and let stand for at least an hour to allow the flavors to develop. If you have used garlic, remove and discard it. This sauce keeps for at least 2 weeks if stored, well covered, in the refrigerator.

Sweet-and-Sour Sauce

 WESTERNERS TEND TO think "sweet-sour" is a single sauce, but actually, it's a family of sauces with many variations, each one tailored to the food it is meant to accompany. This one is appropriate for any fried chicken.

MAKES ABOUT 2 CUPS

one Combine ¾ cup cold water and the sugar in a nonreactive saucepan and stir until dissolved. Over medium heat, bring to a steady simmer. Add the vinegar, garlic, and ginger and simmer for 10 minutes.

two In a separate bowl, combine the wine, soy sauce, cornstarch, and ¼ cup cold water. Stir until the cornstarch is dissolved and smooth. Add to the saucepan, stirring constantly, and simmer until the sauce is thickened, about 3 minutes more.

½ cup Demerara, turbinado, or light brown sugar

½ cup rice vinegar or Chinese dark vinegar

2 garlic cloves, minced

2 quarter-sized fresh ginger slices, minced

1 tablespoon rice wine or extra-dry sherry

1 tablespoon soy sauce

1 tablespoon cornstarch

2 tablespoons tomato paste

three Remove from the heat and beat in the tomato paste. Cool completely before serving at room temperature. Sweet-and-Sour Sauce will keep for several weeks if stored, well covered, in the refrigerator.

Tempura Sauce

THE SALTY-SWEET, SLIGHTLY fishy dipping sauce need not be limited to tempura. It can be used with any chicken nuggets, fingers, and fried wings in this book.

As is true of all cooking, the key to a good tempura sauce is good broth, or *dashi*. *Dashi* is made from dried kelp and bonito tuna flakes. Many modern Japanese cooks use instant *dashi* (*dashi-no-moto* or *hon-dashi*), and this product is widely available at Asian markets in our country. However, the raw materials are also widely available, and making good homemade *dashi* is not difficult. When buying the seaweed for *dashi*, look for thick, irregular squares labeled *kombu* or *konbu* (kelp) and not *nori*—the thin sheets used for making sushi; nori is too delicate and will disintegrate when it is simmered in water.

The other key ingredient to this sauce is mirin, a sweet Japanese rice wine widely used in sauces and marinades. Mirin is available in Asian markets, specialty grocers, and some wine shops. If you can't find it, you can approximate it by adding a little sugar to dry sake or dry sherry. Grated daikon (giant white radish) is frequently stirred into tempura sauce, but sometimes it is omitted. If you prefer, you may pass the radish in a separate bowl and allow each diner to add it to suit their own tastes. Daikon can be found in many vegetable markets.

MAKES ABOUT 1½ CUPS
(OR 2½ CUPS WITH DAIKON)

3-inch square dried kelp (kombu)

3 tablespoons dried bonito flakes (hana-katsuo)

¼ cup mirin, or sake or dry sherry mixed with 1 tablespoon Demerara, turbinado, or light brown sugar

¼ cup light Japanese soy sauce

2 teaspoons grated fresh ginger

1 cup grated daikon (optional)

one To make the *dashi,* combine the kelp and 1 cup cold water in a saucepan. Over medium heat, bring it slowly to the boiling point. Do not let it boil. Reduce the heat to a slow simmer and simmer for 1 to 2 minutes, or until the kelp is softened. Remove and discard the kelp. Add the bonito flakes and raise the heat to medium. Bring the liquid to a full rolling boil and remove it from the heat at once. Let the bonito flakes settle and soak for 5 minutes, skim any foam from the top, and filter the liquid through a fine wire mesh sieve into a glass mixing bowl, pressing on the solids to extract all the flavor. Set aside and allow the *dashi* to cool completely before proceeding.

two Add the wine, soy sauce, and grated ginger to the *dashi* and stir well. Just before serving, stir in 1 cup grated daikon root, if using. Serve at room temperature. Tempura Sauce will keep for up to a week if stored, tightly covered, in the refrigerator. Do not, however, add the daikon until you are ready to serve it.

NOTE: To make Quick Tempura Sauce using instant *dashi,* bring 1 cup water to a boil. Remove it from the heat and stir in ½ teaspoon instant *dashi* granules. Let it cool completely and proceed with step 2.

BREAD, RICE, GRITS, POTATOES, AND SALADS

Whether it is a Southern biscuit or hoe cake, a bowl of fluffy rice or creamy mashed potatoes, there are many starchy sides that are traditional with fried chicken throughout the world. Not only do these dishes stretch the main course, allowing the cook to feed a relatively large number of people on a small bird, they provide an apt vehicle for the accompanying sauce and contrasting texture. Some of them are so closely linked to the chicken that no native cook would think of serving one without the other. And no matter what kind of fried chicken you are serving, you cannot go wrong if it is followed by a refreshing salad, whether the salad is traditional or not.

Single-Acting Baking Powder: **You can use commercial double-acting baking powder for the recipes in this book, but look for one that is aluminum free (such as Rumford). I prefer single-acting powder, because many double-acting ones have a chemical aftertaste. Unfortunately, single-acting powder isn't made commercially, but making your own is easy**

3 tablespoons cream of tartar
3 tablespoons baking soda
3 tablespoons rice flour or all-purpose flour

Combine all ingredients in an airtight container and shake well. Shake well before each use, and use the powder up within a month. Makes about ½ cup.

Hoe Cakes

HOE CAKES ARE a traditional Southern cornmeal pan-cake that are supposed to have been so-named because they were originally cooked on the blade of a hoe over an open fire. Though many modern Southern cooks add wheat flour and sugar to the batter, I think either one in corn bread is an aberration. Hoe cakes are the perfect accompaniment for just about any family meal and needn't be limited to the Southern recipes in this book. They're great with an Italian, Indian, or French sauté.

MAKES ABOUT 12 CAKES

2 cups fine stone-ground cornmeal

2 teaspoons baking powder, preferably single-acting (see page 167)

1 teaspoon salt

2 large eggs, lightly beaten

2 cups whole milk, buttermilk, or plain, all-natural yogurt

Oil, melted butter, or lard, for the griddle

one Position a rack in the center of the oven and preheat the oven to 150°F (or Warm setting). Sift together the meal, baking powder, and salt in a large bowl. In a separate bowl, combine the eggs and milk or yogurt and beat until they are smooth. Stir this quickly into the dry ingredients, using as few strokes as possible.

two Heat a griddle or cast-iron skillet over medium heat. When it is hot, brush it lightly with the fat. Using a large, pointed kitchen spoon, take up about 2 tablespoons of the batter and pour it onto the griddle from the pointed end of the spoon (this helps insure that a round cake will form). Repeat until the griddle is full, but not crowded.

three Cook the cakes until the bottoms are nicely browned and air holes form in the tops, about 4 minutes. Turn, and cook until the second side is browned, 3 to 4 minutes longer.

four Transfer them to the warm oven and repeat with the remaining batter until all the cakes are cooked. Serve hot, with or without additional butter.

Spoon Bread

THIS LOVELY, SOFT soufflé-like bread has become a hall-mark of Southern baking. Its picturesque name evolved in the nineteenth century, from the way the bread must be served—literally, with a spoon. Some traditional cooks add baking powder to this bread, but this is one place where it does not belong. A small dose does help insure that the bread will rise, but it is superfluous when the eggs are well beaten and carefully incorporated.

SERVES 4

3 cups half-and-half
1 cup fine stone-ground cornmeal
3 tablespoons unsalted butter
1 teaspoon salt
3 large eggs, separated

one Preheat the oven to 350°F. Lightly butter an 8-inch soufflé dish or round casserole (or an 8-inch square one that is at least 2 inches deep). Prepare a double boiler with water in the bottom half well below the top pot. Bring it to a boil and lower the heat to medium-low. Add the half-and-half to the top boiler and scald it over the simmering water.

two Stirring constantly with a whisk, gradually add the meal to the liquid in a thin but steady stream, either from your clenched fist or from a pitcher. When all the meal is incorporated, cook, stirring constantly, until a thick mush forms, about 5 minutes. Take the top boiler from the heat and beat in the butter and salt. Set it aside to cool slightly.

three Separate the eggs, placing the whites in a clean stainless steel or glass bowl. Beat the yolks until they are light and smooth, then stir them into the mush. Using a clean wire whisk or hand-held mixer, beat the egg whites until they form stiff, but not dry, peaks. Gently fold them into the batter. Pour the batter into the prepared baking dish and place it in the center of the oven. Bake the bread until it is puffed and golden brown on the top, about 45 minutes. It should be set, but still soft, like a soufflé. Serve at once from the baking dish.

Skillet or Chicken Biscuits

IN RURAL SOUTHERN families, where appetites have always been large and budgets small, chicken biscuits were once a common way of stretching a chicken to go as far as possible. They are nothing more than traditional Southern biscuits fried in the fat leftover from frying the chicken. Rich, golden brown, and infused with the full flavor of the chicken, they are, yes, full of fat, and yet they are light and fluffy—and absolutely delicious.

MAKES ABOUT 24 TO 30 SMALL BISCUITS

10 ounces (about 2 cups) unbleached all-purpose flour or pastry flour

2 teaspoons baking powder, preferably single-acting (see page 167)

¹/₂ teaspoon salt

2 tablespoons (1 ounce) lard or unsalted butter

Enough fat left over from frying a chicken to come halfway up the sides of a skillet or Dutch oven

1 cup buttermilk or plain all-natural yogurt

one Sift together the flour, baking powder, and salt into a mixing bowl. Add the shortening and cut it in with a pastry blender or two knives until the flour resembles coarse meal.

two Reheat the fat over medium-high heat. Make a well in the center of the flour and pour in the buttermilk or yogurt. Quickly stir it in until a smooth dough is formed, working it as little as possible. Lightly flour the dough and gather it into a ball.

three Lightly flour a work surface and put the dough on it. Gently pat it out into a flat cake about ½ inch thick. Fold it over, give it a quarter turn, and gently pat it out again. Lightly flour it again if it begins to stick. Do not knead it—use as light a hand as you can manage. Repeat this maneuver twice more and then pat out the dough to a ½-inch thickness.

four Quickly cut the dough with a knife into squares or with a cookie or biscuit cutter into rounds or fanciful shapes. When the fat is hot (around 325°F), add the biscuits one at a time until the pan is full but not crowded. Fry, turning once, until the biscuits are risen and are a uniform golden brown, 3 to 5 minutes.

five Drain briefly on absorbent paper and serve at once.

Carolina-Style Rice

THOUGH IN OTHER parts of the South fried chicken is always served with mashed potatoes or grits, in the Carolina and Georgia Lowcountry, fried chicken without rice is not considered to be a complete meal. When properly prepared, Carolina-style rice literally rattles when it hits the plate. Each grain is distinct, separate, and firm, and yet tender and fluffy. The only time it is creamy is when there is cream gravy poured over it.

The two basic rules to remember when cooking rice by the Carolina method are: first, to always wash the rice before cooking it, and second, to never stir it while it is cooking. When it is done, the rice is fluffed by picking it with a fork, but never stirred—as this would break up the grains and make them sticky.

SERVES 4

one Put the rice in a large bowl filled with water. Gently pick it up and rub it between your hands. Even prewashed rice will get milky. Let it soak for a few minutes, then pour the rice into a large, tightly woven wire sieve. Rinse it briefly under cold running water until the water running from it is clear, and set it aside in the sink to drain.

1 cup long-grain rice, preferably basmati
Salt

two Combine 2 cups cold water, a large pinch of salt, and the drained rice in a 2-quart pot over medium-high heat and bring it to a good boil. Stir it to make sure that the rice is not sticking, then put the spoon away.

three Reduce the heat to low and set the lid askew on the top. Let the rice simmer for 12 minutes. After that time, there should be clear, dry steam holes formed on the surface, and most, if not all, of the water should be absorbed. Gently fold the top rice under with a fork, "fluffing" not stirring it.

four Put the lid on tight and let it sit over the heat for a minute more to rebuild the steam, then turn off the heat. Move the pot to a warm part of the stove (if you have an electric stove, leave it where it is; the residual heat in the burner should be just right.) If you don't have a warm spot, put the pan in a larger pan of hot water.

five Let it steam for 12 more minutes. You can hold it like this for up to an hour without harm, but 12 minutes is the minimum. When you are ready to serve the rice, fluff it by picking it with a fork, then turn it out into a serving bowl. Serve at once.

Chinese-Style Rice

 THOUGH THE IDEAL for plain Chinese rice is fluffy, distinctive grains much like Indian, African, and Carolina-Style Rice (previous recipe), the rice is just slightly sticky so that it is easier to manage with chopsticks. This is not to be confused with Chinese sticky rice, a short-grained, glutinous rice which is used for croquettes, sweets, and stuffings.

SERVES 4

one Wash the rice as for Carolina-Style Rice (page 171).

1 cup long-grain rice

two Combine the rice and 2 cups cold water in a heavy-bottomed saucepan, loosely cover it, and place it over medium-high heat. Bring it to a boil and boil for 5 minutes, until the water is mostly absorbed. Gently stir the rice, shake the pan to level it, and tightly cover. Reduce the heat as low as possible. Steam the rice for 20 minutes. Do not lift the lid for any reason during this time.

three Turn off the heat. Gently fluff the rice with a large carving fork or with chopsticks. Replace the lid and set the pot in a warm spot for 15 minutes more. Fluff again and serve.

Grits

GRITS IS A good basic accompaniment for any fried food. It was once popular with both fried chicken and fish and is still a common side dish at many fish camps (fried fish restaurants) all over the South. During the harvest season, when temporary workers and neighbors came to help bring in the crop, fried chicken and grits were frequently the fare for a hearty breakfast that sent everyone into the field with a full and happy stomach.

There are no exact measurements for the proportion of grits to water. The usual is four to one, but the amount of water needed can vary, depending on the grits, so keep a teakettle of water simmering close at hand in case you find the grits need more water before they get tender. Never add cold water to the pot, or the grits will not be good.

1 cup corn grits (preferably whole corn grits)

SERVES 4

Salt

one Bring 4 cups water to a good boil in a stainless steel or enameled saucepan and stir in the grits. Add a pinch of salt, but not too much; you can adjust it later. Bring back to a boil.

two Reduce the heat to a bare simmer and cover the pan. Cook, stirring occasionally, until the grits absorb all the moisture and has the consistency of a thick cornmeal mush, about 1 hour. Taste and adjust the seasoning. Serve hot.

Mashed or Creamed Potatoes

THOUGH LOWCOUNTRY CAROLINIANS and Georgians expect rice with their chicken, where rice is not the staple in the local diet, serving fried chicken without mashed potatoes could cause a mutiny at the table. You can make the potatoes richer by using heavy cream instead of light cream, or lighter by using whole milk. Don't, however, go nutso with the low-fat business and use low-fat milk. They need some fat for body and texture.

SERVES 4

2 pounds medium russet potatoes
1 cup light cream or half-and-half
Salt
2 tablespoons unsalted butter

one Scrub the potatoes well under cold, running water. Put them into a pot that will comfortably hold them all at once and cover them with cold water by about ½ inch. Lift out the potatoes and set them aside. Cover the kettle and place it over high heat. Bring the water to a rolling boil and add the potatoes. Let it come back to a boil, then reduce the heat to medium, loosely cover the kettle, and simmer until the potatoes are tender—from 12 to 30 minutes, depending on the size and age of the potatoes.

two Drain the potatoes thoroughly and while they are still fairly hot, peel them. Put them through a potato ricer and return them to the pot, or put them in the pot and mash them smooth with a potato masher. Add the cream or half-and-half and a healthy pinch of salt. Over medium-low heat, warm the potatoes, beating constantly with the masher or a wooden spoon (or, for really fluffy potatoes, with a hand-held electric mixer) until the cream is absorbed and the potatoes are fluffy and smooth.

three Turn off the heat and stir in the butter, or melt the butter in a separate pan, transfer the potatoes to a warm serving bowl, and pour the melted butter over them. Serve at once.

Creamed Sweet Potatoes

A LOVELY TWIST on the usual potato side dish for fried chicken, this is also a great accompaniment for just about any other fowl or for pork, venison, or other game meat. Try it instead of candied or souffléed sweet potatoes with the Thanksgiving turkey.

SERVES 4 TO 6

2 pounds sweet potatoes

2 tablespoons unsalted butter

Salt

Whole nutmeg

Grated zest of 1 lemon

1 tablespoon bourbon or dry sherry

Demerara, turbinado, or light brown sugar

½ cup light cream

one Scrub the potatoes under cold running water. They can be baked in the oven or cooked on the stovetop. To bake them, position a rack in the upper third of the oven and preheat the oven to 400°F. Rub the potatoes with a little butter, wrap them in foil, and bake, turning occasionally, until they are soft and yield easily when pressed with your finger, 45 to 60 minutes, depending on how large the potatoes are. To cook them on the stovetop, put them into a large pot and add enough cold water to cover them by 1 inch. Lift out the potatoes, cover the pot, and place it over high heat. When the water begins to boil, add the potatoes and bring the liquid back to a vigorous boil. Reduce the heat to medium and cook until the potatoes are soft and easily pierced with a carving fork or skewer, 20 to 30 minutes. Drain thoroughly.

two Peel the potatoes and put them through a ricer into a large mixing bowl, or cut them into large chunks, put them in a bowl, and mash them with a potato masher until they are smooth. Beat in the butter and season with a small pinch of salt, several liberal gratings of nutmeg, the lemon zest, and the bourbon or sherry. Stir them, then taste and add just enough sugar to bring up the natural sweetness of the potatoes—about a tablespoon or so, depending on how sweet the potatoes are already. Beat until the sugar is dissolved. Beat in the cream a little at a time until light and fluffy. You may not need all the cream. Taste and adjust the seasonings and serve while hot.

NOTE: You can vary the basic recipe by substituting the grated zest of 1 orange for the lemon zest and 1 teaspoon of ground cinnamon for the nutmeg. This combination is especially successful when paired with gamy fowls, pork, or turkey.

175

ON THE SIDE

The potatoes can also be made ahead and reheated in the oven. Put them in a 9-inch square casserole, smooth out the top with a spatula, and reheat them in a 400°F oven until hot and beginning to brown. Or you can top the casserole with 1 cup of dry bread crumbs or chopped pecans mixed with 2 tablespoons melted butter. Bake until the topping is browned and crunchy, 20 to 30 minutes.

Granny's Hot Potato Salad

THE INDISPENSABLE ACCOMPANIMENT for Granny Fowler's Sunday Fried Chicken (page 108)—or for just about any Sunday dinner at her table. This is not a potato salad the way we nowadays think of them. It is more like creamed potatoes—in fact, Granny usually put a little gravy on hers. Mashed potato salads of this type have been around in the South for the better part of two hundred years. Wait until you taste it.

SERVES 4 TO 6

2¹/₂ pounds boiling potatoes

¹/₂ cup mayonnaise (preferably homemade)

Cream

¹/₂ cup chopped scallions or other green onions, including the green tops

Salt and freshly milled black pepper

one Scrub the potatoes well under cold running water. Put them into a pot that will comfortably hold them all at once and cover them with cold water by about ½ inch. Lift out the potatoes and set them aside. Cover the pot and place it over high heat. Bring the water to a rolling boil and add the potatoes. Let it come back to a boil, then reduce the heat to medium, loosely cover, and simmer until the potatoes are tender—from 12 to 30 minutes, depending on the size and age of the potatoes.

two Thoroughly drain the potatoes, and while they are still hot, peel them. Put them in a mixing bowl and mash them well with a potato masher or press them through a ricer into the mixing bowl.

three Quickly beat in the mayonnaise until they have the consistency of creamed potatoes, adding a little cream if they appear too dry. Stir in the scallions and salt and pepper to taste, and mound them in a warm serving bowl. You could save out some of the scallion tops or sprinkle chopped chives or parsley over the top, but Granny would have thought it prissy.

176

French Potato Salad

LIGHTER, FRESHER, AND cleaner-tasting than our mayonnaise-based versions, this potato salad is well mated with any fried food. You can vary it by changing the acid from wine vinegar to lemon juice, or by using an herb-flavored vinegar, or by adding a small handful of chopped fresh herbs such as tarragon, basil, or dill, or 2 tablespoons of capers.

SERVES 4

2 pounds small, waxy red potatoes (or a waxy yellow variety, such as Yukon Gold)

Dry vermouth, preferably French

4 scallions or other green onions, thinly sliced

2 tablespoons chopped parsley

Red wine vinegar or 1 lemon

Salt and freshly milled black pepper

Extra virgin olive oil

one Put the potatoes into a pot that will comfortably hold them in no more than 2 layers. Add enough water to cover them by 1 inch and lift the potatoes out of the pot. Cover and bring the water to a rolling boil over high heat. Return the potatoes to the pot, replace the cover, and bring it back to a vigorous boil. Reduce the heat to medium-high and boil until the potatoes are just tender, 12 to 20 minutes, depending on their size and age.

two Drain the potatoes thoroughly and while they are still hot, peel them (the skins will slip right off). Slice them into ¼-inch-thick rounds and spread them on a platter. Sprinkle generously with vermouth and let them stand until it is absorbed, about 5 minutes. They should still be quite warm. Add the scallions and parsley. Give them a light sprinkling of vinegar (or split the lemon and squeeze half its juice over the potatoes), a healthy pinch or so of salt, and a few liberal grindings of pepper. Gently toss until they are evenly seasoned. Taste and adjust the seasonings. Sprinkle generously with olive oil and toss until the potatoes are all coated. Let stand at room temperature until cool. Do not refrigerate. Serve at room temperature.

NOTE: The salad can be varied by omitting the oil and vinegar and dressing it with ½ cup Aïoli (page 160) instead. Thin the sauce with a little cream or cold water to the consistency of thick cream.

Other vegetable are sometimes added to a French potato salad, including boiled artichoke hearts, quick-cooked French beans, raw sliced tomatoes, julienned red bell peppers, and small black Niçoise olives.

Mixed Salad with Oil and Lemon Dressing

WE CALL THIS "mouthwash" salad in my house because it never fails to cleanse and refresh the palate. I serve it after the main course for just that reason. It's especially appropriate to serve after any fried food and will complement any chicken dish in this book—even the stir-fries. You can go in your own direction with it, adding herbs such as dill or basil, rubbing the bowl with a cut clove of garlic, or tossing in another blanched or raw vegetable, such as small zucchini.

SERVES 4

1 head romaine lettuce, torn into bite-size pieces

4 small scallions or other green onions, thinly sliced

2 medium cucumbers

4 small red radishes, thinly sliced (optional)

Extra virgin olive oil

Salt

1 lemon

Freshly milled black pepper

one Put the romaine in a salad bowl that will give you plenty of tossing room. Add the scallions. Lightly peel the cucumber, leaving a light faint blush of green on the outside, and cut it in half. If the center seeds are tough and woody, split the halves lengthwise, scoop out and discard the seeds, and thinly slice each quarter. If the seeds are tender, slice the cucumber without splitting it. Add it to the salad bowl. Add the radishes to the salad bowl, if using.

two Drizzle the salad generously with olive oil and toss until it is glossy. Taste and add more oil if needed; it should taste distinctly but not heavily of oil. Sprinkle in a large pinch of salt and toss until it is distributed. Again, taste and adjust, tossing until the seasoning is distributed. Cut the lemon in half and squeeze the juice from one of the halves through a strainer over the salad. Toss and taste again. If it isn't tart enough to suit you, add more juice until it is blanched. Finally, add a few generous grindings of black pepper, give it a final toss, and serve at once.

178

Cucumber and Fennel Salad

 THIS IS A refreshing salad that goes nicely with any sort of fried chicken, especially the Southern and Mediterranean ones, as well as with all fish and shellfish dishes and any roasted poultry or game. It's one of my favorites for Chicken Kentuckian (page 113).

SERVES 4 TO 6

1 large fennel

1 large or 2 medium cucumbers

1 large sweet onion, preferably Vidalia, very thinly sliced

2 hard-cooked large egg yolks

1 tablespoon Dijon mustard

Salt, sugar, and freshly milled black pepper

2 tablespoons freshly squeezed lemon juice

⅓ cup extra virgin olive oil

one Trim the root end from the fennel bulb and cut off the stalks. Clip enough of the feathery leaves to make about ½ cup and set them aside. Discard the stalks. Cut the fennel bulb crosswise into the thinnest slices you can manage and put them in a salad bowl.

two Wash the cucumbers and, only if they have been waxed, lightly peel them; otherwise, peeling them isn't necessary. Cut them crosswise into the thin rounds and add them to the salad bowl along with the onion. Chop the reserved fennel leaves and add them to the mixture, then toss until the vegetables are uniformly mixed.

three In a separate bowl, combine the egg yolks, mustard, a pinch of salt, a small pinch of sugar, and a few grindings of black pepper, mashing it with a fork until it is a smooth paste. Gradually rub the lemon juice into the paste, then, a few drops at a time, beat in the olive oil until the dressing is emulsified.

four Pour the dressing over the salad and toss until the vegetables are evenly coated. Taste and adjust the seasonings, adding salt and pepper if needed.

179

ON THE SIDE

Boiled Zucchini Salad

LIKE ITS COUSIN, the cucumber, zucchini has a refreshing, cleansing effect on the palate, making it an especially appropriate vegetable to serve with fried foods. Zucchini is Italian for "little squash" and that's what you should be after when selecting the vegetable for this salad. Look for firm, glossy young zucchini that are no more than 1 inch in diameter and 6 to 8 inches in length. Pass over the baseball-bat-sized variety.

SERVES 4

Salt

2 pounds small green zucchini, or a mix of green and yellow zucchini

1 large garlic clove, crushed but left in one piece

Freshly milled black pepper

Extra virgin olive oil

Red wine vinegar or freshly squeezed lemon juice

8 to 10 fresh basil leaves, or 2 tablespoons chopped fresh mint

1 tablespoon chopped parsley

2 small scallions or other green onions, white and green parts, thinly sliced (optional)

4 to 8 romaine lettuce leaves

one Bring 2 quarts of water to a boil in a large pot over high heat. Add a small handful of salt, let it return to the boil, and add the zucchini. Cover and bring the water back to a vigorous boil, then uncover it and cook until the zucchini are barely tender, 10 to 15 minutes. Do not overcook; they should be firm and still bright green.

two Drain the zucchini and, while still hot, slice them into ½-inch-thick rounds. Put them on a large platter lying flat in 1 layer. Rub each round gently but thoroughly with the crushed garlic. Discard the garlic and set the zucchini aside to cool.

three Drain off any accumulated moisture from the zucchini, and sprinkle them with a few liberal grindings of black pepper and a pinch or so of salt. Drizzle generously with olive oil until they have a nice gloss. Toss gently and sprinkle with vinegar or lemon juice, adding it gradually until it is tart enough to suit you. Tear the basil into small pieces and add it with the parsley and scallions. Toss gently until it is evenly mixed.

four Lay the lettuce on a platter or on individual serving plates and distribute the salad over the lettuce. Serve at once or it will continue throwing off moisture and get soggy.

NOTE: Though Italians don't usually add scallions to this salad, they are a nice addition. I will also frequently substitute half a thinly sliced Vidalia sweet onion for the scallions. Where I live, mint thrives in the fall, winter, and spring and I use it when fresh basil is out of season.

Orange and Onion Salad

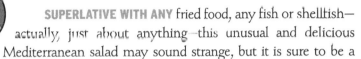 **SUPERLATIVE WITH ANY** fried food, any fish or shellfish—actually, just about anything—this unusual and delicious Mediterranean salad may sound strange, but it is sure to be a favorite after you taste it.

SERVES 4

one Peel the oranges, cutting all the way through to the fruit. Slice crosswise into rounds about ¼ inch thick, so that the connective membranes between the sections show in a cartwheel pattern. Thinly slice the onion and separate it into rings. Gently press the olives under your thumb until you feel them "give" to loosen the flesh from the pit. Slit them down one side and pit them, then cut them lengthwise into quarters.

6 navel oranges
1 medium red onion
8 to 10 dry-cured olives
Extra virgin olive oil
Red wine vinegar
Salt and freshly milled black pepper
10 to 15 fresh mint leaves

two Spread the oranges on a serving platter in one slightly overlapping layer. Scatter the onion and olives over them. Sprinkle generously with olive oil, then sprinkle lightly with the vinegar, a stingy pinch of salt, and a few liberal grindings of pepper. Cut the mint into fine shreds and scatter it over the salad. Serve at once.

181

Bibliography

Acton, Eliza. *Modern Cookery for Private Families.* London: Longman, Brown, Green and Longmans, 1845 and 1855. Reprint. Lewis, England: Southover Press, 1993.

Andrews, Coleman. *Flavors of the Riviera.* New York: Bantam Books, 1996.

Andrews, Mrs. Lewis R., and Mrs. J. Reaney Kelly, eds. *Maryland's Way: The Hammond-Harwood House Cook Book,* 14th ed. Annapolis, Md.: The Hammond-Harwood House Association, 1995.

Bailey, Lee. *Lee Bailey's Southern Food and Plantation Houses.* New York: Clarkson Potter, 1990.

Belk, Sarah. *Around the Southern Table.* New York: Simon & Schuster, 1991.

Bennani-Smires, Latifa. *Moroccan Cooking.* Casablanca: Société d'Edition et de Diffusion, Al Madrariss, 1984.

Brennan, Jennifer. *The Original Thai Cookbook.* New York: The Berkeley Publishing Group, 1981.

Bronz, Ruth Adams. *Miss Ruby's American Cooking.* New York: HarperCollins Publishers, 1989.

Bryan, Lettice. *The Kentucky Housewife.* Cincinnati, Ohio: Shepard and Sterns, 1839.

Bugialli, Giuliano. *The Fine Art of Italian Cooking.* New York: Times Books, 1977.

Casas, Penelope. *The Foods and Wines of Spain.* New York: Alfred A. Knopf, 1988.

Chang, Wonona W. and Irving, with Helene W. and Austin H. Kutscher. *An Encyclopedia of Chinese Food and Cooking,* New York: Crown Publishers, Inc., 1970.

Charlton, Windsor, ed. *The Good Cook: Poultry.* Alexandria, Va.: Time-Life Books, Inc., 1979.

Child, Julia. *From Julia Child's Kitchen.* New York: Alfred A. Knopf, 1982.

Colquitt, Harriett Ross. *The Savannah Cook Book.* Charleston, S.C.: Walker Evans, & Cogswell Co., 1933.

Copage, Eric V. *Kwanzaa: An African American Celebration of Culture and Cooking.* New York: William Morrow, 1991.

Crawford, William, and Kamolmal Pootaraksa. *Thai Home-Cooking from Kamolmal's Kitchen.* New York: Penguin Books USA Inc., 1985.

The Creole Cook Book. New Orleans: *The New Orleans Picayune,* 1900. Reprint, 2nd ed., *The Picayune's Creole Cook Book.* New York: Random House, 1987.

La cucina di Genova e della Liguria. Genoa, Italy: Valenti editore, 1978.

Cusick, Heidi Haughy. *Soul & Spice: African Cookery in the Americas.* New York: Chronicle Books, 1995.

David, Elizabeth. *Elizabeth David Classics* (collection incorporating *Mediterranean Food, French Country Cooking,* and *Summer Cooking*). New York: Alfred A. Knopf, 1980.

———. *Italian Food.* Baltimore, Md.: Penguin Books, 1963.

Del Conte, Anna. *The Gastronomy of Italy.* New York: Prentice Hall Press, 1987.

Delfs, Robert A. *The Good Food Szechwan.* Tokyo: Kodansha International Ltd., 1974.

Dewitt, Antoinette, and Anita Borghese. *The Complete Book of Indonesian Cooking.* Indianapolis, Ind.: Bobbs Merrill, 1973.

Dull, Henrietta Stanley. *Southern Cooking.* Atlanta, Ga.: Ruralist Press, 1928. Facsimile. Atlanta, Ga.: Cherokee Press, 1989.

Duong, Binh, and Marcia Kiesel. *The Simple Art of Vietnamese Cooking.* New York: Prentice Hall Press, 1991.

Dupree, Nathalie. *New Southern Cooking.* New York: Alfred A. Knopf, 1986.

Egerton, John, *Southern Food.* New York: Alfred A. Knopf, 1987.

Fisher, Mrs. Abby. *What Mrs. Fisher Knows About Old Southern Cooking.* San Francisco: Women's Co-operative Printing Office, 1881. Reprint, Karen Hess, ed., Bedford, Mass.: Applewood Books, 1995.

Fobel, Jim. *Jim Fobel's Big Flavors.* New York: Clarkson Potter, 1995.

Fowler, Damon Lee. *Classical Southern Cooking.* New York: Crown, 1995.

Fu, Pei-Mei. *Pei Mei's Chinese Cook Book.* Taipai, Taiwan: n.p., 1969.

———. *Pei Mei's Chinese Cook Book,* Volume II. Taipai, Taiwan: n.p., 1974.

Glenn, Camille. *The Heritage of Southern Cooking.* New York: Workman Publishing, 1986.

Grosvenor, Vertemae. *Vertemae Cooks in America's Family Kitchen.* San Francisco: KQED Books, 1996.

Harris, Jessica B. *Iron Pots and Wooden Spoons.* New York: Atheneum, 1989.

———. *The Welcome Table.* New York: Simon & Schuster, 1995.

Hawkes, Alex D. *The Flavors of the Caribbean & Latin America.* New York: Simon & Schuster, 1978.

Hazan, Marcella. *Essentials of Classic Italian Cooking.* New York: Alfred A. Knopf, 1992.

———. *Marcella Cucina.* New York: HarperCollins Publishers, 1997.

Hill, Annabella P. *Mrs. Hill's New Cook Book.* New York: James O'Kane, Publishers, 1867.

Howard, Mrs. B. C. *Fifty Years in a Maryland Kitchen.* Baltimore, Md.: n.p., 1873.

Idone, Christopher. *Brazil: A Cook's Tour.* New York: Clarkson Potter, 1995.

Indra, Majupuria. *Joys of Nepalese Cooking.* Madhoganj, India: Smt. S. Devi, 1983.

Jaffrey, Madhur. *An Invitation to Indian Cooking*. New York: Alfred A. Knopf, Inc., 1973.

———. *A Taste of India*. New York: Atheneum, 1986.

Kasper, Lynne Rossetto. *The Splendid Table*. New York: William Morrow, 1992.

Kuo, Irene. *The Key to Chinese Cooking*. New York: Alfred A. Knopf, 1977.

Lee, Jim. *Jim Lee's Chinese Cook Book*. New York: Harper & Row, 1968.

Lew, Judy. *Enjoy Chinese Cuisine*. Tokyo: Joie, Inc., 1984.

Lewis, Edna. *The Taste of Country Cooking*. New York: Alfred A. Knopf, 1978.

Liles, Jean W., ed. *The Southern Heritage Plain and Fancy Poultry Cookbook*. Birmingham, Ala.: Oxmoor House, Inc., 1983.

Lundy, Ronni. *Shuck Beans, Stack Cakes and Honest Fried Chicken*. New York: Atlantic Monthly Press, 1991.

Mallos, Tess. *The Complete Middle East Cookbook*. New York: McGraw-Hill Book Company, 1979.

Martinez, Zarela. *The Food of Oaxaca*. New York: Macmillan, 1997.

Miller, Gloria Bley. *The Thousand Recipe Chinese Cookbook*. New York: Grosset & Dunlap, 1970.

Montagne, Prosper. *The New Larousse Gastronomique* (Am. Ed.). New York: Crown Publishers, Inc., 1977.

Moore, Isabel, and Jonnie Godfrey, eds. *Foods of the Orient: South-east Asia*. London: Marshall Cavendish Books, 1978.

Nathan, Joan. *Jewish Cooking in America*. New York: Alfred A. Knopf, 1994.

Neal, William F. *Bill Neal's Southern Cooking*. Rev. ed.. Chapel Hill, N.C.: The University of North Carolina, 1989.

Ortiz, Elisabeth Lambert. *The Book of Latin American Cooking*. New York: Vintage Books, 1980.

———. *The Complete Book of Caribbean Cooking*. New York: M. Evans and Company, Inc., 1973.

Ortiz, Elisabeth Lambert, and Mitsuko Endo. *The Complete Book of Japanese Cooking*. New York: M. Evans and Company, Inc., 1976.

Puladitmontri, Rut, with Judy Lew *Thai Cuisine: Lemon Grass Cookbook*. Tokyo: Joie, Inc., 1991.

Prudhomme, Paul. *Chef Paul Prudhomme's Louisiana Kitchen*. New York: William Morrow & Co., Inc., 1984.

Randolph, Mary. *The Virginia House-Wife*. Washington: Davis and Forth, 1824. Rev. and enl. editions, 1825 and 1828. Facsimile, Karen Hess, ed. Columbia, S.C.: University of South Carolina Press, 1984.

Roden, Claudia. *The Book of Jewish Food*. New York: Alfred A. Knopf, 1996.

———. *A Book of Middle Eastern Food*. New York: Alfred A. Knopf, 1972.

Rudisill, Marie. *Sook's Cookbook*. Atlanta, Ga.: Longstreet Press, 1989.

Rutledge, Sarah. *The Carolina Housewife, or House and Home.* Charleston: W. R. Babcock & Co., 1847. Facsimile. Columbia, S.C.: University of South Carolina Press, 1979.

Scicolone, Michele. *A Fresh Taste of Italy.* New York: Broadway Books, 1997.

Solomon, Charmaine. *The Complete Asian Cookbook.* New York: McGraw-Hill Book Company, 1976.

Taylor, John Martin. *The Fearless Frying Cookbook.* New York: Workman, 1997.

Toklas, Alice B. *The Alice B. Toklas Cook Book.* 1954. New York: Harper & Row, Publishers, 1984.

Tsuji, Shizuo. *Japanese Cooking: A Simple Art.* Tokyo: Kodansha International, 1980.

Tyree, Marion Cabell, ed. *Housekeeping in Old Virginia.* Louisville, Ky.: John P. Morton and Company, 1879.

Uvezian, Sonia. *The Cuisine of Armenia.* New York: Harper & Row, 1974.

Valldejuli, Carmen Aboy. *The Art of Caribbean Cookery.* Garden City, N.Y.: Doubleday, 1957.

Voltz, Jeanne, and Caroline Stuart. *The Florida Cookbook.* New York: Alfred A. Knopf, Inc., 1995.

Wilson, Justin. *Louisiana Home Grown.* New York: MacMillan Publishing Company, 1990.

Wolfert, Paula. *The Cooking of the Eastern Mediterranean.* New York: HarperCollins Publishers, 1994.

Yan, Martin. *A Wok for All Seasons.* New York: Doubleday, 1988.

Index

All recipes are listed by their English titles as well as their foreign titles, which are included in italicized type. Recipes are also listed by country (except by region in the cases of "South America" and "Southern-fried chicken"). Within each country, recipes are listed by their English titles, with the foreign titles following. In addition, recipes are organized by the cuts of chicken, manner of preparation, and by major ingredients.

accompaniments. *See* side dishes
Africa. *See* Egypt; Morocco; Nigeria; South Africa
Almond Chicken Cutlets, 48–49
animal fat, 13
Apricot Sauce, Quick Plum or, 164
Armenian recipe: Butter-Fried Chicken with Eggplant (*Tapaka*), 60–61
Asia. *See* Cambodia; China; India; Indonesia; Israel; Japan; Mongolia; Russia; Singapore; Thailand
Asparagus and Long Onions, Chicken with (*Toriniku To Asparagasu*), 142–143
Austrian recipe: Viennese Fried Chicken (*Wiener Backhendl*), 38–39
Ayam Goreng Asam (Indonesian Curry Fried Chicken), 53–54
Ayam Pecel (Chicken Shreds with Coconut-Shrimp Sauce), 144–145

Backhendl, Wiener (Viennese Fried Chicken), 38–39

baking powder, 167
bamboo shoots, 148
Barbadian recipe: Bajan Fried Chicken, 29–30
basil
    Chicken Breasts with Fresh Mozzarella and (*Petti di Pollo alla Margherita*), 70–71
    in *Pesto alla Genovese* (Genovese Pesto), 128
battered chicken, 19–28
    about, 15–16, 19–20
    Beer-, Drumettes, 88–89
    Florentine (*Pollo Fritto alla Fiorentina*), 20–21
    French Marinated (*Poulet en Marinade, Frit*), 22–23
    General Tsao's, 24–25
    Golden Coin (*Jin Chin Ji*), 80–81
    Livers Beijing-Style, 26–27
    Sesame, Fingers, 84–85
    Southern, 100–101
    Tempura, 27–28
batters and doughs, 15–16
Bean Sauce, Mongolian Chicken with (*Mong Ku Gai Pan*), 134–135

Beer-Battered Chicken Drumettes, 88–89
Biscuits, Skillet or Chicken, 170
Boiled Zucchini Salad (*Insalata di Zucchini*), 180–181
boning, 10, 11–12, 40. *See also* cutting; disjointing
Bread, Spoon, 169
bread crumbs, 49
breaded chicken, 29–49
    about, 15, 16, 29
    Bajan, 29–30
    Buttermilk, 102–103
    Cajun Popcorn, 76–77
    Creole, 107–108
        Poor Boy, 81–82
        à la Mediatrice, 82
    Cuban, Creole Style (*Pollo Fritto a la Criolla*), 31–32
    cutlets
        Almond, 48–49
        Breasts with Fresh Mozzarella and Basil (*Petti di Pollo alla Margherita*), 70–71
        Cordon Bleu (*Suprêmes de Volaille Cordon Bleu*), 65–66

breaded chicken (cont'd)
Georgia, 42
Indian, 43–44
Kiev, 67–68
Milanese (Cotolleta di Pollo
alla Milanese), 41–42
Savannah, with Curry
Sauce, 44–45
South African, in Curry
Sauce, 46–47
with Spinach and Feta,
68–69
Fingers, Coconut, 78–79
Granny Fowler's Sunday,
108–109
Greek Marinated (Kotopoulo
Tiganito Marinato), 34–35
Herb-and-Spice Southern,
104–105
Israeli, with Sesame (Off Sum-
Sum), 36
Japanese (Toriniku Tatsuta-age),
83
Jewish Georgia, 110–111
Kentuckian, 113–114
livers
Cajun-Style, 106
Southern, 105–106
Maryland, 112–113
Nepali (Kukhurako Bhutuwa),
37
South American (Chicharrones
de Pollo), 33–34
Southern, 100–101
Basic, with Cream Gravy,
99–100
thighs
Hunter-Style, with Sweet
Potato Stuffing, 72–73
"Saltimbocca," 74
Viennese (Wiener Backhendl),
38–39
breasts
in Brown Butter (Suprêmes de
Volaille à Brun or à la

Meuniere, or Petti di Pollo alla
Fiorentina), 126
Cajun Popcorn, 76–77
Cantonese, Curry (Yea tsup
Ga Li Gai), 136–137
coconut
Fingers, 78–79
Shrimp Sauce, Shreds
with (Ayam Pecel),
144–145
Cordon Bleu (Suprêmes de
Volaille Cordon Bleu), 65–66
Creole
Poor Boy, 81–82
à la Mediatrice, 82
with Fresh Mozzarella and
Basil (Petti di Pollo alla
Margherita), 70–71
Ginger and Mint (Gai Khing),
139–140
Golden Coin (Jin Chin Ji),
80–81
Indonesian, and Coconut
Croquettes (Rempah Ayam),
95–96
Kiev, 67–68
Mongolian, with Bean Sauce
(Mong Ku Gai Pan),
134–135
with Pesto (Petti di Pollo con
Pesto), 127
Sesame, 84–85
with Spinach and Feta,
68–69
Szechwan, with Red Pepper
Shreds (La-jiao Zi Ji),
137–138
broth
about, 16
Chicken, 18
dashi, 166
Quick, 17
brown sugar, 25
butter
about, 13–14

Brown, Chicken Breasts
in (Suprêmes de Volaille à
Brun or à la Meuniere, or
Petti di Pollo alla
Fiorentina), 126
-Fried Chicken with
Eggplant, Armenian
(Tapaka), 60–61
buttermilk
about, 102, 105
Fried Chicken, 102–103
in Southern Fried Chicken
Livers, 105–106

Cajun
Popcorn Chicken, 76–77
-Style, Deep-Fried Livers, 106
Cambodian recipe: Fried
Chicken with Mushroom and
Cilantro (Moan Chua Noeung
Phset Kream), 140–141
candlenuts, 145
Cantonese Chicken Curry (Yea
tsup Ga Li Gai), 136–137
Caribbean. See Barbados; Cuba
Carolina-Style Rice, 171–172
Cashew Chicken (Yao Go Ji-ding),
132–133
cast-iron skillets, 2–3
cheese
Blue, Dressing, Garlicky-
Green, 87
Feta, Chicken with Spinach
and, 68–69
Gruyère, in Chicken Cordon
Bleu (Suprêmes de Volaille
Cordon Bleu), 65–66
mozzarella
and Basil, Chicken
Breasts with Fresh (Petti
di Pollo alla Margherita),
70–71
in Chicken Breasts with
Pesto (Petti di Pollo con
Pesto), 127

Parmigiano-Reggiano, in *Pesto alla Genovese* (Genovese Pesto), 128

Chicharrones de Pollo (South American Fried Chicken), 33–34

chile paste, how to make, 96

China
Almond Chicken Cutlets, 48–49
Cantonese Chicken Curry (*Yea tsup Ga Li Gai*), 136–137
Cashew Chicken (*Yao Go Ji-ding*), 132–133
Chicken Livers in Oyster Sauce (*Ho-yu Feng-gan*), 147–148
Chinese Style Rice, 172
Crispy Skin Chicken (*Cui-pi Ji*), 63–64
Deep-Fried Chicken Livers Beijing-Style, 26–27
Five Fragrance Chicken (*Wu Xiang Ji*), 50–51
General Tsao's Chicken, 24–25
Golden Coin Chicken (*Jin Chin Ji*), 80–81
Hot Chinese Mustard, 162
Plum Sauce, 163
Quick, or Apricot Sauce, 164
Sesame Chicken Wings, 89–90
Sweet-and-Sour Sauce, 165
Szechwan Chicken with Red Pepper Shreds (*La-jiao Zi Ji*), 137–138
Chinese-style disjointing, 11
choosing chicken, 9
cilantro
Mushroom and, Fried Chicken with (*Moan Chua Noeung Phset Kream*), 140–141
in Thai Fried Chicken (*Gai Tord*), 52
clarifying butter, 14
coatings for frying, 15–16
Cocktail Sauce, Horseradish, 77
coconut
about, 79
Chicken Fingers, 78–79
Croquettes, Indonesian Chicken and (*Rempah Ayam*), 95–96
Milk, Rich, 151–152
-Shrimp Sauce, Chicken Shreds with (*Ayam Pecel*), 144–145
color of chicken, 9
cooking techniques, 5–8
deep-frying, 6–8
pan-frying, 6
sautéing, 5–6, 118
stir-frying, 6, 129–131
Cordon Bleu, Chicken (*Suprêmes de Volaille Cordon Bleu*), 65–66
cornmeal
Hoe Cakes, 168
Spoon Bread, 169
Cotolleta alla Bolognese (Bolognese Cutlets), 41–42
Cotolleta alla Siciliana (Sicilian Cutlets), 41–42
Cotolleta di Pollo alla Milanese (Milanese Cutlets), 41–42
Country Captain, Chicken, 115–116
cracklings (*chicharrones*), 33
Cream Gravy (Milk Pan Gravy), 154
Creamed Potatoes (or Mashed), 174
Creamed Sweet Potatoes, 175–176
Creole chicken, 107–108
Poor Boy, 81–82
à la Mediatrice, 82
Style, Cuban (*Pollo Frito a la Criolla*), 31–32
Creole Sauce, Raw (*Salsa Criolla Cruda*), 156
Crispy Skin Chicken (*Cui-pi Ji*), 63–64
Croquettes, Indonesian Chicken and Coconut (*Rempah Ayam*), 95–96
crumb breadings, 15
Cuban recipe: Fried Chicken, Creole Style (*Pollo Frito a la Criolla*), 31–32
Cucumber and Fennel Salad, 179
Cui-pi Ji (Crispy Skin Chicken), 63–64
curry(ied)
Cantonese Chicken (*Yea tsup Ga Li Gai*), 136–137
in Chicken Country Captain, 115–116
in Fried Chicken Malabar, 119
Hot, Livers, Nepali Style, 150–151
Indonesian, Fried Chicken (*Ayam Goreng Asam*), 53–54
Livers (*Murgh Kaleja Kari*), 149
Sauce, 157
Savannah Cutlets with, 44–45
South African Cutlets in, 46–47
cutlets, 40–49
about, 40
Almond, 48–49
Creole
Poor Boy, 81–82
à la Mediatrice, 82
Georgia, 42
Indian, 43–44

189

cutlets (*cont'd*)
    Milanese (*Cotolleta di Pollo alla Milanese*), 41–42
    with Pesto (*Petti di Pollo con Pesto*), 127
    Savannah, with Curry Sauce, 44–45
    South African, in Curry Sauce, 46–47
cutting, 10, 11. *See also* boning; disjointing

dashi (broth), 166
deep-frying technique, 6–7
Demerara sugar, 25
disjointing, 10–11. *See also* boning; cutting
draining fried food, 8
Dressing, Garlicky-Green Blue Cheese, 87
drumettes
    about, 85
    Beer-Battered, 88–89
    Spicy, 90–91
Dutch oven, 3

Eggplant, Armenian Butter-Fried Chicken with (*Tapaka*), 60–61
Egyptian recipe: Chicken Fritters (*Koftit Ferakh*), 94
equipment
    for frying, 2–4
        outdoors, 62
    and safety, 7–8
Europe. *See* Armenia; Austria; France; Greece; Italy; Russia

fat for frying, 7, 13–14, 99
Fennel Salad, Cucumber and, 179
Feta, Chicken with Spinach and, 68–69
fingers
    about, 75
    Coconut, 78–79

mustard for, 162
    Sesame, 84–85
fire, how to put out, 7
fish sauce, 140
five-spice powder, 51
Florentine Fried Chicken (*Pollo Fritto alla Fiorentina*), 20–21
France
    Aïoli (garlic mayonnaise), 160
    Butter-Browned New Potatoes (*Pommes des Terre à la Noisette*), 125
    Chicken Breasts in Brown Butter (*Suprêmes de Volaille à Brun* or *à la Meuniere*), 126
    Chicken Cordon Bleu (*Suprêmes de Volaille Cordon Bleu*), 65–66
    Chicken Sauté with Morels and White Wine (*Poulet Sauté à la Forestière*), 124–125
    Chicken Sauté with Onions (*Poulet Sauté à la Lyonnaise*), 121–122
    French Marinated Batter-Fried Chicken (*Poulet en Marinade, Frit*), 22–23
    French Potato Salad, 177
    Herb Mayonnaise, 160
    Mayonnaise, 159
    Tartar Sauce, 160
Frank's Louisiana Hot Sauce, 87
Frank's Original Red Hot Cayenne Pepper Sauce, 87
"free-range" chicken, 9
freezing chicken, 9–10
Fresh Mango Sauce, 158
fritters
    Egyptian (*Koftit Ferakh*), 94
    and Green Tomato, 92–93

Ga Xao Xa Ot (Chicken with Lemongrass), 145–146

Gai Khing (Chicken with Ginger and Mint), 139–140
Gai Tord (Thai Fried Chicken), 52
garlic(ky)
    -Green Blue Cheese Dressing, 87
    Sauce, Thai Sweet and Hot (*Nam Jim Gratiem*), 53
General Tsao's Chicken, 24–25
Georgia Cutlets, 41–42
Ginger and Mint, Chicken with (*Gai Khing*), 139–140
gizzards, 147
    as substitute in Hot Curried Chicken Livers, Nepali Style, 150
Golden Coin Chicken (*Jin Chin Ji*), 80–81
Granny Fowler's Sunday Fried Chicken, 108–109
Granny's Hot Potato Salad, 176
gravy
    Cream (Milk Pan), 154
    Southern Tomato, 155
grease control in frying, 2
Greece
    Chicken with Spinach and Feta, 68–69
    Greek Marinated Fried Chicken (*Kotopoulo Tiganito Marinato*), 34–35
Green Tomato Fritters, Chicken and, 92–93
Grits, 173

handling chicken, 9–10
hearts, 147
    as substitute in Hot Curried Chicken Livers, Nepali Style, 150
Hoe Cakes, 168
hors d'oeuvres. *See* party chicken
Horseradish Cocktail Sauce, 77
Hot Chinese Mustard, 162

hot sauce
    with Buffalo Wings, 87
    in Deep-Fried Livers Cajun-
        Style, 106
    Frank's Louisiana, 87
    Frank's Original Red Hot
        Cayenne Pepper, 87
how to fry, 5–8
Ho-yu Feng-gan (Chicken Livers in
    Oyster Sauce), 147–148

India
    Curried Chicken Livers
        (*Murgh Kaleja Kari*), 149
    Fried Chicken Malabar, 119
    Hot Curried Chicken Livers,
        Nepali Style, 150–151
    Indian Chicken Sauté with
        Yogurt Sauce, 120–121
    Indian Cutlets, 43–44
    Nepali Fried Chicken
        (*Kukhurako Bhutuwa*), 37
Indonesia
    Indonesian Chicken and
        Coconut Croquettes
        (*Rempah Ayam*), 95–96
    Indonesian Curry Fried
        Chicken (*Ayam Goreng
        Asam*), 53–54
ingredients for frying, 9–18
Insalata di Zucchini (Boiled
    Zucchini Salad), 180–181
Israeli recipe: Fried Chicken with
    Sesame (*Off Sum-Sum*), 36
Italy
    Boiled Zucchini Salad
        (*Insalata di Zucchini*),
        180–181
    Chicken Breasts in Brown
        Butter (*Petti di Pollo alla
        Fiorentina*), 126
    Chicken Breasts with Fresh
        Mozzarella and Basil (*Petti
        di Pollo alla Margherita*),
        70–71

Chicken Breasts with Pesto
    (*Petti di Pollo con Pesto*), 127
Chicken Sauté with Olives
    (*Pollo alla Franceschiello*), 123
Chicken Thighs
    "Saltimbocca," 74
Florentine Fried Chicken
    (*Pollo Fritto alla Fiorentina*),
    20–21
Genovese Pesto (*Pesto alla
    Genovese*), 128
Milanese Cutlets (*Cotolleta di
    Pollo alla Milanese*), 41–42

Japan
    Chicken Tempura, 27–28
    Chicken with Asparagus and
        Long Onions (*Toriniku To
        Asparagasu*), 142–143
    Japanese Fried Chicken
        (*Toriniku Tatsuta-age*), 83
    Tempura Sauce, 166–167
Jewish Georgia Fried Chicken,
    110–111
Jin Chin Ji (Golden Coin
    Chicken), 80–81

katakuri-ko (potato starch), 83
Kentuckian, Chicken, 113–114
Kiev, Chicken, 67–68
Koftit Ferakh (Egyptian Chicken
    Fritters), 94
kosher chicken, 110
Kotopoulo Tiganito Marinato (Greek
    Marinated Fried Chicken),
    34–35
Kukhurako Bhutuwa (Nepali Fried
    Chicken), 37

La-jiao Zi Ji (Szechwan Chicken
    with Red Pepper Shreds),
    137–138
lard (pork fat), 13
    in Southern-fried chicken,
    99

in Viennese Fried Chicken
    (*Wiener Backbendl*), 38–39
Lemongrass, Chicken with (*Ga
    Xao Xa Ot*), 145–146
lemons, preserved, 57
livers
    Beijing-Style, Deep-Fried,
        26–27
    Cajun-Style, Deep-Fried, 106
    Curried (*Murgh Kaleja Kari*), 149
    Hot curried, Nepali style, 150
    in Oyster Sauce (*Ho-yu Feng-
        gan*), 147–148
    Southern, 105–106

Malabar, Fried Chicken, 119
Mango Sauce, Fresh, 158
marinated chicken
    about, 4, 10, 22, 98
    Almond, Cutlets, 48–49
    buttermilk
        about, 102, 105
        recipe for, 102–103
        in Southern Fried
            Chicken Livers,
            105–106
    Coconut, Fingers, 78–79
    Creole, 107–108
        Poor Boy, 81–82
        à la Mediatrice, 82
    Crispy Skin (*Cui-pi Ji*),
        63–64
    Five Fragrance (*Wu Xiang Ji*),
        50–51
    French (*Poulet en Marinade,
        Frit*), 22–23
    General Tsao's, 24–25
    Golden Coin (*Jin Chin Ji*),
        80–81
    Greek (*Kotopoulo Tiganito
        Marinato*), 34–35
    Herb-and-Spice Southern,
        104–105
    Indonesian Curry (*Ayam
        Goreng Asam*), 53–54

marinated chicken (cont'd)
Japanese (*Toriniku Tatsuta-age*), 83
Jewish Georgia, 110–111
livers
Beijing-Style, 26–27
Cajun-Style, 105–106
Southern, 105–106
Mexican, with Oregano (*Pollo con Oregano*), 55–56
Mongolian, with Bean Sauce (*Mong Ku Gai Pan*), 134–135
Nepali (*Kukhurako Bhutuwa*), 37
Sesame, Wings, 89–90
South American (*Chicharrones de Pollo*), 33–34
Southern, 100–101
Spicy, Drumettes, 90–91
Thai (*Gai Tord*), 52
Viennese (*Wiener Backbendl*), 38–39
Maryland Fried Chicken, 112–113
Mashed Potatoes (or Creamed), 174
mayonnaise
about, 158–159
Aïoli (garlic), 160
basic recipe, 159
Herb, 160
Tartar Sauce, 160
Mediterranean. *See* Greece; Italy
Mexican recipe: Fried Chicken with Oregano (*Pollo con Oregano*), 55–56
M'Hammer (Moroccan Fried Chicken), 56–57
Middle East. *See* Egypt; Israel
Milk Pan Gravy (Cream Gravy), 154
Mint, Chicken with Ginger and with (*Gai Khing*), 139–140
mirin (rice wine), 27

Mixed Salad with Oil and Lemon Dressing, 178
Moan Chua Noeung Phset Kream (Fried Chicken with Mushroom and Cilantro), 140–141
Mongolian recipe: Chicken with Bean Sauce (*Mong Ku Gai Pan*), 134–135
Morels and White Wine, Chicken Sauté with (*Poulet Sauté à la Forestière*), 124–125
Moroccan recipe: Fried Chicken (*M'Hammer*), 56–57
Mozzarella and Basil, Chicken Breasts with Fresh (*Petti di Pollo alla Margherita*), 70–71
Murgh Kaleja Kari (Curried Chicken Livers), 149
mushroom(s)
in Chicken Kentuckian, 113–114
in Chicken Sauté with Morels and White Wine (*Poulet Sauté à la Forestière*), 124–125
and Cilantro, Fried Chicken with (*Moan Chua Noeung Phset Kream*), 140–141
mustard
about, 161
Honey, 161–162
Hot Chinese, 162

Nam Jim Gratiem (Thai Sweet and Hot Garlic Sauce), 53
Nepal
Fried Chicken (*Kukhurako Bhutuwa*), 37
Hot Curried Chicken Livers, 150
Nigerian recipe: Fried Chicken, 58–59
North Africa. *See* Egypt; Morocco
North America. *See* Mexico;

Southern-fried chicken; United States
nuggets
about, 75
Golden Coin (*Jin Chin Ji*), 80–81
Japanese Fried (*Toriniku Tatsuta-age*), 83

Off Sum-Sum (Israeli Fried Chicken with Sesame), 36
Olives, Chicken Sauté with (*Pollo alla Franceschiello*), 123
onion(s)
Chicken Sauté with (*Poulet Sauté à la Lyonnaise*), 121–122
Chicken with Asparagus and Long (*Toriniku To Asparagasu*), 142–143
Salad, Orange and, 181
orange(s)
about, 32
in Coconut Chicken Fingers, 78–79
in Cuban Fried Chicken, Creole Style (*Pollo Fritto a la Criolla*), 31–32
and Onion Salad, 181
Oregano, Mexican Fried Chicken with (*Pollo con Oregano*), 55–56
outdoor deep-frying, 62
Crispy Skin Chicken (*Cui-pi Ji*), 63–64
Oyster Sauce, Chicken Livers in (*Ho-yu Feng-gan*), 147–148

palm sugar, 25
pan-frying technique, 6
pans
for frying, 2–4
and safety, 7–8
party chicken, 75–96
about, 75
Cajun Popcorn, 76–77
Creole, Poor Boy, 81–82

192

INDEX

à la Mediatrice, 82
drumettes
    Beer-Battered, 88–89
    Spicy, 90–91
fingers
    Coconut, 78–79
    Sesame, 84–85
fritters
    Egyptian (*Koftit Ferakh*), 94
    and Green Tomato,
        92–93
    Golden Coin (*Jin Chin Ji*),
        80–81
    Indonesian, and Coconut
        Croquettes (*Rempah Ayam*),
        95–96
    Japanese (*Toriniku Tatsuta-age*),
        83
wings
    Buffalo, 86–87
    Sesame, 89–90
peanut oil, 14
pepper vinegar, how to make,
    93
pesto
    Chicken Breasts with (*Petti di
        Pollo con Pesto*), 127
    Genovese (*Pesto alla Genovese*),
        128
    storing, 128
Petti di Pollo alla Fiorentina
    (Chicken Breasts in Brown
    Butter), 126
Petti di Pollo alla Margherita
    (Chicken Breasts with Fresh
    Mozzarella and Basil), 70–71
picnic chicken
    Buttermilk, 102–103
    Herb-and-Spice Southern,
        104–105
    Plum Sauce, 163
    Quick, or Apricot Sauce, 164
Pollo alla Franceschiello (Chicken
    Sauté with Olives), 123
Pollo con Oregano (Mexican Fried

Chicken with Oregano),
    55–56
Pollo Fritto alla Fiorentina
    (Florentine Fried Chicken),
    20–21
Pollo Frito a la Criolla (Cuban Fried
    Chicken, Creole Style), 31–32
Pommes des Terre à la Noisette
    (Butter-Browned New
    Potatoes), 125
pork fat (lard), 13
    in Southern-fried chicken, 99
    in Viennese Fried Chicken
        (*Wiener Backhendl*), 38–39
potato salad
    French, 177
    Granny's Hot, 176
potato(es)
    Butter-Browned New
        (*Pommes des Terre à la
        Noisette*), 125
    Mashed or Creamed, 174
Poulet en Marinade, Frit (French
    Marinated Batter-Fried
    Chicken), 22–23
Poulet Sauté à la Forestière (Chicken
    Sauté with Morels and White
    Wine), 124–125
Poulet Sauté à la Lyonnaise
    (Chicken Sauté with Onions),
    121–122
preserved lemons, 57

Quick Broth, 17

raw sugar, 25
Red Pepper Shreds, Szechwan
    Chicken with (*La-jiao Zi Ji*),
    137–138
Rempah Ayam (Indonesian
    Chicken and Coconut
    Croquettes), 95
rendering lard, 13
rice
    Carolina-Style, 171–172

Chinese-Style, 172
rice wine, 27
Rich Coconut Milk, 151–152
Russian recipe: Chicken Kiev,
    67–68

safety
    and chicken, 9, 10
    fire, how to put out, 7
    and frying, 7–8
        outdoors, 62
    salmonella, 9, 10
    washing equipment and
        hands, 9
sake (rice wine), 27
salad
    Mixed, with Oil and Lemon
        Dressing, 178
    Orange and Onion, 181
    potato
        French, 177
        Granny's Hot, 176
    Zucchini, Boiled (*Insalata di
        Zucchini*), 180–181
salmonella, 9, 10
Salsa Criolla Cruda (Raw Creole
    Sauce), 156
"Saltimbocca," Chicken Thighs,
    74
sambal oelek or *ulek* (chili paste),
    96
sandwiches
    Creole Chicken Poor Boy,
        81–82
        à la Mediatrice, 82
sauce
    about, 154
    Apricot, 164
    Creole, Raw (*Salsa Criolla
        Cruda*), 156
    Horseradish Cocktail, 77
    Mango, Fresh, 158
    Pesto alla Genovese (Genovese
        Pesto), 128
    Plum, 163

sauce (cont'd)
    Quick, or Apricot Sauce,
      164
    Sweet-and-Sour, 165
    Tartar, 160
    Tempura, 166–167
    Thai Sweet and Hot Garlic
      (Nam Jim Gratiem), 53
sautéed chicken, 118–128
    about, 5–6, 118
    Indian, with Yogurt Sauce,
      120–121
    with Morels and White
      Wine (Poulet Sauté à la
      Forestière), 124–125
    with Olives (Pollo alla
      Franceschiello), 123
    with Onions (Poulet Sauté à la
      Lyonnaise), 121–122
    technique for, 5–6, 118
Savannah Cutlets with Curry
  Sauce, 44–45
sesame
    Chicken Fingers, 84–85
    Israeli Fried Chicken with
      (Off Sum-Sum), 36
    Wings, 89–90
sesame oil, 135
shallow frying, 118
Shrimp Sauce, Chicken Shreds
  with Coconut- (Ayam Pecel),
  144–145
side dishes, 154–181
    bread
      about, 167
      Spoon, 169
    Cakes, Hoe, 168
    gravy
      about, 154
      Cream, 154
      Milk Pan, 154
      Southern Tomato, 155
    grits
      about, 167
      recipe for, 173

mayonnaise
    about, 158–159
    Aïoli (garlic), 160
    basic recipe, 159
    Herb, 160
    Tartar Sauce, 160
mustard
    about, 161
    Honey, 161–162
    Hot Chinese, 162
potatoes
    about, 167
    Butter-Browned New
      (Pommes des Terre à la
      Noisette), 125
    Mashed or Creamed, 174
rice
    about, 167
    Carolina-Style, 171–172
    Chinese-Style, 172
salad
    about, 167
    Cucumber and Fennel,
      179
    Mixed, with Oil and
      Lemon Dressing, 178
    Orange and Onion, 181
    potato
      French, 177
      Granny's Hot, 176
    Zucchini, Boiled (Insalata
      di Zucchini), 180–181
sauce
    about, 154
    Apricot, 164
    Creole, Raw (Salsa Criolla
      Cruda), 156
    Curry, 157
    Mango, Fresh, 158
    Plum, 163
      Quick, or Apricot
      Sauce, 164
    Sweet-and-Sour, 165
    Tartar, 160
    Tempura, 166–167

Sweet Potatoes, Creamed,
  175–176
Singaporean recipe: Chicken
  Shreds with Coconut-Shrimp
  Sauce (Ayam Pecel), 144–145
size of chicken, 9
Skillet or Chicken Biscuits, 170
skillets for frying, 2–3
skin, 50
sous prik (chili paste), 96
South African recipe: Cutlets in
  Curry Sauce, 46–47
South American recipe: Fried
  Chicken (Chicharrones de Pollo),
  33–34
Southeast Asia. See Cambodia;
  Indonesia; Singapore; Thailand
Southern-fried chicken, 97–116.
  See also United States
    about, 97–98
    Basic, with Cream Gravy,
      99–100
    Batter-, 100–101
    Buttermilk, 102–103
    Country Captain, 115–116
    Creole, à la, 107–108
    Granny Fowler's Sunday,
      108–109
    Herb-and-Spice, 104–105
    Jewish Georgia, 110–111
    Kentuckian, 113–114
    Livers, 105–106
      Cajun-Style, 106
    Maryland, 112–113
soy sauce, 133
Spicy Chicken Drumettes,
  90–91
Spinach and Feta, Chicken with,
  68–69
Spoon Bread, 169
stir-fried chicken, 129–152
    about, 6, 129–131, 147
    with Asparagus and Long
      Onions (Toriniku To
      Asparagasu), 142–143

Cantonese, Curry (*Yea tsup Ga Li Gai*), 136–137
Cashew (*Yao Go Ji-ding*), 132–133
Chinese, 131
Coconut-Shrimp Sauce, Shreds with (*Ayam Pecel*), 144–145
with Ginger and Mint (*Gai Khing*), 139–140
ingredients for, 131
with Lemongrass (*Ga Xao Xa Ot*), 145–146
livers
    Curried (*Murgh Kaleja Kari*), 149
    Hot Curried, Nepali Style, 150–151
    in Oyster Sauce (*Ho-yu Feng-gan*), 147–148
Mongolian, with Bean Sauce (*Mong Ku Gai Pan*), 134–135
with Mushroom and Cilantro (*Moan Chua Noeung Phset Kream*), 140–141
pieces and parts, 147
Szechwan, with Red Pepper Shreds (*La-jiao Zi Ji*), 137–138
technique for, 6, 129–131
storing chicken, 9
stuffed chicken, 65–74
about, 65, 71
Cordon Bleu (*Suprêmes de Volaille Cordon Bleu*), 65–66
with Fresh Mozzarella and Basil, Breasts (*Petti di Pollo alla Margherita*), 70–71
Kiev, 67–68
with Spinach and Feta, 68–69
thighs
    Hunter-Style, with Sweet Potato Stuffing, 72–73

"Saltimbocca," 74
sugar, 25
Suprêmes de Volaille à Brun or *à la Meuniere* (Chicken Breasts in Brown Butter), 126
Suprêmes de Volaille Cordon Bleu (Chicken Cordon Bleu), 65–66
sweet potato(es)
    Creamed, 175–176
    Stuffing, Thighs Hunter-Style, with, 72–73
Szechwan Chicken with Red Pepper Shreds (*La-jiao Zi Ji*), 137–138

tamarind, in Indonesian Curry Fried Chicken (*Ayam Goreng Asam*), 53
tamarind paste, 54
Tapaka (Armenian Butter-Fried Chicken with Eggplant), 60
Tartar Sauce, 160
techniques for cooking, 5–8
    deep-frying, 6–8
    pan-frying, 6
    sautéing, 5–6, 118
    stir frying, 6, 129–131
temperature
    of chicken, 9, 10
    of fat, 2, 4
Tempura, Chicken, 27–28
tenders
    Coconut, Fingers, 78–79
    Sesame, 84–85
Thailand
    Chicken with Ginger and Mint (*Gai Khing*), 139–140
    Thai Fried Chicken (*Gai Tord*), 52
    Thai Sweet and Hot Garlic Sauce (*Nam Jim Gratiem*), 53
thermometer for frying, 4, 7–8
thighs

with Asparagus and Long Onions (*Toriniku To Asparagasu*), 142–143
Cajun Popcorn, 76–77
Cantonese, Curry (*Yea tsup Ga Li Gai*), 136–137
coconut
    Fingers, 78–79
    -Shrimp Sauce, Shreds with (*Ayam Pecel*), 144–145
Hunter-Style, with Sweet Potato Stuffing, 72–73
Japanese Fried (*Toriniku Tatsuta-age*), 83
"Saltimbocca," 74
Sesame, 84–85
tomato(es)
    in Chicken Country Captain, 115–116
    Gravy, Southern, 155
    in Raw Creole Sauce (*Salsa Criolla Cruda*), 156
tools for frying, 4
    outdoors, 62
Toriniku Tatsuta-age (Japanese Fried Chicken), 83
Toriniku To Asparagasu (Chicken with Asparagus and Long Onions), 142–143
toung ot (chili paste), 96
turbinado sugar, 25
types of chicken, 9

United States. *See also* Southern-fried chicken
    Beer-Battered Chicken Drumettes, 88–89
    Buffalo Wings, 86–87
    Cajun Popcorn Chicken, 76–77
    Carolina-Style Rice, 171–172
    Chicken and Green Tomato Fritters, 92–93

United States (*cont'd*)
    Chicken Thighs Hunter-
       Style, with Sweet Potato
       Stuffing, 72–73
    Cream Gravy (Milk Pan
       Gravy), 154
    Creamed Sweet Potatoes,
       175–176
    Creole Chicken Poor Boy,
       81–82
       à la Mediatrice, 82
    Cucumber and Fennel Salad,
       179
    Curry Sauce, 157
    Fresh Mango Sauce, 158
    Georgia Cutlets, 41–42
    Granny's Hot Potato Salad,
       176
    Grits, 173
    Hoe Cakes, 168
    Honey Mustard, 161–162
    Horseradish Cocktail Sauce,
       77
    Mashed or Creamed
       Potatoes, 174

    Mixed Salad, with Oil and
       Lemon Dressing, 178
    Orange and Onion Salad,
       181
    Raw Creole Sauce (*Salsa
       Criolla Cruda*), 156
    Savannah Cutlets with Curry
       Sauce, 44–45
    Sesame Chicken Fingers,
       84–85
    Skillet or Chicken Biscuits,
       170
    Southern Tomato Gravy,
       155
    Spicy Chicken Drumettes,
       90–91
    Spoon Bread, 169

vegetable oils, 14

washing
    chicken, 10
    equipment and hands, 9
West Africa. *See* Nigeria
Western-style disjointing, 11

whole chicken, 62
    Crispy Skin (*Cui-pi Ji*),
       63–64
Wiener Backhendl (Viennese Fried
    Chicken), 38–39
Wine, Chicken Sauté with
    Morels and White (*Poulet
    Sauté à la Forestière*), 124–125
wings
    about, 85
    Beer-Battered, 88–89
    Buffalo, 86–87
    Sesame, 89–90
    Spicy, 90–91
wok, 3–4
Wu Xiang Ji (Five Fragrance
    Chicken), 50

Yao Go Ji-ding (Cashew Chicken),
    132–133
Yea tsup Ga Li Gai (Cantonese
    Chicken Curry), 136–137
Yogurt Sauce, Indian Chicken
    Sauté with, 120–121